SENTIMENTAL FABULATIONS,
CONTEMPORARY CHINESE FILMS

FILM AND CULTURE SERIES

JOHN BELTON, GENERAL EDITOR

SENTIMENTAL FABULATIONS, CONTEMPORARY CHINESE FILMS

ATTACHMENT IN THE AGE OF GLOBAL VISIBILITY

REY CHOW

COLUMBIA UNIVERSITY PRESS

NEW YORK

COLUMBIA UNIVERSITY PRESS
Publishers Since 1893
New York   Chichester, West Sussex

Library of Congress Cataloging-in-Publication Data

Chow, Rey
   Sentimental fabulations, contemporary Chinese films : attachment in the age of global
visibility / Rey Chow
     p. cm. — (Film and culture)
   Includes bibliographical references and index.
   ISBN-10: 0-231-13332-4 (cloth : alk. paper) — ISBN-10: 0-231-13333-2 (pbk. : alk. paper)
   ISBN-13: 978-0-231-13332-6 (cloth) — ISBN-13: 978-0-231-13333-3 (paper)
   1. Motion pictures—China.   2. Motion pictures—Social aspects—China.   I. Title.   II. Series.

PN1993.5.C4C467 2007
791.430951—DC22

2006039237

⊖ Columbia University Press books are printed on permanent and durable acid-free paper.

Printed in the United States of America

c 10 9 8 7 6 5 4 3 2 1
p 10 9 8 7 6 5 4 3 2 1

A portion of the materials in the introduction has been adapted, with modifications, from the essay "A Phantom Discipline" *PMLA* 116.5 (2001): 1386–95.

An early and shorter version of chapter 1 was published under the title "The Seductions of Homecoming: Place, Authenticity, and Chen Kaige's *Temptress Moon*," *Narrative* 6.1 (January 1998): 3–17.

An early and shorter version of chapter 2 was published under the title "Nostalgia of the New Wave: Structure in Wong Kar-wai's *Happy Together*," *Camera Obscura*, no. 42 (1999): 31–48.

An early and shorter version of chapter 3 was published under the title "Sentimental Returns: On the Uses of the Everyday in the Recent Films of Zhang Yimou and Wong Kar-wai," *New Literary History* 33.4 (Autumn 2002): 639–54.

Early versions of some sections of chapter 7 were published under the titles "Toward an Ethics of Postvisuality: Some Thoughts on the Recent Work of Zhang Yimou," *Poetics Today* 25.4 (Winter 2004): 673–88; and "*Not One Less*: The Fable of a Migration," in *Chinese Films in Focus: 25 New Takes*, ed. Chris Berry (London: British Film Institute, 2003), 144–51.

A considerably shorter version of chapter 8 is forthcoming in *Traces* in 2007.

An early and shorter version of chapter 9 was published under the title "A Pain in the Neck, a Scene of 'Incest,' and Other Enigmas of an Allegorical Cinema: Tsai Ming-liang's *The River*," *New Centennial Review* 4.1 (Spring 2004): 123–42.

All previously published materials have been substantially rewritten and reorganized for the purposes of this book.

FOR MICHAEL SILVERMAN

Contents

Preface and Acknowledgments

A couple of decades ago, the field of English-language Chinese film studies as we know it today had not yet come into being. Other than a handful of dedicated scholars who had been quietly doing their historical research for years, the field was wide open—and unformed. In the short period since, as though by the "fast forward" command on some remote control, settlers of different stripes, all with publications under their belts, have taken up abode in what has by now become a busy and populous terrain, home to a steady stream of migrants from Chinese, English, and Asian American literary studies, non-Chinese-speaking/reading film enthusiasts, cultural studies critics, and global media experts, as well as to academically trained researchers and experienced teachers of Chinese film.

This collectively opportunistic movement into a newly fashionable academic enclave is, of course, a sign of our times, marked as it is by a declining patience for older, time-consuming forms of humanistic learning such as language and literature (especially in Asian areas) and a fascination with the glamour and speedy recognition associated with the visual media (especially contemporary Asian cinemas). While opportunism is often a professional necessity—one that can come with its own positively innovative momentum, especially when the "raw materials" or primary texts that can be accessed seem in such abundant and convenient supply—what is more disturbing is how smoothly the new field of Chinese film studies seems to have adapted itself to established patterns of normative knowledge production and management rather than assuming the critical task of challenging them. For instance, even as the adjectives "global" and "transnational" are invoked everywhere, the field is quickly being compartmentalized—and monumentalized—into distinct local archives and genealogies, which are typically arranged by way of chronological divisions and geopolitical boundaries such as the People's Republic of China, Taiwan, Hong Kong, and Shanghai. What may be at stake here?

Among specialists of various disciplines such as history, literature, religion, and philosophy, it is a known fact that for a long time, when non-Western cultures were studied in comparison with the leading European ones, they were judged as not having attained the levels of certain forms of knowledge. Accordingly, cultures such as India, China, and Africa were presumed not to have history, literature, religion, or philosophy. What they had, or were thought to have, were phenomena of social or anthropological interest, in the form of mass or nonindividuated beliefs, customs, rituals, and practices. Properly speaking, the high ends of human civilization, having to do with the capacities for abstract, speculative, and imaginative endeavors, pertained only to select cultures of the West. The much more recent history of the study of film has not exactly departed from this traditional and increasingly challenged, though clearly not defunct, way of thinking. Hence, on the one hand (for those specializing in Western European and North American films), there is film in the singular and generic, while, on the other hand, there are Chinese films, Japanese films, Korean films, Iranian films, Indian films, Algerian films, and so forth. Non-Western cultures can be acknowledged as producers of film, in other words, only insofar as their national or ethnic labels remain in the picture. Such labels are reminders of the mass or nonindividuated socioeconomic realities to which the study of non-Western films, much like the study of non-Western cultures in general, is consigned as a rule, so that understanding non-Western films—nowadays often grouped under the rubric of "world cinemas"—becomes a matter of returning the films to the so-called local specifics, known summarily as contexts. In brief, understanding non-Western films remains an exercise in instrumentalist knowledge gathering and dissemination, aimed at producing and authenticating an object that is conceptualized a priori as a horde and granted intelligibility only in the plural (except for the occasional appearances of individual "geniuses"—in this case, the auteurs).

While they undoubtedly have much to teach us, the trends toward geo-political and chronological determinism in the new field of Chinese film studies are, in this light, perhaps unwittingly partaking of a larger ideo-logical legacy, one that is reinforced in part by the post–Second World War U.S. academic establishment of area studies. This legacy would have one believe that it is much more pertinent to study a modern non-Western rep-resentational form—deemed not to be high art or high culture to begin with—in accordance with empirical data such as realpolitik, geographi-cal origins, production figures, market statistics, box office records, and so forth, rather than in terms, say, of conceptual, theoretical, or aesthet-ic problematics. When used appropriately, empirical data are, of course, seldom categorically irrelevant, but the seemingly innocuous, reverential processes of information retrieval, accumulation, and classification in this instance mask a more fundamental question: why, when the subject hap-pens to be Chinese films, must critical language itself become preoccupied with the positivistic—with what is called the real, actual, concrete, nu-merically verifiable, and so forth—as though positivism itself (often mis-named as history) were an incontrovertibly superior, indeed moral, virtue? This question, underscored here as a way to argue the intellectual merits of Chinese films—of Chinese films as abstract, speculative, and imaginative endeavors; as artifacts with logics and purposes of their own that are not reducible to socioeconomic factoids—is behind all my readings in the fol-lowing pages.

ACKNOWLEDGMENTS

The completion of this book was facilitated by a resident research fellow-ship at the Radcliffe Institute for Advanced Study, Harvard University, in 2005–6. I am grateful to the Radcliffe Fellowship Program and to the office of the dean of the faculty, Brown University, for enabling me to take advan-tage of the opportunity to devote a year to writing. My sincere thanks to the audiences at the many institutions in North America, Asia, Australia, and Europe where I have presented small segments of the book over the years and to the colleagues who have engaged with my previous work on Chinese cinema in a generous spirit and/or adopted it for their classes.

A number of colleagues and friends—Réda Bensmaïa, Chris Berry, Yomi Braester, Brian Carr, Chang Hsiao-hung, Yvonne Leung, Kien Ket Lim, Song Hwee Lim, Kwai-cheung Lo, Liang Luo, Christopher Lupke, Fiona Ng, Laikwan Pang, and Emilie Yue-Yu Yeh—deserve special mention for the help they offered at various stages, pointing me to or tracking down important people and source materials on my behalf. Sam Geall was a godsend, and I thank him for his good will, cyberspace expertise, and admirable sense of responsibility. As always, Austin Meredith patiently put up with all the inconveniences created by my technological incompetence.

I am indebted as well to Harry Harootunian and Kathleen Woodward, who have endorsed this project and my work in general with magnanimous enthusiasm, and to William Mills Todd III, who, as teacher, adviser, colleague, and friend, has been exemplary in the gracious manner in which he has been providing counsel for more than a quarter of a century. Jennifer Crewe, my splendid editor, who persuaded me to write my first book on Chinese cinema years ago, has been instrumental in making this book happen at each and every level. It was my good fortune to have her oversee the book's preparation, a process that was handled with superb efficiency by Columbia University Press's production staff. (A special note of thanks to Sarah St. Onge for her excellent copyediting.) The perceptive and constructive comments of two anonymous reviewers, who firmly supported the manuscript even as they helped me see my mistakes and inadequacies, contributed to the revised and, I believe, improved, final version.

Last but not least, I would like to thank Michael Silverman, whose DVD-copious knowledge of film (among other things) is infinitely humbling and who, despite my initial reluctance, encouraged me to teach my first course ever on Chinese cinema, during the spring semester of 2002, at Brown. It was the research and thinking I did for that course, together with my students' contagiously effusive responses to the films we were watching together, that gave me the inspiration to write this book. I dedicate it to Michael with heartfelt gratitude and love.

Note on Transcription

Transcriptions of Chinese-language words, quotations, and sources are mostly provided according to the *pinyin* system, though Wade-Giles transliterations of Mandarin (in use in Taiwan) and loose English transliterations of Cantonese pronunciations (in Hong Kong and Asian American films) are also present throughout the book. Unless otherwise specified, spellings of film characters' names have been adopted from the official English subtitles. In those cases where I believe it would make a difference to see the original Chinese characters, I have provided the latter as well.

SENTIMENTAL FABULATIONS,
CONTEMPORARY CHINESE FILMS

Introduction

Where is the movie about me?

In the academic study of cinema, this is one of the most commonly encountered questions in recent years. Versions of it include some of the following: Where in this discipline am I? How come I am not represented? What does it mean for me and my group to be unseen? What does it mean for me and my group to be seen in this manner—what has been left out? These questions of becoming visible pertain, of course, to the prevalence of the politics of identification, to the relation between representational forms and their articulation of subjective histories and locations. It is one reason the study of cinema, like the study of literature and history, has become increasingly caught up in the study of group cultures: every group (be it defined by nationality, class, gender, ethnicity, sexual orientation, religion, or disability), it seems, produces a local variant of the universal that is cinema, requiring critics to engage with the specificities of particular collectivities even as they talk about the generalities of the filmic apparatus. According to one report, for instance, at the Society of Cinema Studies Annual Conference of 1998, "nearly half the over four hundred papers (read from morning to night in nine rooms) treated the politics of representing ethnicity, gender, and sexuality."[1] Western film studies, as Christine Gledhill and Linda Williams write, is currently faced with its own "impending dissolution . . . in . . . transnational theorization."[2] How

did this state of affairs arise? How might we approach it not simply empirically, by way of numerical classifications, but also theoretically, by prob-
ing visibility as a problematic, to which film, because of its palpably visual
modes of signification, may serve as a privileged point of entry?

Transnational theorization was, in fact, already an acute part of the reflections of non-Western authors on film experiences during the 1900s,
1910s, and 1920s. When contemplating the effects of the filmic spectacle,
for instance, Lu Xun and Tanizaki Junichiro, writing self-consciously as
Chinese and Japanese nationals, readily raised questions of what it meant
to be—and to be visible as—Chinese and Japanese in the modern world.
The visual immediacy of Chinese and Japanese figures and faces, conveyed
on the screen as they had never been before, was experienced by these
authors not only as scientific advancement but simultaneously as a type
of racially marked signification—specifically, as representations in which
their own cultures appeared inferior and disadvantaged vis-à-vis a newly
global, mediatized gaze.[3]

In light of these early reflections—reflections that are, strictly speaking,
part of the history of film but which have hitherto been relegated to the
margins of the West—the current preoccupation with group identities in
film studies is perhaps only a belated reenactment of a longstanding set of
issues pertaining to the fraught relationship between film and cultural identity. This book, which examines some Chinese films from the period of the
late 1980s to the early 2000s, will be an approach to some of these issues.

HIGHLIGHTS OF A WESTERN DISCIPLINE

When film captured the critical attention of European theorists in the early
twentieth century, it did not do so in terms of what we now call identity
politics. Instead, it was film's novelty as a technological invention, capable
of reproducing the world with a likeness hitherto unimaginable, that fascinated cultural critics such as Walter Benjamin, Siegfried Kracauer, and
Ernst Bloch. Unlike photography, on which film and the early theorization
of film depended, cinema brought with it the capacity for replicating motion in the visual spectacle. But as the motion picture ushered in a new
kind of realism that substantially expanded on that of still photographic
mimesis, it also demanded a thorough reconceptualization of the bases on
which representation had worked for centuries. In this regard, few studies could rival Benjamin's oft-cited essay "The Work of Art in the Age of

Mechanical Reproduction" (1936) in its grasp of the challenge posed by film to classical Western aesthetics. Along with his work on Charles Baudelaire's lyric poetry, this essay defines that challenge in terms of what Benjamin calls the decline of the aura, the sum of the unique features of works of art that is rooted in the time and place of the works' original creation.[4] For Benjamin, film's thorough permeation by technology, a permeation that led to its modes of apparent visual transparency, meant that a new kind of sociological attitude, one that associates representation more with repro-ducibility than with irreplaceability, would henceforth shape the expecta-tions about representation: the repeatable copy, rather than the singular original, would now be the key. Benjamin viewed this fundamental icono-clasm (or irreverence toward the sacredness of the original) as a form of emancipation. No longer bound to specific times, places, and histories, the technically reproducible filmic image is now ubiquitously available, secu-larized, and thus democratized.

In retrospect, it is important to note the kind of emphasis critics such as Benjamin placed on the cinematic spectacle. This is a kind of emphasis we no longer seem to encounter in contemporary cinema studies. For the crit-ics of Benjamin's era, film's faithful yet promiscuous realism—it records everything accurately yet also indiscriminately—announced the triumph of the camera's eye over human vision. The origins of cinema, they under-stood, are implicated in a kind of inhumanism even as cinema serves the utilitarian end of telling human stories. This inhumanism, rooted in the sophistication, efficiency, and perfection of the machine, was seen in over-whelmingly positive terms in the early twentieth century. By expanding and extending the possibilities of capturing movement, registering color, enlarging, speeding up, or slowing down the transitory moments of life, and rewinding time past, cinema was regarded first and foremost as an ad-vancement, an overcoming of the limitations inherent in human percep-tion. As in the theorizations and practices of early Soviet filmmakers such as Sergei Eisenstein, Dziga Vertov, and Lev Kuleshev, in Benjamin's think-ing, the cinematic was a power to transform what is visible—to enhance, multiply, and diversify its dimensions. Cinema was the apparatus that en-abled the emergence of what he called the optical unconscious—the sur-facing of the optical that had hitherto been unconscious, on the one hand, and the surfacing of the unconscious in optical form, on the other.

These relatively early theorizations of the cinematic spectacle had to account in some rudimentary way for spectators' responses. And yet, although early cinema was closely affined with representational realism, it was, as Tom Gunning writes, not necessarily accompanied by the stability of viewer position: "the appearance of animated images, while frequently invoking accuracy and the methods of science, also provoked effects of astonishment and uncanny wonder. Innovations in realist representation did not necessarily anchor viewers in a stable and reassuring situation. Rather, this obsession with animation, with super-lifelike imagery, carries a profound ambivalence and even a sense of disorientation."[5]

Again, it is necessary to remember how such spectatorial ambivalence and disorientation were theorized at the time when cinema was seen, by European theorists at least, predominantly as a type of scientific and technological progress. Even though the audience was in the picture, as it were, its lack of stability (or uniformity) tended to be configured in terms of a general epochal experience rather than by way of specific histories of reception. For this reason, perhaps, Benjamin made ample use of the notion of shock, the high modernist sensibility he identified with montage and traced back to the artistic work of Baudelaire and the analytic work of Sigmund Freud (among others). While other critics saw cinematic shock in more existential-aesthetic terms, as the product of the abruptness, intensity, and ephemerality of fleeting moments,[6] for Benjamin, shock had a determinedly political significance. As is evident in his discussion of Bertolt Brecht's epic theater, in which the equivalent of cinematic montage could be located in the theatrical tableau (the moment in which ongoing gestures and movements are interrupted and suspended by the entry of an outsider in such a way as to become a frozen and thus quotable spectacle), Benjamin relied for some of his most suggestive insights on a capacity for defamiliarization (that is, for unsettling habitual perception) often associated with aesthetic form,[7] a capacity to which he then attributed the purpose of critical reflection. (His notion of the dialectic image in the unfinished *Arcades Project* arguably belongs as well in this repertoire of visual figures for mobilizing historical change.)[8] It was by engaging with film as shock—a quality of the cinematic spectacle that, by extension, he assimilated to the spectators' general response—that Benjamin wrote of film as a forward-looking medium.[9] He was, of course, deeply aware of the political danger that this entailed—by the 1930s film just as easily lent itself to manipulation by the Nazis and the Fascists for propaganda purposes—but his emphasis remained a utopian one, whereby the cinema stood for liberatory and transformative possibilities.

By contrast, André Bazin, writing in France in the 1950s, was not drawn to the elusive and shocking effects of the cinematic spectacle but instead theorized the filmic image in terms of its ontology, its function as a preserve of time: "photography . . . embalms time, rescuing it simply from its proper corruption. . . . [In film,] for the first time, the image of things is likewise the image of their duration, change mummified as it were."[10] If film was in an earlier era associated with time as progress, Bazin's theoretical emphasis was decidedly different. The cinema was by his time no longer a novelty but more a mundane fact of mass culture, and the political potentiality of cinematic shock that energized theorists in the 1930s had given way in Bazin's writings to phenomenologically oriented reflections, which were, paradoxically, also about the arrest and suspension of time. But whereas for Benjamin the filmic image as halted time provided an impetus for historical action, for Bazin it signaled rather retrospection, the act of looking back at something that no longer exists. The hopefulness and futurism of the earlier film theorizations were now superseded by a kind of nostalgia, one that results from the completion of processes. Accordingly, because time has fossilized in the cinematic spectacle, time is also redeemed there.[11]

In spite of his critics, Bazin's understanding of the cinematic image as time past does not mean that his film theory is by necessity politically regressive or conservative. Indeed, his grasp of the filmic image as (always already) implicated in retroaction enabled Bazin to analyze astutely how it was exploited in the Soviet Union for a political purpose different from that of capitalist Hollywood.[12] Describing the propaganda films in which Joseph Stalin always appeared not only as a military genius and an infallible leader but also as an avuncular, neighborly friend, filled with personal warmth and eagerness to help the common people, Bazin observed that the cinematic spectacle had become, in the hands of the Soviet filmmakers, a completed reality—a perfect image against which the real-life Stalin must henceforth measure himself. Although Stalin was still alive, Bazin wrote, it was as though he had already been rendered dead; beside his own glowing image, he could henceforth only live nostalgically, attempting in vain to become like himself over and over again. The real-life Stalin had become a somewhat inferior version of the Stalin image. Interestingly, in this cynical but perceptive account of Soviet propaganda, the theory of the cinematic image offered by Bazin was derived not so much from its effect of shock, potential for change, or hope for the future as from its effect of stability, permanence, and immobilization. The cinematic image here takes on the status of a monumentalized time, which compels one to look retroactively at something better, larger, and more glorious that no longer is. The remarkable lesson offered by Bazin is that, as much as the futurity imputed to the cinematic image, nostalgia, too, can be a profoundly political message; it, too, can inspire action.

These continental European negotiations with temporality as implied in the cinematic image, negotiations that tended, in a classical manner, to concentrate on film's representational relation to the external world it captured, shifted to a different plane as film gained status as an academic subject in Britain and the United States in the 1960s, 1970s, and 1980s. As a field of intellectual inquiry that sought institutional legitimation, film had to elaborate its own set of disciplinary specificities. At one level, it was, of course, possible to continue with the more abstract theorizations of the cinematic spectacle: as semiotics acquired critical purchase, film was accordingly rendered as a type of signification. Christian Metz's works, notably *Language and Cinema* and *Film Language*, led the way for the kind of inquiry that asks if film could indeed be seen as a kind of language in the Saussurean sense and, even if not, what its governing logic might be.[13] The point of Metz's project was to configure the perceptual possibility of a structuration, a network of permutations, that had a materiality all its own, a materiality that meanwhile was not to be confused with the vulgar materiality of the flesh. From Benjamin's and Bazin's adherence to the visual spectacle, then, with Metz and his followers, theorization moved rigorously into film's internal principles for generating and organizing meanings. As such theorization became increasingly idealist and rationalist, film critics, including Metz himself (in *The Imaginary Signifier*),[14] eventually found themselves returning to psychoanalysis as a remedial means of gauging the more intractable but undeniable issues of human fantasy and desire, and with them the politics of sexuality, to compensate for what had been typically left out of the semiotic explication.[15] In retrospect, it is tempting to see semiotics and psychoanalysis as the two inward turns—and disciplining moments—symptomatic of a process in which *the study of film itself was caught up in its own identity formation.* Be it through the labor of the filmic signifier or the labor of subjectivities interpellated around the cinematic apparatus, film studies was seeking its mirroring, so to speak, by the profession at large.

This is the juncture at which the old question of time, at one point debated in terms that were more or less exclusively focused on the cinematic image per se, splintered. Time could no longer be grasped in the abstract, as the future or the past, but demanded to be understood in relation to the mental, cultural, and historical processes by which the seemingly self-evident cinematic image was produced in the first place. Accordingly, the givenness of the cinematic image was increasingly displaced onto the politics of spectatorship. In the Anglo-American studies of film in the 1970s and 1980s, such as those being published in the influential British journal *Screen*, the continental European focus on the cinematic image was steadily supplemented, and supplanted, by modes of inquiry that were concurrently informed by Marxist, structuralist and poststructuralist, and psychoanalytic writings (the master figures being Jacques Lacan and Louis Althusser). But it was feminist film theory, described by Dudley Andrew as "the first and most telling Anglo-American cinema studies initiative,"[16] that brought about a thorough redesign of the European focus.

In her groundbreaking essay of 1975, "Visual Pleasure and Narrative Cinema," Laura Mulvey turned the question of the cinematic image (and its implications of time) into a story, one that, she revealed, was far from being sexually neutral or innocent.[17] Rather than treating the cinematic image as a single entity, Mulvey approached it in a deconstructive move, in which what seems visually obvious and unified is taken apart by the reintroduction of narrative. The part of the narrative that determines how specific images are looked at while remaining itself hidden and invisible, Mulvey called the gaze. Most critically, Mulvey gave the temporal differential between image and gaze the name of patriarchy, so that, in the case of classical Hollywood melodrama at least, she charged, masculinist scopophilia underwrote the imperative of gazing, while women were cast, as a result, as passive, fetishized objects, as beautiful images to be looked at. Mulvey was formidably direct about her goal: "It is said that analysing pleasure, or beauty, destroys it. That is the intention of this article."[18] As Maggie Humm puts it, "Mulvey's essay marked a huge conceptual leap in film theory: a jump from the ungendered and formalistic analyses of semiotics to the understanding that film viewing always involves gendered identities."[19] By arguing that cinema is irreducibly structured by (hetero) sexual difference, Mulvey succeeded in doing something that her fellow male critics were uninterested in doing—prying the filmic image open and away from its hitherto spontaneous, reified status and reinserting in it the drama of the ongoing cultural struggle between men and women, the drama of narrative coercions and ideological interpellations.

In its justifiable distrust of the cinematic image as deceptive and usur-patory and in its courageous effort to forge a politics that would prevent the woman spectator from completely collapsing, at her own peril, into the cinematic image of femininity produced by men, was feminist film theory, in spite of itself, an unwitting ally to an intellectual tradition that is, to borrow a term from Martin Jay's study of modern French theory, icono-phobic?[20] I tend to think so, but it is necessary to add that this iconopho-bia was a theoretically and institutionally productive one.[21] (Among other things, it posed a crucial question within the politics of film production: how could one make a differently narrativized kind of film?) It was pre-cisely its momentum of negativity, manifested in the belief that the cin-ematic image has somehow repressed something existing beyond it, that became the characteristic force with which the study of film has since then spread—first to English departments, in which film is often accepted as a kind of pop culture; then to foreign language and literature departments, in which film becomes yet another method of learning about other cultures; and finally to the currently fashionable discussions, in social science as well as humanities programs across the university, of so-called global media.

Feminist film theory, in other words, inaugurated the institutional dis-semination of cinema studies in the Anglo-American world with some-thing akin to what Michel Foucault, in his work on the history of sexuality in the West, called the repressive hypothesis, whereby the conceptualiza-tion of what is repressive—together with its investment in lack and cas-tration—is reinforced simultaneously by the incessant generation and proliferation of discourses about what is supposedly repressed.[22] (It was no mere coincidence that the political weapon on which Mulvey relied for attacking phallocentrism was Freudian psychoanalysis.)[23] But what was unique—and remarkable—in this instance was the articulation of the re-pressive hypothesis to the visual field, an articulation wherein the visually full (presence and plenitude of the) cinematic image has become itself the very evidence/sign of repression and lack.

IMAGE, TIME, IDENTITY:
TRAJECTORIES OF BECOMING VISIBLE

Because it was underwritten with the push of the repressive hypothesis, the paradigm shift within the cinematic visual field toward the study of narrativity and ideology led to consequences that have gone considerably beyond (the Western parameters of) film studies. Such a paradigm shift harked back to the heightened sense of group self-consciousness already felt by non-Western writers such as Lu Xun and Tanizaki about film technology in the early twentieth century and logically made way, in academia, for the study of differences dispersed along multiple lines of inquiry. In the decades since Mulvey's essay was first published,[24] film and cultural critics have been extending the implications of her work (often in simplified terms) by devoting themselves to problematizing the naturalness of the cinematic image. Rather than being on the image itself, its magic, or its tendency toward monumentalization, the focus in theorizing and analyzing film has increasingly been on identifying and critiquing the multiple narrative and ideological processes that go into the image's production. Bill Nichols sums up this general trend succinctly: "The visual is no longer a means of verifying the certainty of facts pertaining to an objective, external world and truths about this world conveyed linguistically. The visual now constitutes the terrain of subjective experience as the locus of knowledge, and power."[25] Whereas feminist critics, following Mulvey, elaborate and refine women-centered modes of interrogating patriarchy, other critics, equipped with other types of social queries, would complicate the differential between gaze and image in terms of class, race, ethnicity, nationality, and sexual preference in order to expose the repressive effects of dominant modes of visuality and identification. (Think, for instance, of the numerous critiques in postcolonial studies of orientalist representations.) Concurrently, they also theorize the ambiguities inherent in various forms of spectatorship and, by implication, in various forms of seeing and subjectivity.[26]

In these collective endeavors to destroy the pleasure of the beautiful image, what has happened to the problematic of time? At one level, time is infinitely diversified and relativized: as every group of spectators comes forward with its demands, interrogations, and political agendas, one can no longer speak of the image as such but must become willing to subject the image to processes of re-viewing, reimaging, and reassembling. This is perhaps one reason there are so many publications on filmmaking and film reception in different cultures (Brazilian, Chinese, French, German, Hong Kong, Indian, Iranian, Israeli, Italian, Japanese, Korean, and Spanish, just to name some commonly encountered examples). At the same time, in this culturally pluralized way of theorizing the filmic image, one cannot help feeling that a certain predictability has set in and that, despite their local differences, the theoretical moves made by different cultural groups vis-à-vis the cinematic image often share a similar kind of critical prerogative. Borrowing again from Nichols, we may describe this prerogative in this manner: "The rise of distinct cultures to a condition of visibility accompanies a radical shift away from democratic ideals of universalism (equality under the law for all regardless of gender, color, sexual orientation and so on) toward a particularism that insists on equality precisely in relation to differences of gender, color, sexual orientation and the like."[27] "Differences of gender, color, sexual orientation and the like," it follows, all generate research agendas, competition for institutional space and funding, and self-reproductive mechanisms such as publications and the training and placing of students. The questions of identity politics with which I began this discussion are therefore, arguably, some of the *temporal* outcomes of the proliferating and disseminating mechanisms that characterize the repressive hypothesis as it has been mobilized around the cinematic visual field.

In this light, the ambivalent logics exemplified by feminist film theory from the very beginning may be seen as constitutive, perhaps paradigmatic, of the process of a subordinated group's rise to visibility. When feminist film theory alerted us to the cinematically fetishized status of women, its apparent iconophobia shared important affinities with the moral charge that accompanied Western political activisms of the 1960s and early 1970s, with their demands for an end to imperialism and military violence and for the granting of civil rights to disenfranchised populations. At the same time, like the mass protests so self-consciously staged during that era, feminist film theory was delivering another message. This was the message that the politics of gender and sexuality (together with the politics of race, class, and ethnicity) was, in fact, none other than the politics of commodified media spectacles, a politics constituted by the demonstrative forces of public display.[28] Indeed, the determination with which feminist critics sought to subvert the widespread "false" representations of women—by actively competing for the right to transform, possess, and manage the visual field; to fabricate women's images; to broadcast women's stories—suggested that the dynamics of late capitalist simulacra was assuming center stage. The mechanically and then electronically produced images; the instantly transmitted, spectacular "reality" shows: these were henceforth going to be the actual, ubiquitous political battleground.

The attempt to anchor one's identity definitively in what Mulvey called to-be-looked-at-ness (on the screen as well as off) is, in view of this history, a newly fetishistic practice in an exponentially expanding and accelerating virtual field of global visibility. (This is, I believe, one reason that those who traditionally would have concentrated on the study of prose fiction have been migrating steadily toward the study of film and visual cultures.)[29] Moreover, this fetishistic practice and its countless simulacra—in so many varieties of "Look at me! Look at us!"—are no longer confined to the realm of gender politics but also repeated and reproduced widely across the disciplines, in which the morally impassioned rebuke of images always goes hand in hand with the massive production and circulation of more images—be those images about classes, races, nations, or persons of different sexual orientations.

Pursued in close relation to a controversial visual medium, feminist film theory since Mulvey hence reveals (in a handy manner) something crucial about the condition of visibility in general. In the course of feminist critique, the immediately present, visible object—the image of woman in classical Hollywood narrative cinema—is delimited or bracketed in an intervention that, notably, cannot abandon the visible as such but instead moves it into a different frame (women's world). This move makes it possible to include that which has hitherto remained invisible and thereby to reinvent the very terms of the relation between the visible and the invisible. In this process, however, becoming visible is no longer simply a matter of becoming visible in the visual sense (as an image or object) but also a matter of participating in a discursive politics of (re)configuring the relation between center and margins, a politics in which what is visible may be a key but not the exclusive determinant. *There is, in other words, a visibility of visibility—a visibility that is the condition of possibility for what becomes visible, that may derive a certain intelligibility from the latter but cannot be simply reduced to it.* It is to this other, epistemic sense of visibility—of visibility as the structuration of knowability—that Gilles Deleuze alerts us in his fascinating study of Foucault. As Deleuze writes in different passages, "Visibilities are not to be confused with elements that are visible or more generally perceptible, such as qualities, things, objects, compounds of objects. . . . Visibilities are not forms of objects, nor even forms that would show up under light, but rather forms of luminosity which are created by the light itself and allow a thing or object to exist only as a flash, sparkle or shimmer"; "Visibilities are neither the acts of a seeing subject nor the data of a visual meaning"; "Visibilities are not defined by sight but are complexes of actions and passions, actions and reactions, multisensorial complexes, which emerge into the light of day."[30]

If we follow Deleuze's thinking along these lines, the question of any-one's or any group's rise to the condition of visibility would turn out to be much more complicated than an attainment of quantifiable image time or even of the empirical status of being represented or seen. Instead, such a question would need to involve a consideration of the less immediately or sensorially detectable elements helping to propel, enhance, or obstruct such visibility in the first place and, even where visibility has occurred, a consideration of the often vacillating relations between the visible and the invisible that may well continue at different levels.

Tied as it is to the problematic of becoming visible (understood in these terms), the fetishization of identity as it is currently found in the study of cinematic images thus tends to proceed with a Janus-faced logic. There are those who, mistaking simple visual presence for (the entirety of) visibility, will always insist on investing artificial images with an anthropomorphic realism—the very thing that the iconoclasm of film, as its early theorists observed, fundamentally undid—and moreover to equate such images with the lives and histories of "real" cultural groups. ("National allegory" readings are one good example of this.) This line of thinking has its produc-tive moments, to be sure, but it is ultimately limited in what it can offer. Meanwhile, for those who remember that what is on the screen are not real people but images, a suspension of such insistence on literal, positivistic identifications can mean a turn, more interestingly, to the specific mate-rialities of image, affect, and fantasy, on the one hand, and the fraught complexities of globalized visibility, on the other.

With respect to the recent Western European and North American fas-cination with East Asian cinema,[31] the first question to ask, then, is this: should we try to direct such fascination back at some authentic, continu-ous Asianness lying beyond the alluring cinematic images, or would it not be more pertinent to see Asianness itself as a commodified and reproduc-ible value, made tantalizingly visible and accessible not only by the filmic genres of the action or martial arts comedy, the love story, and the histori-cal saga but also by an entire network of contemporary media discourses—economic rivalry, exotic cuisine, herbal medicine, spiritual and physical exercise, sex trade, female child adoption, model minority politics, illegal immigration, and so on—that are at once sustained by and contributing to the flows of capital? Part of my goal in this study is to argue that Chinese cinema since the 1980s—a cinema that is often characterized by multina-tional corporate production and distribution, multinational cast and crew collaboration, international award competition activity, and multicultural, multiethnic reception, as well as being accompanied by a steady stream of English-language publications, written (not infrequently by those who do not speak or read Chinese or consult Chinese-language sources) for an English-reading market—is an inherent part of a contemporary global problematic of becoming visible. As much as belonging in the history of Chinese culture, the films involved should also, I contend, be seen as belonging in the history of Western cinema studies, in the same manner that modern Asia, Africa, and Latin America, properly speaking, belong in the history of modern European studies.[32]

DEFINING THE SENTIMENTAL IN RELATION TO CONTEMPORARY CHINESE CINEMA

To the extent that one implicit aim of her criticism of classical Hollywood cinema was to eradicate conventional Western images altogether, Mulvey's early work can be seen as a British rejoinder to the political aspirations of the French nouvelle vague filmmakers (such as Jean-Luc Godard) and the theorists associated with the French journal *Tel quel*, who in the 1960s and 1970s mobilized critiques of Western thinking, often by way of looking east, especially to Mao Zedong's China.[33] Just as Mao and his cohort, following a native revolutionary tradition that began with the May Fourth Movement of 1919, sought to radicalize Chinese society by attacking its most basic social unit—the Chinese family[34]—so, too, did Anglo-American feminist film theory of the mid-twentieth century leave some of its most pronounced critical marks on melodrama, the film genre that is, arguably, most intimately linked to the middle-class nuclear family and its demands for female self-sacrifice.[35] But the Chinese connection, if it may be so called, did not stop at the attempt to deconstruct the family, East or West. As the consequences of Chinese communism began to be questioned by organic intellectuals in China—and as the disasters spawned by Mao's political idealism (which reached its frenzied heights during the Cultural Revolution of 1966–76) became a subject of reflective critique by those who had spent their formative youthful years living under the mainland Chinese regime—Chinese cinema became, for the first time, globally visible. In the astonishing films made by mainland Fifth Generation directors such as Chen Kaige, Zhang Yimou, Tian Zhuangzhuang, and their classmates, as well as by their contemporaries in Hong Kong and Taiwan such as Tsui

Hark, Hou Hsiao-Hsien, Ann Hui, Ang Lee, Edward Yang, Stanley Kwan, Clara Law, Wong Kar-wai, and Tsai Ming-liang, Chinese cinema has since the 1980s become an event with which the entire world has to reckon.[36] Appearing first in international film festivals and art house theaters, then gradually in undergraduate curricula across college campuses in the English-speaking world, and finally in mainstream Hollywood productions, China—in the form of films, directors, actors and actresses, cinematographic techniques, and special effects—has helped to revitalize cinematic discourse in the West and made it necessary, once again, for Western intellectuals to come to terms with aspects of what in so many ways still remains an exotic culture.

What does this becoming-visible of contemporary Chinese cinema signify in light of the small history of the discipline of film studies that I eclectically outlined above, including the critical moment of Anglo-American feminist critique? Many things can be said in response to this question,[37] but I'd like to foreground something that is central to my readings in some of the chapters to follow. Whereas contemporary cultural theory in the West, including feminist film theory, has thrived on an inextricable linkage (itself a legacy from Bertolt Brecht) between political consciousness raising, on the one hand, and an aesthetic-cum-theoretical avant-gardism,[38] on the other, the emergence of Chinese cinema renders this particular linkage a historical—and culturally specific—occurrence rather than a universal or absolute necessity. That is to say, although for left-leaning Western intellectuals since the post–Second World War period, "China" has often stood for a set of political aspirations alternative to the right, when China enters the world picture in the form of a contemporary cinema, it does not necessarily comply with such presumptions. Consciousness raising, contemporary Chinese cinema suggests, does not have to take the route of the avant-garde; conversely, aesthetic and theoretical avant-gardism, so valued in certain academic sectors for purposes of intellectual renewal and regeneration, does not necessarily lead to a progressive or democratic politics. In particular, the persistence of a predominant affective mode,[39] a mode I will describe as the sentimental, indicates that contemporary Chinese cinema, even as its contents fully partake of contemporary film and cultural problematics such as explicit sex, women's lives, gay male relationships, extramarital liaisons, immigrant tragedies and comedies, reproduction, and so forth, simultaneously brings with it fundamental challenges to the cornerstones of Western progressivist theoretical thinking. To engage productively with the global visibility of contemporary Chinese cinema, it is therefore important to work conceptually and speculatively, at a level beyond the (obviously invaluable) documenting and inventorying efforts and the geographical and chronological compartmentalization exercises that currently seem to dominate developments in this fledgling field. To put it bluntly, it is important to aim at goals other than information retrieval and canonization, and other than a monumentalizing of film periods (as tradition) and film directors (as individual talents).

What do I mean, then, by the recurrent sentimental in contemporary Chinese films? It would be helpful to begin with a conventional understanding—namely, of the sentimental as an affective orientation/tendency, one that is often characterized by apparent emotional excess, in the form of exaggerated grief or dejection or a propensity toward shedding tears.[40] But when examined closely, such emotional excess is only a clue to a much broader range of issues.

In his famous discussion, in 1795–96, of naive and sentimental poetry, the German-speaking philosopher and writer Friedrich Schiller defined the sentimental as a modern creative attitude marked by a particular self-consciousness of loss. To reiterate Schiller's statements in simple terms: while the poet who writes "naively" *is* nature, the poet who writes "sentimentally" *seeks* nature; the latter's "feeling for nature is like the feeling of an invalid for health."[41] The sentimental relation to nature (the condition of simple and sensuous wholeness that, because it is lost, will henceforth become a moral ideal) is, in other words, no longer spontaneous but reflexive—suffused with feelings of longing and characterized by the imaginative infiniteness of thought. What remains instructive in this classic European account is its attempt to understand the sentimental not only as an instance of affect but also as a relation of time: as an affective state triggered by a sense of loss, sentimentalism was, for Schiller, the symptom of the apprehension of an irreversible temporal differentiation or the passing of time. As well, this symptom was mediated by and accessible through aesthetic and cultural form: it was poetry (or "the poetic mood"), which Schiller considered "an independent whole in which all distinctions and all shortcomings vanish,"[42] that seemed generically appropriate for conveying the moral rigor pertaining to the naive and sentimental as contrastive but deeply bonded spiritual states.

Although Schiller's writings are typically classified under the rubric of German romanticism—he wrote about the sentimental belatedly, at a time

when the term had already become pejorative in connotations; his formulation of the sentimental (as the awareness of the loss of spontaneous feeling) was also quite distinct from the views advanced in previous decades,
as for instance in mid-eighteenth century England—his emphasis on the
reflexive character of the sentimental—that is, the character whereby the
mind does not receive any impressions without simultaneously observing
its own activity and reflection—was illustrative of the general tenets of the
well-established debates in eighteenth-century European moral philosophy and literature about the sentiments.[43] Conducted in the vocabulary of
sensibility, pity, sympathy, compassion, virtue, refined and delicate feeling,
and so forth,[44] some of these debates have also evolved around what in retrospect might be called a dialectical relationship between sentimentality
and its darker underside, as discourses about the philanthropic function
of benevolence were shown to be regularly underpinned by a fascination
with monstrosity, cruelty, violence, and the pleasures of inflicting pain on
others. For some scholars, this dialectical relationship constitutes a definition of humanity that is ridden with ambiguity and puts the European
Enlightenment's presumed (arrival at) rationality into serious question.[45]

In Anglo-American literary and cinematic studies, this rich historical
backdrop of intellectual controversies over the unresolved tensions between compassion and cruelty, between altruism and sadism gave way to
a type of articulation about the sentiments that links them explicitly with
the dynamics of social power struggles. When studied in relation to modern narrative fiction and film melodrama, in particular, the sentimental,
which for many still carries derogative meanings such as effeminacy and
sensationalist self-indulgence, often becomes a means to focalize issues
about the politics of identity. From the novels of Samuel Richardson and
Charlotte Brontë to those of Toni Morrison, to the woman-centered narrative films of Hollywood, and to the media representations of nonwhite
peoples, sentimentalism has, beginning with feminist revisionist scholarship of the 1970s and 1980s, increasingly been analyzed in conjunction with
the agency of those (most typically, white middle-class women confined to
domesticity) who occupy a marginalized social status and read as an alternative form of power attainment based, ironically, on the emotional cathexes produced by experiences of social deprivation, subordination, and
exclusion.[46] In such reversal of social hierarchy, what used to be considered
trivial and weak is accordingly reread as dazzle and strength: the seeming passivity or minoritization of those who are inmates of their environ-

ments are thus reconceptualized as possessing a manipulable potentiality that was previously dismissed or ignored. In this manner, sentimentalism, rather than designating the passing of time or the melancholy sensitivity of a lone lyric consciousness, becomes instead a vindicated instrument in (the reinterpretation of) social entanglements, often providing new clues as to who is actually in control.

Although far from being a unitary or unified concept, the sentimental in modern Euro-American humanistic studies clearly occupies a place that has much to do with *the enduringly fraught ethics of human sociality as mediated by art and fiction*, be that ethics conceived negatively, in the form of an individual consciousness's satirical or elegiac longing for an ideal whose attainment is always deferred, or affirmatively, in the form of (collective) identity empowerment and the fight for social justice.[47] And even where the sentimental reveals itself to be much more intimately entwined with sadism and malevolence than the feeble-minded would prefer, its function in gauging the textures and nuances of a society's moral duplicity seems indisputable. The pertinent question to be derived from these cross-cultural considerations is not exactly how to apply them to Chinese film or how such "Western theory" does not fit "Chinese reality" but rather the question of a particular discursive relation: how can the symptoms of prominent affective tendencies, as detectable in certain films, be theorized in relation to the foundations and practices of social interaction? With this question in the foreground, the sentimental, instead of being equated with the occurrence of affective excess per se, can more fruitfully be rethought as a discursive constellation—one that traverses affect, time, identity, and social mores, and whose contours tend to shift and morph under different cultural circumstances and likely with different genres, forms, and media.[48] To this extent, this book could perhaps be seen as participating in a larger trend in recent film studies of a (re)turn to the historical relationship between medium and ontology, a (re)turn that has been triggered in part by digitization's radical altering and obsoleting of film's materiality and that has led scholars to rethink the medium-specific and oftentimes somatic, as well as imaginary, effects of cinematic signification itself.[49]

In the Chinese language, as can be expected, more than one term has been used for "sentimentalism," but the term *wenqing zhuyi* (溫情主義)— literally, "warm sentiment-ism"[50]— seems to me to shed light on something unique to the Chinese discursive constellation. "Warm sentiment," of course, does conjure up all the touchy-feely, lachrymose effusiveness that is conventionally associated with the sentimental. At the same time, a rather different connotation is being evoked: being warm, to be exact, is being in the middle between the extremes of hot and cold, bespeaking a kind of moderation that is, interestingly, not quite the affective outpour that is the typical definition of sentimentalism. This alternative emphasis on being moderate, which readily translates into affiliate notions of being mild, tender, tolerant, obliging, and forbearing, was the reason *wenqing zhuyi* used to be targeted for criticism as bourgeois ideology by the Chinese communists. *Wenqing* was suspect because it signals an accepting attitude that is the opposite of a clear-cut determination to reject and expel.[51]

With this crucial sense of moderation in the foreground, the sentimental may thus be specified as *an inclination or a disposition toward making compromises and toward making-do with even—and especially—that which is oppressive and unbearable*. Whereas a Freudian or proto-Freudian approach to the emotions often sees them in hydraulic terms (in what Foucault has called the repressive hypothesis), as an overflow of what has been repressed, the sentimental is rather about what keeps and preserves, what holds things together. For this reason, the sentimental is perhaps best described as *a mood of endurance*, a mode whose contours tend to remain fuzzy rather than sharply delineated and whose effects may more easily be apprehended as (a prevailing) *tone*.[52] From this perspective, it is not at all surprising that the film hailed by contemporary Chinese directors and audiences alike as the sentimental masterpiece *sans pareil* is Fei Mu's *Xiaocheng zhichun* (*Springtime in A Small Town*, 1948; remake, 2002, by Tian Zhuangzhuang), a story in which disruptive emotional energies, triggered by the entry of an outsider (the wife's former intimate male friend), come into play only to result, finally, in the restoration of the status quo of a familial situation already in ruins. (Fei Mu's remarkably stylized film, now considered a classic, was denounced as decadent and reactionary at the height of communist orthodoxy in the People's Republic.)

Still, why does so much of the drama of the sentimental have to do with domesticity, the household, and the home?

Borrowing from Harry Harootunian's discussion of the twentieth-century Japanese philosopher Watsuji Tetsuro's writings on *fudo* (climate, culture, and history), I believe the interior of the house may help illuminate things at this juncture. As Harootunian writes (in explication of Watsuji), "The house constitutes the spatial container of the most primordial relationships guiding conduct in the everyday. . . . It calls attention to the space of relationality among the members of the household and to a form that derived from the most archaic experience."[53] As the material structure basic to human existence, the house is lived, we may say, as a boundary differentiating an inside holding the comfortable apart from the uncomfortable, and hence as a home—a refuge from a tyrannical world. Because it functions as a refuge, this inside also tends to take on the import of a timeless, undifferentiated, and infinitely adaptable (interpersonal) time/space whereby conflicts ought to be resolved and opposites ought to be reconciled. The modes of human relationships affectively rooted in this imagined inside—an inside whose depths of feeling tend to become intensified with the perceived aggressive challenges posed by modernity—are what I would argue as sentimental.

The English-language lexicon "accommodation" provides a felicitous encapsulation of the issues involved: as *wenqing* or moderation, the sentimental is ultimately about being accommodating and being accommodated, about the delineation and elaboration of a comfortable/homely interiority, replete with the implications of exclusion that such delineation and elaboration by necessity entail. Accordingly, what is excluded, what is banished to the outside, is believed to be antagonistic, dangerous, and evil. Reformulated in this manner, the affective excess usually attributed to the sentimental should be grasped, more precisely, as a symptom of the emotional demands—alternating between the polarized extremes of forbearance and xenophobia—exacted by the imaginary, and very much lived, relations to such interiority and its outside. The gravest problems arise, of course, when the homely—what is inside—too, is revealed to be oppressive and unbearable—indeed, uninhabitable—as we will see in the stories of some of the films to be discussed.

THE SENTIMENTAL IN THE AGE OF GLOBAL VISIBILITY

Among the various films featured in this book, a list of the situations in which the sentimental typically occurs includes some of the following, most of which are refracted through that important imagined relationship between the interior and the outside:

FILIALITY, including especially the imputed indebtedness to elders and the explicit or implicit demand for filial piety (*Temptress Moon*, *The Road Home*, *Song of the Exile*, *Eat a Bowl of Tea*, *The Wedding Banquet*, *Blind Shaft*, *The River*);

DOMESTICITY, the household or partnership arrangement in which human interactions often assume the form of caring for loved ones' physical well-being,
including performing menial chores for them, urging them to rest and relax,
and nursing them when they are sick (*Happy Together, The Road Home, In the
Mood for Love, Song of the Exile, Comrades, Almost a Love Story, Eat a Bowl of Tea,
The Wedding Banquet, Happy Times, The River*);

THE PREPARATION, CONSUMPTION, SHARING AND/OR OFFERING
OF FOOD, when food is often still a reminder of possible material scarcity
and thus a source of intimacy, pathos, and/or sinocentrism (*Happy Together, The
Road Home, In the Mood for Love, Song of the Exile, Comrades, Almost a Love Story,
Eat a Bowl of Tea, The Wedding Banquet, Happy Times, Blind Shaft, The River*);

POVERTY, or the condition of economic deprivation and social powerlessness
that sets some groups of people apart from others (*Temptress Moon, Happy Together, Comrades, Almost a Love Story, Eat a Bowl of Tea, Happy Times, Not One
Less, Blind Shaft*); in close relation to poverty is the valorization of frugality and
the practice of having savings;

CHILDHOOD AND OLD AGE, the two life stages in which people are deemed
worthy of consideration and sympathy because they are physically dependent
or frail and often helpless (*Temptress Moon, The Road Home, Song of the Exile, Eat
a Bowl of Tea, The Wedding Banquet, Happy Times, Not One Less*);

THE SIGHT OR KNOWLEDGE OF THE EXERTION OF PHYSICAL
LABOR, a condition associated alternately with poverty, hardship, undeserved
cruelty, misfortune, and low-class or subservient status (*Happy Together, The
Road Home, Comrades, Almost a Love Story, Eat a Bowl of Tea, Happy Times, Not
One Less, Blind Shaft*);

TOGETHERNESS AND SEPARATION, including departure on a journey,
migration, and physical illness (with its threat of death), as well as the appre-
hension of the transience of life itself and of fateful affinities (*Temptress Moon,
Happy Together, The Road Home, In the Mood for Love, Song of the Exile, Comrades,
Almost a Love Story, Eat a Bowl of Tea, The Wedding Banquet, Happy Times, Not
One Less, Blind Shaft*);

A PREFERENCE FOR FAMILIAL/SOCIAL HARMONY AND RECON-
CILIATION, as opposed to family/social discord and conflict—a preference
that is underwritten with demands for self-restraint and self-sacrifice, qualities that are essential to group unity (*Temptress Moon, Happy Together, Song of
the Exile, Comrades, Almost a Love Story, Eat a Bowl of Tea, The Wedding Banquet,
Blind Shaft*);

THE PASSING OF TIME, the irreversibility of which typically leaves one feeling defenseless and irrelevant and/or leads to nostalgic ruminations as ways
to reconjure or reinhabit the past (*Temptress Moon, Happy Together, The Road
Home, In the Mood for Love, Song of the Exile*);

MANIFESTATIONS OF NATURE, such as the elements, flowers in bloom,
leaves falling, rivers flowing or stagnating, and so forth—classic visual meta-
phors for change, transience, decline, loss, and other inevitable conditions that
often have the effect of taming human beings and that human beings must learn
to accept (*The Road Home, In the Mood for Love, Song of the Exile, The River*);

THE NON-NEGOTIABLE IMPERATIVE TO REPRODUCE BIOLOGI-
CALLY, a legacy of responsibility handed down from generation to generation
for the preservation and continuation of the family line (*Eat a Bowl of Tea, The
Wedding Banquet, Blind Shaft*).

In a cinema in which even renegade directors are given their places in a
hierarchical filial system (as the names "Fifth Generation," "Sixth Generation," and so forth clearly indicate),[54] the oft-encountered affective excesses surrounding domestic and familial stories would seem at first to amount
to an obvious case of ideological manipulation. As the list above suggests,
the heart-wrenching situations that many films dramatize include poverty,
interpersonal and intergenerational conflicts, separation, exile, illness,
death, and loneliness—situations in which quotidian living itself can take
on the weight of imprisonment or assault, and the most ordinary scenarios
(the memory of a pond filled with lotuses in the autumn sun; an illegal immigrant accidentally shot to death by gangsters in a cold foreign land; the
glimpse of a proud but aging father dozing off before breakfast in his son's
apartment; a hungry country boy wandering in the streets of the big city,
staring at shop windows . . .)[55] can become imbued with melancholy connotations of helplessness, loss, belatedness, or regret. From the perspective of a stringent ideology critique, such focalizations on physical or material deprivation and psychological destitution can easily be read as ways to
(re)affirm the necessity and virtue of the interior, the organic connected-
ness that is the patriarchal family, clan, village, nation, or ethnic group,
whose demands often give rise to a profound sense of entrapment yet
whose dispersal and disunity are dreaded as a kind of invasive otherness,
to be dispelled at all costs. As tragicomic stories of human fragility unfold
with moving effects, what seems perpetuated sentimentally is the myth of
the continuous growth, expansion, and reproductive power of an indomi-

table collective will, above and beyond individual difference and dissent. This is why it is possible to argue that *at the heart of Chinese sentimentalism lies the idealization of filiality*: as a predominant mode of subjectivization, filial piety is not simply a matter of respecting one's biological or cultural elders but also an age-old moral apparatus for interpellating individuals into the hierarchy-conscious conduct of identifying with—and submitting to—whatever preexists them—from the ancestral family to the ancestral land, the province, the country, and the ethnic community in a foreign nation—as authoritative and thus beyond challenge.

Although such sentimental situations are readily identifiable in the films, however, my objective is not merely to subject sentimentalism to yet another barrage of criticism by simply exposing its ideology-ridden assumptions. Rather than offering a strictly demythifying approach to the sentimental, I am also invested in articulating the ideological assumptions with the fictive but intense processes of identity negotiation. In other words, much as I am, like many of my fellow academics, suspicious of the maudlin extravagances and containment strategies that are considered a hallmark of the sentimental, my readings of the selected films are really attempts to think through the fantasy structures of accommodation and endurance that develop and multiply around such extravagances and strategies: the economic and moral forms of submission and subjectivization they solicit, the imaginary resolutions they supply to social antagonisms, and, most important, the formal and cognitive ruptures within them that, however tangentially or even unnoticeably, signal possibilities for perversion, subversion, and diversion.

Let me also formulate my interest in the sentimental in closer relation to the preceding parts of this introduction. If contemporary cultures are caught up in what I have been referring to as global visibility—the ongoing, late capitalist phenomenon of mediatized spectacularization in which the endeavor to seek social recognition amounts to an incessant production and consumption of oneself and one's group as images on display, a phenomenon in which subjectivity has become, willy-nilly, object-ivity—how do we come to terms with older—or increasingly estranged—forms of interpellations such as self-restraint, frugality, filial piety, compliance with collective obligations, inconspicuous consumption, modesty about exhibiting and thrusting oneself (including one's body parts and sexual interests) forward as a cause in public, and so forth, wherein the key is not exactly—perhaps exactly not—becoming visible? How might we go about handling the tenacity, in the midst of global visibility—itself a new kind of aggressive, oftentimes oppressive, reality—of residual significatory traces of a different kind of social behavioral order? Such traces, often emergent in the form of a vaguely anachronistic affect whose mere survival points to another modality of attachment and identification—and whose noncontemporaneity stands in mute contrast to the glamour of global visibility—are among the things I would like to see encompassed within the conceptual parameters of this study.[56]

Defined in these terms, the sentimental is thought-provoking not exactly because it allows us to rediscover something old. It is rather that the old, now lingering in the enigmatic form of an intensity (in the form of some emotionally guarded and clung-to inside) that seems neither timely nor fully communicable—especially not across cultures—should nonetheless also be acknowledged as an inherent link to the nexus of becoming visible—in the specific sense of visibility that Deleuze argues. In other words, more than simply a matter of excavating historical layers of meaning embedded in cinematic images, what I would like to get at is the process in which this second, epistemic sense of visibility—that is, a trajectory of objectification, recognition, and knowledge that may be made palpable by visual objects such as filmic images but cannot in the end be reduced to them—materializes not only in relation to the visible that is the images but also in the very sentimental interstices—the remains of a collective cultural scaffold—that lend the images their support.

The films featured in the various chapters include both popular and iconoclastic works by nine directors (Chen Kaige, Wong Kar-wai, Zhang Yimou, Ann Hui, Peter Chan, Wayne Wang, Ang Lee, Li Yang, and Tsai Ming-liang), based in the People's Republic, Hong Kong, the United States, and Taiwan. The films are grouped in three parts, each highlighting a particular articulation of the sentimental: (1) films in which the past, in the form of a time, place, or relationship, is consciously or imaginatively invoked and idealized; (2) films in which the experiences of migrancy, so often aggravated by economic hardships and ethnic discrimination, are staged against the demands of the traditional kinship family with its inordinate emphasis on genealogical continuity, financial stability, filial loyalty, and the subordination of women; (3) films in which disenfranchised populations—migrant workers, impoverished schoolchildren, and those who are handicapped, unemployed, sexually deviant, and lonesome—are explored in such manners as to make way for unconventional affective connections, which emerge, at certain junctures, simultaneously as innovative epistemic possibilities.

What engage me analytically in my readings are the manners and implications of the collision, as well as collaboration, between the multifaceted manifestations of the sentimental as I have tried to define it, on the one hand, and the narrative and visual modes found in contemporary Chinese films, on the other. Is there something about the sentimental that makes it particularly adaptable for cinematic visual display and narrative negotiation even as its meanings remain hybrid, messy, and elusive? Conversely, is there something about film as a medium—with its mechanisms of fetishistic imaging and magnification, its capacities for experimenting with narrative temporalities, and its methods of conjuring interiorities beyond verbal language—that makes it well-suited for the elaboration of sentimentalism in the late twentieth century (as the digressive and dilatational English novel, for instance, was in the eighteenth and nineteenth)? In what ways can some of the scenarios of contemporary Chinese films be construed as cinema-defining events?

Since some of the chapters originated as essays, I have left them in the form of independent discussions that can be read on their own, while stressing, whenever it is appropriate, their relevance in relation to one another and their implications for the book as a whole. In assembling the chapters together, I have also—in a manner that goes against the trends of the times—refrained from categorizing the directors and films by geopolitical determinants and particularisms such as "mainland Chinese," "Hong Kong," "Taiwan," and "Chinese diaspora" cinemas. With the uninhibited surge of mainland Chinese nationalism, fueled this time not by conditions of scarcity and deprivation (as was the case in the first three-quarters of the twentieth century) but by China's imminent ascendance to the status of an economic superpower in the twenty-first century, it is important that the term "Chinese" not be invoked in such ways as to become, automatically and at all times, the equivalent of the People's Republic. To be sure, the populations in Hong Kong, Taiwan, and other diasporic Chinese communities have been keen on affirming their autonomies, but their concurrent claims to being Chinese—in numerous historical and linguistic connections, in alternately venerational and repudiative registers—must also, I believe, be granted their legitimacy.[57] And, even where it has been made to seem entirely natural by territorial propriety, linguistic hegemony, cultural centrism, global attention, or sheer demographic stupendousness, any particular group's attempt to appropriate the term "Chinese" for itself would be best served, in the long run, not by monopoly and exclusivity but by having to coexist with similar attempts by other groups. Only in that contentious manner, whereby even a term of origin is understood as a matter of appropriation rather than as any one group's natural possession, can the competitive claims to Chineseness evolve into an open-ended, rather than a predetermined, discursive event.

In naming this book, I have borrowed the notion of fabulation in part from Nietzsche, who wrote about "How the True World Finally Became a Fable," and in part from Deleuze, who defined fabulation as a mythmaking function, central to minor cinemas, that brings together archaic and contemporary, as well as documentary and fictional, elements in the production of collective modes of storytelling, and that in turn constitutes the visionary basis for a people to come (or in the process of becoming).[58] Amid the polyphonic and polyvalent claims to Chineseness—traversed by temporalities, languages, media, and diasporic routes or grounded in stable localities and prideful chauvinisms—the sentimental (in) contemporary Chinese films, with a worldwide accessibility unprecedented among Chinese cultural forms, may yet strike the most resonant chord.

Part I

REMEMBRANCE OF THINGS PAST

FIGURE 1.1 The image of the three children gazing at the audience at the end of *Fengyue / Temptress Moon* (Copyright Shanghai Film Studios / Tomsen Films [Hong Kong], 1996)

The Seductions of Homecoming

Temptress Moon and the Question of Origins

That sentiment accompanying the absence of home—homesickness—can cut two ways: it can be a yearning for the authentic home (situated in the past or in the future) or it can be the recognition of the inauthenticity of all homes.

—ROSEMARY MARANGOLY GEORGE,
"Traveling Light: Of Immigration, Invisible Suitcases, and Gunny Sacks"

Even though it has been an overwhelmingly successful phenomenon worldwide since the late 1980s, contemporary Chinese cinema is habitually greeted by Chinese-speaking audiences with cynicism if not hostility. It is as if the accomplishments of this cinema have an impossible task in returning home. The simple fact that it has traveled abroad and been gazed at with enthusiasm by foreigners is apparently enough to cause it to lose trustworthiness as wholly and genuinely Chinese. This sentimental relation to what is firmly held as the boundary between the outside and the inside of a community and, with it, the imagined inviolable origin of a culture constitutes perhaps the single most thorny problem in the reception of this cinema among its native consumers, even as what is native itself has become an increasingly porous and unstable phenomenon.

For instance, the films of Chen Kaige and Zhang Yimou, arguably the two most well-known contemporary directors from the People's Republic, have continued to be attacked for their tendencies to pander to the tastes of Western audiences eager for the orientalized, exotic images of a China whose history they ignore, falsify, or misrepresent.[1] This problematic, with its impassioned insistence on what is authentic, is familiar to all those engaged in cross-cultural studies.[2] In the 1990s, when filmmaking and film watching were obviously global events involving ineluctable interactions with the foreign, how might a film come to terms with such insistence? Chen's 1996 film *Fengyue* (*Temptress Moon*) is, I believe, highly instructive in this regard,[3] perhaps not least because of the director's own unresolved cultural complexes. A discussion of the film may begin with the significance of place in its narrative. Place, as I shall show, is not only the setting that helps shape characters in action; it is also the locus where, in specifically filmic terms, the notions of homecoming and originality unravel as questions rather than resolutions.

THE FLIGHT FROM HOME

Topographically, *Temptress Moon* shifts back and forth between the countryside of Jiangnan (the location of the wealthy Pang clan) and the metropolis of Shanghai, which was among the first Chinese cities to be opened to foreign trade in the mid-nineteenth century (under the Treaty of Nanking, signed between China and Britain as a result of the Opium War of 1839–42). In the film, visual and architectural details combine to convey the sharp differences between the two locations, respectively, as traditional native culture and fashionable foreign enclave. The Pang family house, situated by a river, is a well-endowed ancient estate with an air of unbreakable heritage and kinship order; the solemnity and reticence typical of tribal bondage find their expression in darkish interiors with austere, muted decor. Shanghai, by contrast, is a world of gaudy kaleidoscopic colors, loud and vibrant dance-hall music, fast-moving vehicles, and ruthless, mercenary human relations. Contrary to the mood of languid eternality that shrouds the old books, arcane utensils, and antique furnishings, as well as opium-smoking habits, of the Pang household, Shanghai's living spaces are characterized by a much less permanent, because much newer, sense of time. In an apartment rented for the purpose of an illicit relationship, for instance, commodified Western artifacts such as a vase of roses, a rocking chair, a windowpane, a closet mirror, and the occasional music of a piano from afar all suggest the aura of a larger culture in the process of change. For the inhabitants of the countryside, meanwhile, everything from the port city, including clothes, shoes, hairstyles, and personal possessions such as pocket watches, slippers, razors, soaps, hats, and photographs, takes on the historic fascination of a progressive modernity—the legend, sign, and imprint that separates Shanghai from the rest of China's hinterland.

It is in Shanghai that we meet the adult figure of the leading male character, Yu Zhongliang. Zhongliang is by profession a special kind of gigolo. A key member of a Shanghai mafia in the 1910s, Zhongliang's work involves the seduction and blackmail of rich married women who are eager for amorous attention. Using the pseudonym Xiao Xie, Zhongliang would entice a woman into a secret affair; after the affair had gone on for a while, a typical scene was staged by the mafia: while Zhongliang was making love with the woman during one of their trysts, gangsters of the mafia would burst in on the scene, blindfold the woman, and threaten to report the affair to her husband unless the woman agreed to pay them a large sum of money. In the process, the woman would be told that her lover, Xiao Xie, was dead. After she was thus psychologically devastated, Zhongliang would leave quietly with his cohorts and move on to the next target.

Zhongliang's professional success is the result of his familiarity with topography of another kind—a particular strategic spot on a woman's body. Typically, as he gained intimacy with a woman, he would kiss her on one ear, nibbling at the ear until the earring came off. The earring, like Denis Diderot's "bijoux indiscrets," is therefore the site of a female sexual confession.[4] For the mafia, this memento of a single earring exists as a repeated symbol of Zhongliang's invincibility. Although every case of extortion is carried out with the announcement that Xiao Xie is dead, in the next shot Zhongliang is usually alive and well, speedily departing from the scene of destruction for the next scene of conquest. Zhongliang's ease at the two subplaces that govern his life in Shanghai—married women's earlobes and the boudoirs of clandestine affairs—makes him indispensable to the mafia. Dada (or Boss), the head of the mafia, openly speaks of Zhongliang as someone he cannot do without.

To the audience, however, the smoothness with which Zhongliang moves about in Shanghai carries a different set of connotations. When the film begins, years before his Shanghai career, Zhongliang has just arrived at the residence of the Pangs in the countryside of Jiangnan after both his parents have died. His only relative is his sister, Xiuyi, who is married to the young master Pang. Despite being officially the brother-in-law of the young master, Zhongliang is in effect treated like a servant. Between the lowly task of serving opium to his decrepit and perverse brother-in-law and the intimate, incestuous affection of his sister, the young boy is plunged into a confusing encounter with the adult world. The twin experiences of a cruel adult male and a desirous adult female culminate in a scene in which

Zhongliang's brother-in-law orders him to kiss his sister, who, sitting on the side of her bed, acquiesces smilingly by opening her arms to the boy. Fearful and reluctant, Zhongliang approaches the older woman while holding the opium-serving tray, his hands shaking violently. Amid the unforgettable sound of the opium utensils rattling against one another, his gaze arrests on one of Xiuyi's earrings.

The place that is supposed to be a home for the displaced orphan child thus serves, in terms of narrative structure, as the unbearable site of infantile seduction (in the etymological sense of the word "infant" as *in-fans*, the state of speechlessness).[5] Like many first encounters with sexuality, the meaning of his experience with the sadomasochistic relationship of the two adults eludes Zhongliang and leaves him speechless. Architecturally, the traumatic nature of this seduction is mirrored by the circular, labyrinthine structure of the Pang estate, where a seemingly infinite series of doors and chambers, each connected with and indistinguishable from the others, precludes any clear notion of entry or exit. Unable to comprehend (that is, to enter fully or leave fully behind) this primary encounter with sexuality, Zhongliang retains it through a certain repeated pattern of behavior. Having illicit relationships with married women that begin with the stealing of a single earring becomes his symptom and trademark, which turns a painful remembrance virtually into an industry. Although Zhongliang is a successful seducer, therefore, his success is presented from the beginning as a facade—a cover-up and a displacement of the uncomprehended trauma of his own seduction.

Meanwhile, there is another incident that makes it impossible for him to remain with the Pang family. Filled with resentment, he uses his opportunity of serving opium to poison his brother-in-law with a dose of arsenic, which causes the man to become brain-dead. Fearing that his murderous act will be discovered, Zhongliang escapes. This escape clarifies the teleological tendency of the narrative of *Temptress Moon*. As an adopted home for Zhongliang, the backward, decadent countryside of the Pangs is significant as the site of a sexual primal scene that has shaped his character negatively: in order to be, Zhongliang must leave. His existential autonomy, in other words, has to be established as a flight from the shock that is supposedly home—but where will he flee from there?

Zhongliang intends to head for Beijing, the site of the historic, student-led May Fourth Movement of 1919, which sought, among other things, to revolutionize and modernize the Chinese written language, literature, and culture. To make sure that the audience does not miss this point, Chen Kaige inserts a scene in which Zhongliang, like other passengers, is hurrying along the railway, shouting: "Is this the train to Beijing?" Crucially, this intention is intercepted when Zhongliang, robbed of his luggage before boarding the train, is picked up by Dada's gangsters and transported to Shanghai instead. Rather than Beijing, the enlightened capital city of modern China, in which he might have been able to receive a proper education, Zhongliang is literally abducted into a new home, the depraved underground world of Shanghai, where he soon emerges as the favorite son. He is so at home in this corrupt, commercial city that Dada, who may be regarded as Zhongliang's adopted father, says to him: "You belong to Shanghai; Shanghai cannot do without you."[6]

The escape from "home" leads not to liberation and enlightenment but rather to another type of entrapment. In the decadence of Shanghai, Zhongliang remains enslaved to an autocratic, violent, and immoral patriarchal community. His two masters, the poisonous Pangs in the countryside and the poisonous mafia in the metropolis, echo each other in the control they exert over him, and his life in Shanghai, despite its glamour and success, becomes a symmetrical double to his life in Jiangnan. One may even go so far as to say that, in fact, it is precisely as he becomes existentially autonomous and acquires agency as an adult human being that the shadow of the past begins to loom the darkest. He may have physically left "home," but psychically "home" has never left him.

This unfinished relationship with home is evident, for instance, in Zhongliang's affair with a nameless woman. In one scene, in which he is waiting for her in her apartment on Tianxiangli (Heavenly Lane) in Shanghai, we as well as he are transported by hallucinatory images from his current surroundings back to his former home: first, the woman's picture, which bears a striking resemblance to Xiuyi; then, a flashback to the scene of Zhongliang's childhood seduction; finally, the woman herself appearing, putting her hands over Zhongliang's eyes from behind—a gesture that once again reminds us of the games Xiuyi used to play with her younger brother. This attachment to a figure who visually conjures the past constitutes an obstacle in Zhongliang's job: despite Dada's urging, Zhongliang is unable to bring himself to destroy this woman. He tries to delay her destruction by prolonging their relationship. In this postponement, this reluctance to execute, we recognize the prelude to his ultimate return home.

THE HOMECOMING . . . AS YOU WISH

Dada's new target is Pang Ruyi, Xiuyi's sister-in-law, whom he wants Zhongliang to seduce. After Xiuyi's husband becomes brain-dead and leaves the clan without a male to succeed the old master, the Pang elders decide to appoint Ruyi as the head of the clan. Since Ruyi is female, they also appoint Duanwu, Ruyi's younger cousin from a poor, distant branch of the family, as her male companion.

Upon receiving instructions for his new task, Zhongliang's first reaction is a firm refusal: "As you know," he says to Dada, "I will never go to the town of the Pangs." The next thing we know, he is there against his conscious will.

Strictly speaking, Ruyi is merely the latest in Zhongliang's series of targets, but what distinguishes her from the other women is precisely her topographical location. The fact that this wealthy and powerful woman lives in his former home means that his seduction of her is inevitably commingled with a fateful revisiting of the scene of his own seduction. In the course of the film, we are made to understand that Ruyi is topographically distinctive in another sense. Unlike the women in Shanghai, Ruyi is a virgin, a "place" yet untouched by the rest of the world because, having been raised in an opium-filled house, she remains unwanted by most families looking for a prospective daughter-in-law. Despite her poisonous history, moreover, Ruyi comes across as a beautiful person with a refreshing, untainted sense of personal integrity.

Like her name, which means "as you wish," Ruyi likes to act according to her own wishes, which are, contrary to her conservative upbringing, entirely independent and liberatory. After becoming the head of the clan, for instance, she orders the retirement of her father's concubines, much to the anger of the clan elders. Then, after meeting Zhongliang, she is direct in her expression of interest in him: one day, she even asks him to teach her how to ride a bicycle. This occasion gives Zhongliang the opportunity to become intimate with her, but when he kisses her on the ear and comes away as usual with one of the earrings, Ruyi reacts by taking off the other earring and offering it to him as well. This unusual event, which epitomizes Ruyi's difference from all the other women Zhongliang has conquered, does not escape the notice of his cohort, who asks: "How come there are two earrings this time?"

If the possession of the single earring is Zhongliang's means of surviving the trauma of an illicit sexual experience, which he does not understand and must thus compulsively keep repeating—through the screening work of fetishization and continual repression—in order to attain a false sense of equilibrium, this equilibrium is now disturbed by the voluntary gift of the other earring by an unsuspecting Ruyi. By giving him the other earring, Ruyi offers Zhongliang something he had never found at home—a love that does not carry with it the connotations of enslavement, illicitness, and humiliation. As such, Ruyi's boldness and spontaneity stand as a force that has the potential of pulling Zhongliang out of the stupor that is his entire existence so far. Through this "virgin territory" that is the independent-minded woman at home, Zhongliang could have found redemption. Yet, in spite of this, he remains unmoved. In a scene following the offer of the second earring, we find him displaying disgust at Ruyi, who, being in love, has secretly gone into his room to look at his belongings. Instead of reciprocating her attention, Zhongliang merely feels resentful and loses his temper. Accusing her of a lack of respect for his privacy, he reminds her bitterly of the class hierarchy that used to separate them—that he was, at one time, a servant at her house.

THE SEDUCTION OF THE SEDUCED

The strong, innocent woman who offers him true love thus remains, topographically, a goal Zhongliang has the potential of reaching but somehow misses. Instead, he continues to aim consciously at the Ruyi that is his professional target—the rich woman to be cheated, blackmailed, and then abandoned. As in the case of his journey toward Beijing, however, Zhongliang's conscious move toward Ruyi is diverted en route, bringing about an unexpected turn in his plan. This turn occurs when Ruyi asks Zhongliang to meet her in the family boathouse by the riverside one evening. For her, it is a rendezvous with a newfound love; for him, it is an opportunity to carry out his duty and finally have sex with her. As they begin to make love, Zhongliang, confident that Ruyi is inexperienced and that he should take control, suddenly hears her confess: in order to please him (who, she believes, likes women more than girls because of the picture of the nameless woman she has seen in his belongings), she says, she has already had sex with Duanwu. She has deliberately gotten rid of her virginity so that he would love her.

Zhongliang's face at this point has nothing of the look of someone who is happy at discovering that he is being loved. Instead, it is contorted with anguish. Since the film narrative does not offer any explanation, we must use the clues we have to speculate. Ruyi's independent behavior overwhelms Zhongliang, we might say, not because she has casually given her virginity to someone whom she does not really love or even because she has performed a selfless deed for his sake. Rather, it overwhelms him because she has unwittingly plunged him into the abyss of his own past. For, in sacrificing her virginity, her integrity, for him, is Ruyi not exactly like the other women and ultimately like Xiuyi? And is Ruyi's incestuous relationship with Duanwu not a frightful mirror image of Xiuyi's incestuous relationship with Zhongliang years ago? With the binding intensity of the unanticipated déjà vu, Ruyi's confession strikes Zhongliang as if it were his own flashback, his own involuntary memory: though (and perhaps precisely as) a picture performed by others, it forces him to recognize himself. Like the character Cheng Dieyi in Chen's popular film *Farewell My Concubine* (1993), who is finally tamed by the sight of a performance of the story he has been resisting, Zhongliang is finally tamed and, instead of seducing others, becomes seduced once again into playing the role that is his destiny.[7]

If this chance (re)seduction of Zhongliang, which constitutes the major narrative turning point, can be described as the ultimate meaning of his homecoming, what is the relationship between seduction and home? Etymologically, "seduction" refers to a leading astray, the opposite of going home. As the paradigm of Odysseus demonstrates, a man must, in order to return home, be determined to stave off seduction—to refuse to succumb to the sirens. In *Temptress Moon*, importantly, this classic opposition between home and seduction has broken down. Consciously, indeed, home is what Zhongliang resists and rejects, and yet in his negative, flighty mode as a professional seducer, he seems nonetheless to keep turning back, to keep clinging to something he does not fully comprehend. And, as he tries to ignore his own feelings about home and ventures forth with the task of seduction in cold-blooded indifference toward everyone at home, including the innocent woman who loves him, what he stumbles upon is none other than the homely (intimate), yet also seduced (gone-astray), part of himself.

Seductions of the former home involve the memory of and attachment to the entire scenario of Zhongliang's early years, a scenario composed by particular configurations of relationships in their enigmatic violence and intensity. Such violence and intensity have remained unrecognized, we may say, until Zhongliang sees them in the form of an other, an image presented by another person. If this imaging of how "others do it" may be described as a visual guide to home, then homecoming itself is, strictly speaking, a second-order seduction, a seduction of the already seduced. Working by the force of memory, which erupts at the sight/site of that which has already been experienced once before, this homecoming can be extraordinarily powerful. In fact, it is lethal.

What is most interesting about this double seduction—this state of being seduced encountering itself at the sight/site of an other—is that it no longer revolves around one particular character. At the point of Zhongliang's discovery of Ruyi's relationship with Duanwu, the story line of *Temptress Moon* is no longer narratologically reducible to the relationship between the leading characters, Zhongliang and Ruyi, but must instead be understood as a compound series of relationships involving differentiations on multiple planes and scales—sexual, familial, class, rural, metropolitan, modern, and feudalist. Such differentiations, moreover, exceed any restrictive hierarchical arrangement. A diagram would help clarify their superimposed nature as follows:

Zhongliang and Xiuyi	:	Duanwu and Ruyi	:	Zhongliang and.Ruyi
Zhongliang and Xiuyi	:	Zhongliang and women in Shanghai	:	Zhongliang and woman at Tianxiangli
Zhongliang and the Pangs	:	Zhongliang and the Shanghai mafia		
Zhongliang and the Shanghai mafia	:	Duanwu and the Pangs		

In these relationship series, every character becomes the narrative hinge for the emergence and development of another character, and every relationship becomes the double of another relationship. The subjectivity of a character is hence no longer a matter of his/her inner world but the result of his/her interactions with others. Accordingly, the significance of each character no longer has an independent value but can only be established through his/her entanglement with other characters. While this point may be obvious, it is still worth emphasizing in consideration of our persistently essentialist ways of thinking about characterization (as real-life persons). In *Temptress Moon*, because meaning cannot stabilize upon such multilayered relationships, characterization takes on a topographical or even archaeological significance: characters themselves become intersecting places or crossroads, digs or ruins, all with multifaceted messages. In the case of Zhongliang, for instance, character is the meeting of a prehistory, in which lie the remnants of a traumatic experience that he does not understand and cannot express, and a posthistory, which is a belated, deferred reimaging, in the form of an other (scene), of that prehistory. If the ineluctability of this meeting is an ineluctable return home, then homecoming itself is always (the repetition of) a going-astray, a departure that already began some time ago.

THE MAN IN FLIGHT, THE WOMEN BOUND, AND THE COUNTRY BUMPKIN TURNED NOUVEAU RICHE

As the film approaches its end, Zhongliang is unsettled by his own feelings for Ruyi but must still fulfill his duty to Dada. Dada has meanwhile sensed that Zhongliang has changed. In order to prevent further harm, he decides to stage a scene in which Ruyi will discover for herself Zhongliang's identity as a gigolo. Dada is convinced that, once Ruyi sees this, she will no longer love Zhongliang, and Zhongliang will have to become once again his professionally cool and efficient self. This exposure of Zhongliang happens in Shanghai. By intricate arrangements, Ruyi is indeed forced to witness Zhongliang's act from the window of an apartment opposite his in Shanghai: he is making love to the woman on Tianxiangli for the last time; the gangsters break in in their usual fashion, threatening the woman, and so forth. Only this time, the woman, who refuses to be blindfolded and insists on confronting Zhongliang, commits suicide on learning the truth.

Contrary to Dada's expectations, Ruyi remains determined in her love for Zhongliang. Even so, she is unable to hear from Zhongliang what she wants the most—the verbal affirmation that he, too, loves her. Heartbroken, Ruyi returns to the countryside and prepares to marry another man. Hearing that Ruyi is to get married, Zhongliang hurries back to his former home once more and confesses that he does, in fact, love her. He even proposes that the two of them elope to Beijing "for real this time." Ruyi refuses to change her mind. In despair, Zhongliang replicates the other critical episode that resides in the "primal scene": just as he used arsenic to poison his brother-in-law, so he now prepares a dose of opium mixed with arsenic for Ruyi, who consumes it unawares and becomes brain-dead as well. This act of poisoning completes the saga of Zhongliang's homecoming. As he tries to escape again from the countryside, he is gunned down by Dada's gangsters. If his initial arrival at the Pangs' family residence—by boat at night, through water—is a kind of birth, then the countryside now serves also as his tomb.

Throughout the film, Zhongliang's character is portrayed with a compelling depth, which is the result, ironically, of his need from the very first to escape. Like many writers of the May Fourth period, during which Chinese literature became self-consciously modern, Chen Kaige relies for the construction of male subjectivity on what may be called the paradigm of fright and flight.[8] Hence, just as in *Farewell My Concubine*, *Temptress Moon* is full of instances of exaggerated music and sound, body movements, close-ups, and dialogues that, together with the cinematography (by Christopher Doyle) featuring fast-moving shots and changes of shots, amplify the effects of a psychologically persecuted male character who seems always on the run.[9] In narratological terms, Zhongliang is hence constituted—visually and aurally as well as through the plot—by patterns of departure that help convey all the questions of his identity—What is Zhongliang running from? Where is he going? Whom will he meet on the way? and so forth. This negative pose of a male character on the run is a kind of fury or resistance that, ultimately, delivers him home against his will. At the same time, if such a male psyche is the legacy of a mainstream modernism that defines itself in opposition to the socius, what is revealed in the seductions of Zhongliang's homecoming is perhaps the fragility of this dissident masculinity as inscribed in the paradigm of fright and flight, a paradigm that is subverted by the network of characters and relationships that sprawl around Zhongliang like a labyrinth. In the light of this unwilling captivity—and demise—of the man in flight, the women characters become very interesting.

Unlike Zhongliang, the women characters are all place-bound, in terms of both their physical and their mental locations: Xiuyi is stuck in the countryside and in her bond to a brain-dead husband; the women of the metropolis are trapped by the Shanghai way of life and by their own illicit sexual desires; even Ruyi, who is the most independent of all, remains a prisoner of her home and her heart. (Even though she is about to get married at the end, she consumes opium one more time simply because it has been prepared by Zhongliang, the man she once loved.)[10] However, if these women are ultimately victimized in various ways by their topographical and bodily confinement (a loveless marriage, psychological destruction, suicide, and brain damage), the bold defiance of patriarchal culture expressed by each of them nevertheless signifies a different concept of flight and departure that may, in due course, not have to lead back to the home that is the original place of captivity. As I have commented elsewhere, Chen is, despite his avowed interest, typically ambiguous and ambivalent in the manner he handles questions regarding women. Here, as always, he has left the implications of the women characters' fates in the form only of a suggestion, a possibility in all its open-endedness.[11]

Indirectly, Zhongliang's homecoming is what causes the power of the Pang clan to pass to Ruyi's servant-companion Duanwu. Like Zhongliang, Duanwu has been exploited by an older female for sexual purposes, but unlike Zhongliang, he seems to be unperturbed by this initiation. He remains loyal to Ruyi until they reach Shanghai, where he discovers, he says, the war between the sexes. After Ruyi fails to confirm that Zhongliang loves her, Duanwu rapes her. Later, as they arrive home, he even exposes her relationships with both him and Zhongliang to the man she is about to marry. At the end, as Ruyi becomes permanently brain-damaged by arsenic, Duanwu logically succeeds her as the head of the clan. Like most characters in the film, that of Duanwu is far from being well-developed (his abrupt transformation in Shanghai, for instance, is unexplained and lacks persuasiveness), but he is thought-provoking as a type. What Duanwu stands for, in contrast to Zhongliang, is a new type of man—a new class perhaps—who has been abused but who somehow manages not to have repressed and internalized such abuse; instead, when the right moment occurs, this type of man turns the violence he has experienced to his own advantage by directing it at fresh victims. Lacking the sensitivity and self-doubt, and hence vulnerability, of Zhongliang, Duanwu makes it to the top through petty cunning, hypocrisy, and opportunism. His success, Chen's film seems to say, is the vulgar success of the country bumpkin turned nouveau riche.[12]

FILMMAKING AS HOMECOMING

For a filmmaker, the paths of seduction lie not only in narrativization or characterization but also in the specifics of film language. Is the movie screen not the ultimate place of an irresistible allure? If China and Chinese history are the home to which Chen attempts to return, what might be said about the particular homecoming that is filmmaking?

The story of *Temptress Moon* takes place at a crucial moment in the historical meeting between East and West—the 1911 Revolution, after which China shifted from the imperial to the republican era. Having been documented, described, debated, and fantasized countless times, this moment can indeed be rewritten—schematically, of course—as a certain primal scene in which violence and progress converge and in which the traditional, imperial patriarchal society gives way, albeit sluggishly, to a Westernized and modernized state, henceforth to be ruled by the will of the people. A contemporary Chinese director's revisiting of this, modern China's critical historical moment, much like Zhongliang's revisiting of his former home at the Pangs, cannot be naive or simplistically nativist. This is probably why, besides the convoluted narrative and the superimposed effects of characterization, Chen's film is also remarkably reminiscent of other films about modern China. To that extent, *Temptress Moon* stands as an assemblage of allusions, often calling to mind previous films that one has seen.[13]

To cite a striking example of pure screen resemblance: in the scene in which Duanwu is to receive the honor of being appointed as the companion to Ruyi, who has just been made the head of the clan, the young boy is shown rushing into the ancestral parlor while the entire clan stands in observation of the ceremony. In a great hurry, Duanwu throws his proper clothes on while running. In the context of the story of *Temptress Moon*, such a demonstration of haste is rather illogical—there is no reason why Duanwu should need to rush in the manner he does—until we realize that the scene is probably an allusion to a scene in the prolific Chinese director Li Hanxiang's *Huoshao yuanming yuan* (*Burning of the Imperial Palace*, 1983).[14] In Li's film, which is set during the reign of the late Qing Emperor Xian Feng, there is a scene featuring Prince Gong (Prince Kung), one of the emperor's brothers, as he rushes from Beijing to attend Xian Feng's funeral in Rehe (Jehol) in 1861. Since, by historical account, clothing for different imperial occasions was greatly ritualized and since the prince had been summoned from Beijing on short notice, the character in Li's film is shown to be throwing on the proper funeral garb befitting the brother of the emperor as he dashes into the funeral parlor. Chen probably so liked the compelling ambience of that scene that he decided to re-create it in his own work, even when it is not contextually necessary.

But the film that has left its marks most vividly on Chen's is, interestingly, not one made by a Chinese director but Bernardo Bertolucci's *The Last Emperor*, a film in which Chen was an extra, playing one of the anonymous guards standing at the entrance to the palace. It was from this film that Chen made copious imaginative borrowings, from the construction of characters and narrative episodes to the use of architecture, interior decor, lighting, and individual screen images. For instance, just as the bulk of the story of *The Last Emperor* is historically situated in the transition period between the Qing Dynasty and the Republic of China, so does the story of *Temptress Moon* begin with the 1911 Revolution, when the Qing Dynasty officially ended, and last until around 1920.[15] The poignancy of this epochal moment is in both cases portrayed through the life of a child—Pu Yi, the boy emperor, in one case and Ruyi, the future successor to the "throne" of the Pang clan, in the other. Both children are held captive in a privileged environment that is represented, with fascination, as out of sync with modern times. Like the little Pu Yi, Ruyi is full of mischief. In an early scene, she has to be chased out of the ancestral parlor where girls are not allowed; the doors the elders close in order to shut her inside her quarters are, in terms of cinematographic angles, a clear imitation of the high imperial gates that shut Pu Yi in the Forbidden City.

Like Pu Yi also, Ruyi ascends to power by accident, when a proper male heir has failed to appear at the necessary moment. When she becomes the head of the Pang clan, Ruyi, once again reminding us of Pu Yi, introduces unprecedented policies that cause great consternation. Her order to retire her father's concubines, an act reminiscent of Pu Yi's historic order to retire the palace eunuchs, is shown to be a rather futile attempt at household reform. (The scene in which the concubines leave the family estate is visually reminiscent of the one in Bertolucci's film in which the royal family, led by the grown emperor, is forced to leave the Forbidden City.) Above all, being cloistered in the prisonlike world of her family town, Ruyi is ignorant of and longing for the new, modernized world outside. The arrival of Zhongliang from Shanghai, then, is not unlike the arrival of Reginald Johnston, Pu Yi's Scottish tutor, who brings Western education to the young emperor, including the fashionable item of a bicycle—an important detail that Chen did not neglect to include in his story.

The point of mentioning some of the borrowings Chen has quite obviously made from other films is not to accuse him of plagiarism or lack of originality. Rather, it is to emphasize that, like writing, filmmaking, too, is conditioned by the utterances of others, the references others have made in and of the past. In the case of film, of course, the more accurate word to use would be "gazes," and what I have been referring to as allusions should therefore be understood not simply as plot contents or even simply as images but also as ways of gazing that have been inscribed in previous films. For a contemporary Chinese director making a film about modern China, the questions are daunting: if making a film about one's own culture is a certain kind of homecoming, how does one go about mediating between the desire for portraying that home exactly as one thinks one knows it and the repertoire of ways of seeing it that have already been offered by numerous others and experienced by millions more? In light of the thematics of place, then, the older films of Li, Bertolucci, and others must be regarded as so many versions of a topos in its dual resonance as geography and as knowledge. Capturing the physical place, modern China, on film, these directors' works have also become sites of visual learning—archives of seeing—on which directors such as Chen draw for their own artistic installations of China. As these others' gazes beckon in their orientalist, exoticizing, and/or meticulously historical modes, the homecoming that is filmmaking inevitably becomes a process of citation and re-viewing and— even as one manages to produce a fresh collage of perspectives—of being (re)seduced with the sights/sites of others.

To return to the question of authentic origins raised at the beginning of this chapter, it seems virtually impossible for a director such as Chen to be authentic or original—if by those two words we mean the quality of being bona fide to the point of containing no impurities, no traces of others. Once this is understood, we will realize that, paradoxically, such impossibility is exactly the reason Chen's film can be so provocative. Not being authentic or original here translates into a remarkable filmic self-consciousness, a reflexive visual coming-to-terms with the myriad ways modern China has already been looked at by others, Chinese and non-Chinese, for more than a century and a half.

THE FINAL IMAGE OF HOMESICKNESS

And yet, despite offering a self-conscious statement of what filmmaking amounts to in the postcolonial age by incorporating into his own film others' gazes and perspectives, Chen seemed unwilling or unable to overcome a familiar kind of sentimental emotion in relation to home—nostalgia. As in a number of his other works (notably, *Yellow Earth*, *King of the Children*, *Life on a String*, *Farewell My Concubine*, and *Together*), he expressed this emotion through figures of children. For his concluding image, Chen inserted an early scene from the childhood years of Ruyi, Duanwu, and Zhongliang: Ruyi and Duanwu are playing and running with their backs to the audience; Zhongliang, slightly older, is coming from the opposite

direction, facing us. As Ruyi and Duanwu turn their heads, the three children are looking at us at the same time. This moment is frozen as the final
still (fig. 1.1). This image, recalling similar images (of children looking at the
audience) earlier in the film and placed prominently at the end, stands as
a suggestive rejoinder to an exclamation once made by Zhongliang: "How
nice it would be," he says, "if only we didn't have to grow up!"

In terms of theorizations of the gaze, this visual conclusion conjures the
specific ontological-representational relation that, according to the philosophical critic Slavoj Žižek, may be posited between nostalgia and children.
In the nostalgic mode, Žižek argues, what tends to fascinate one is not so
much a displayed scene (or a visual image) in and by itself as "a certain
gaze, the gaze of the 'other,' of the hypothetical, mythic spectator" who is
still able to "take it seriously." "The innocent, naïve gaze of the other that
fascinates us in nostalgia," he writes, "is in the last resort always the gaze
of the child."[16] The important point to note in Žižek's remarks, I should
emphasize, is not exactly the figure of the child as such but rather that the
child is (simply) the paradigmatic case of the hypothetical or mythic spectator. In other words, the child's putative way of gazing—a way of gazing
that holds such fascination for some—is already a wishful construct on the
part of those who feel nostalgic.

From what/whose perspective, then, are the three children seen/per-
ceived in the way they are seen/perceived at the end of *Temptress Moon*?

In that image, as they gaze at us, the children are mute; we don't know
what they are thinking. What we do know, however, is that, as children,
they were never allowed to be innocent, naive, or happy; childhood for
them was never idyllic but filled with neglect, abuse, and loneliness. Curi-
ously, in spite of the knowledge that his film has presented, this ending
supplied by Chen (in the form of a visual corollary to the verbal wish not to
grow up) seems rather a deliberate erasure/forgetting of such knowledge.
In terms of the thematics of place, what this pivotal image evokes is none
other than utopia, a nonplace. Unidentifiable with any tangible location or
experience (especially not with the children's actually lived lives, as shown),
this nonplace is tantamount to a vanishing point at which a crystallization
and convergence—and thus an imaginary unity—are being forged among
otherwise disparate narrative elements.

By making it necessary to ask: "To whom does childhood look like this?"
this final image also makes us understand various narrative elements for
the first time as tendencies of idealization that have, in fact, been pres-

ent throughout the story from the beginning. Whether by way of plot, characterization, or final screen image, what is persistently idealized is a certain notion of the (authentic) origin—of the origin, moreover, as what is beyond the here and now, as what will remain inaccessible, indeed non-existent. Hence, just as Zhongliang's journey toward Beijing and his designs on Ruyi become derailed, so, too, does the maneuver to "remember" the blissfulness of childhood amount to nothing. The enlightened Chinese capital of Beijing, with its authentic revolutionary modernity (as opposed to the vulgar commercial modernity of Shanghai); the pure virgin girl of the native countryside (as opposed to the unchaste, adulterous women in the debauched Westernized city); and the naive, innocent gazes of children (as opposed to those of scheming, experienced adults) all turn out to be unreachable places—yet precisely because they are unreachable, they are all the more to be longed for. What has become unraveled is the vicious circle of a cultural complex in which idealism leads, as it always does, to homesickness and vice versa, ad infinitum.

Ironically, the implications of Chen's concluding image put him much closer to the critics who like to accuse him and his fellow directors of forsaking the authentic China. In their obstinate adherence to fantasies of the origin as what has not been touched—be it in the form of a mythical Chineseness, a pristine native tradition descending from Beijing, female intactness, or childhood innocence—even as the vices and profanities of Shanghai pose irresistible attraction, the director and his critics are finally united as sentimental perpetrators of a certain type of homecoming with its well-trodden seductive paths. As they probably know only too well, such paths lead nowhere, but that is probably also why their homesickness persists.

FIGURE 2.1 Fai and Bo-wing dancing, *Chunguang zhaxie / Happy Together*
(Copyright Block 2 Pictures / Jet Tone Production / Prénom H / Seowoo Film, 1997)

2 Nostalgia of the New Wave

Romance, Domesticity, and the Longing for Oneness in *Happy Together*

In one of the earliest discussions of poststructuralism to appear in English, "Of Structure as an Inmixing of an Otherness Prerequisite to Any Subject Whatever," Jacques Lacan put across a notion of structure that would henceforth have significant ramifications on the way identity is theorized across the human sciences. This was during the late 1960s, when structuralism, having been an intellectual trend in Europe for some time, had belatedly crossed the Atlantic and become controversial in select North American academic circles. Lacan, like his younger contemporary Jacques Derrida, was working against the more traditional and widely accepted philosophical assumptions about structure, which tended to see structure as the systematic relation between the part and the whole, with the whole being given priority as a unitary or central governing totality. Unity, Lacan wrote, has always been considered "the most important and characteristic trait of structure." Instead of unitariness, Lacan introduced the possibility of thinking about structure in terms of otherness, which he explained in part by appealing to Frege's parsing of numbers. In even the most elementary process of counting, he argued, it is always a subsequent number that holds the meaning of the one preceding it:

> When you try to read the theories of mathematicians regarding numbers you find the formula "n plus 1" ($n + 1$) as the basis of all the theories. It is this ques-

tion of the "one more" that is the key to the genesis of numbers and instead of this unifying unity that constitutes two in the first case I propose that you consider the real numerical genesis of two.

It is necessary that this two constitute the first integer which is not yet born as a number before the two appears . . . the *two* is here to grant existence to the first *one*: put *two* in the place of *one* and consequently in the place of the *two* you see *three* appear.[1]

Lacan's confusion of logical sequence with temporal sequence was a deliberate provocation. Albeit still in the heyday of structuralism, what he was arguing in this passage was, of course, already a poststructuralist way of understanding structure itself as a temporal process governed by nonidentity (or difference). Accordingly, a structure (such as an integer), no matter how integrated (as one) it appears, must be understood to be the effect of retroaction—a belated conferral of meaning on an event (such as the number 1) that does not have such a meaning until it has been repeated in another, subsequent event (the number 2). The nonitalicized word "two," then, stands in Lacan's passage both as the number/integer 2 and as the second, deferred space of a repeated event. The phrase "one more," which Lacan used to describe the genesis of numbers, Jacques Derrida would, in his own equally famous arguments, call "supplementarity" or "play," which tends to be repressed or restricted within the normative understanding of structure. Whereas Lacan problematized the unity or oneness attributed to structure, Derrida would problematize the notions of origin and center and their accompanying metaphysics of presence.[2]

The point of these brief and simplistic recalls of otherness (with its vast implications for subjectivity) and supplementarity (with its vast implications for language and the text) is not to instigate another round of debate about the master theorists of poststructuralism. It is, rather, to use them as a kind of historical and theoretical shorthand with which to argue the critical interest of what may at first appear to be a rather distant event, a contemporary film by Hong Kong director Wong Kar-wai. If the major epistemic rupture introduced by early poststructuralism can be summarized by the formula $1 = 1+$, how might this rupture inform the reading of a cultural work such as a film, a love story between two men?

Lacan and Derrida, in other words, are juxtaposed with Wong Kar-wai here in the manner Wong's screen images are often juxtaposed with one another—by means of a deliberate cut, so as to introduce an unforeseen conceptual relation. This cut is intended as a way to counter the tendency toward reflectionism and analytical reductionism in the reading of non-Western cultural work in general (so that a film made in Hong Kong around 1997, for instance, is invariably approached as having something to do with the factographic, geopolitical reality of Hong Kong's return to the People's Republic of China.)[3] While a detailed analysis of such a tendency and its complicity with a specific type of cross-cultural interpretative politics can only be made on a different occasion,[4] it would be salutary, it seems to me, to attempt an analysis that consciously departs from it. The montage of Lacan and Derrida, then, serves the function of highlighting certain epistemic problems—of structure and its accompanying metaphysics—that often recur in Wong's work in the guises of romance, domesticity, and a longing for happiness. In *Happy Together* (1997), the film that brought Wong the Best Director Award at the Cannes Film Festival of the same year, these epistemic problems come into focus in a remarkable fashion.

"LET'S START OVER AGAIN": NOSTALGIA FOR A MYTHIC BEGINNING

Let me proceed by suggesting that *Happy Together* can be seen as a nostalgic film. This may surprise some readers for the simple fact that nostalgia is most commonly understood as the sentiment of homesickness, which may extend into a tendency to reminisce about old times or to romanticize what happened in the irretrievable past, whereas Wong's film is decidedly a work of Hong Kong's New Wave cinema,[5] both in terms of its technical aspects—its avant-garde, experimental use of image, color, sound, and editing and in terms of its content—a love affair between two men in the 1990s.[6] Unlike many contemporary Chinese films, Wong's work does not seem to be emotionally invested in the usual sites of nostalgia such as rural life or the remote areas of China or, for that matter, in anything having to do with the ideologically oppressive but visually spectacular Chinese cultural tradition. How can a film like this be described as nostalgic, and what is its relationship with the old and with the past as such?

The first clue, I think, lies in the titling of the film itself. The Chinese title, *Chun Gwong Tsa Sit/Chunguang zhaxie* (in Cantonese and Mandarin), literally meaning the "unexpected leakage of scenes of spring," is an idiom for the surprising revelation of erotic sights, and as a film title it is a replication of the Chinese translation of Michelangelo Antonioni's *Blow Up* (a film adapted from a story by the Argentinian author Julio Cortázar), when the latter was shown in Hong Kong in the 1960s.[7] In many ways, of course, the phrase *chun gwong tsa sit* is entirely apt for the sensual aspects of Wong's film, which indeed amount to a revelation of an erotically charged relationship. Although the Chinese title puts the spotlight on the eroticism of the relationship, however, it is, as I will argue, the English title, *Happy Together* (with the subtitle *A Story About Reunion*), that more precisely signals the nostalgia embedded in the story, loosely adapted from the little-known novella *A Buenos Aires Affair* by Manuel Puig. Indeed, the bilingualism and multiway translations of the film title raise some interesting questions: what is this film really about, and what is the relationship between the erotic as such—the so-called scenes of spring—and the state of being happy together? If eros has customarily been construed as "2 becoming 1" (or $1+1 = 1$) in classical philosophy, what does it tell us about the structure of oneness? Do eros and happiness complement each other, or are they incommensurable events?

Like some of Wong Kar-wai's other films, the story here revolves around a melodic popular song with a catchy refrain:[8] the state of being happy together is thus literally a theme both in the musical and in the narrative sense. At the same time, narratologically speaking, this theme is a frustrated one: despite the suggestiveness of the music, it is clear from the narrative that being happy together is a difficult, perhaps impossible, project. In this regard, the music itself, though sensorially familiar, is also a signifier with no real referent; it is as if the more readily we recognize the tune "Happy Together," the more we must notice the actual gap, the discontinuity, between what we hear and what we experience through the narrative.

The film narration begins with the voice-over of Lai Yiu-fai telling us about his ongoing relationship with Ho Bo-wing.[9] The two lovers have traveled from Hong Kong all the way to Argentina, hoping to see with their own eyes the famous Iguazu Falls. Like many lovers, Fai and Bo-wing often quarrel and break up, but after being separated for a while Bo-wing usually suggests: "Let's start over again" (literally, "Let's begin again from the beginning" in the Chinese). In this manner, the tortuous relationship continues.

In terms of this discussion about structure, the plea to start over again bespeaks a desire for a new point of departure. This seemingly simple and innocent plea is, nonetheless, self-contradictory. At the heart of the plea is an "as if": let's start over again as if all that has already happened did not happen. If "1" may be seen as a figure for a new beginning, its firstness, so to speak, is only held together by this wish and haunted from within by "1+," the otherness that is its past. Even as 1 is invoked as a way to clean up/forget that past, therefore, it is inextricably enmeshed in it. "From the beginning," as it were, is always already a repetition and an excess.

This fundamental ambiguity about origins—a theme that *Happy Together* shares with *Temptress Moon*—is staged in the film through the handling of eros. Near the beginning of Fai's narration, a scene of the two men having sex appears. This scene, shot in black-and-white, is the only one in the entire film in which the physical coupling of the two men is presented thoroughly without constraint and in which they seem to climax together. It is entirely possible to interpret this erotic scene as part of an act of recollection—as part of a memory of what has supposedly already receded into the past. Even so, it would be insufficient to conclude that such remembrance alone is what constitutes nostalgia. As I will demonstrate, the nostalgia projected by the film complicates the purely chronological sense of remembering the past as such.

The series of black-and-white shots featuring the physical entanglement of the lovers is, in terms of effects, quite distinct from other scenes in the film. It is, to be sure, a moment of erotic passion, but it is also what we may call a moment of indifferentiation, a condition of perfect unity that was not only chronologically past (perhaps) but also seemingly *before difference and separation*. A moment like this, placed at the beginning of the film, cannot help being evocative. It brings to mind myths of origins such as that of Adam and Eve in the Garden of Eden. Are these images of passionate togetherness, then, indeed a recollection of something that actually happened, or are they part of a fantasy, a conjuring of something that never took place? We do not know. In terms of narrative structure, therefore, these images of copulation constitute not merely a remembered incident but, more important, *an enigmatic beginning in the form of an other time, an otherworldly existence*. The images are unforgettable because their ontological status is, strictly speaking, indeterminable.

But whether or not this series of "primal scenes" actually took place, both men apparently desire to return to the reality they conjure. This desire to return to some other life, imagined as a union that existed once upon a time, is, I believe, the most important dimension of the nostalgia projected by this film. Nostalgia in this case is no longer an emotion attached to a concretely experienced, chronological past; rather, it is attached to a fantasized state of oneness, to a time of absolute coupling and indifferentiation that may nonetheless appear in the guise of an intense, indeed delirious, memory. From this perspective, Wong's style of nostalgia differs significantly in aim from that of other contemporary Chinese directors.

Among the films made in the 1980s and 1990s by the Fifth Generation Chinese directors from the People's Republic, for instance, nostalgia usually assumes the form of cultural self-reflection, by way of stories about traditional China, as represented by rural life or remote geographical areas beyond Han Chinese boundaries. (The conceptualization of the Pang family estate in Chen Kaige's *Temptress Moon* is still within the parameters of such nostalgic cultural self-reflection.) Directors from Taiwan and Hong Kong, on the other hand, often convey nostalgia in the form of a fascination with legendary eras with clear moral divisions, such as are found in martial arts (kung fu) movies. (Ang Lee's international blockbuster *Wohu canglong/Crouching Tiger, Hidden Dragon* [2000] is simply the most famous recent example of a longstanding generic convention.) There are also the works featuring modern and contemporary society with their typically contradictory feelings about the rural or colonized past, which is at once idealized and resented: we may include here not only those films about diasporas, exiles, and emigration to the West and about "home" visits to China (see the discussions in part 2 of this book) but also those films in which a particular form of traditional performing art or craft (such as Beijing or Cantonese opera) is being thematized. Nostalgia, in other words, can be found everywhere in contemporary Chinese cinema, but the object of nostalgia—that which is remembered and longed for—is, arguably, often in the form of a concrete place, time, and event.

The nostalgia that surfaces in Wong's urban films is, of course, also traceable to concrete places, times, and events (for example, the gangsters' haven of Mongkok in *Wangjiao kamen/As Tears Go By*; the protagonist's journey to the Philippines to look for his birth mother or the clock pointing at three in *A fei zhengzhuan/Days of Being Wild*; the derelict, crime-infested Chungking Mansion and the fetishized canned pineapples with their "use by" dates in *Chongqing senlin/Chungking Express*; the claustrophobic tunnels, dark alleys, tiny apartments, and bustling shops and restaurants in Hong Kong in *Duoluo tianshi/Fallen Angels*; the styles of 1960s fashions and household objects in Hong Kong in *Huayang nianhua/In the Mood for Love* and *Er ling si liu/2046*, and so forth).[10] But the concretely identifiable markers in his stories seem at the same time to give way to something more intangible and elusive. As Wong himself puts it, all his works tend to "revolve around one theme: the communication among human beings."[11] With this predominant interest in human communication, the nostalgia expressed in his films is, we may surmise, not simply a hankering after a specific historical past. Instead, the object for which his films are nostalgic is what we may call a flawless union among people, a condition of togetherness in multiple senses of the term. This is a condition that can never be fully attained but is therefore always longed for.

Whereas in *Temptress Moon* the nostalgic pursuit of what is unreachable is recognizable through the idealization of modern Beijing, a rural virgin woman's offer of love, and innocent children's gazes, in *Happy Together* such a pursuit is clearest in the relationship between Fai and Bo-wing. In terms of personalities, the two men are portrayed as opposites: one is earnest and faithful; the other is an irresponsible scumbag. How could there be a long-lasting union between two such different people? And yet it is precisely on their impossible, indeed hopeless, involvement that Wong constructs the theme of being "happy together."[12]

This wishful imagining of, or gesturing back to, an originary state of togetherness—a kind of Edenic perfection in human relationships—against a profound understanding of the tragic differences that divide human beings is characteristic of a certain irreverent romanticist tendency, found also in many modernist works. In this regard, the English title of Wong's film, *Happy Together*, is perhaps more appropriate than the Chinese title because it accurately captures this romanticist and modernist structuring of desire. Etymologically, the word "happy" in English can be traced to roots such as *hap* and *fit*. Apart from its common meaning of feeling good, "happy" also carries connotations of happenstance, coincidence, good luck, and the felicitous fit. These connotations suggest that happiness is, philosophically speaking, an expression of the condition of unitariness—a condition supposedly before separation, difference, and conflict; a condition that is, in biblical terms, before the fall.

Once these implicit connotations of happiness are underscored, we begin to comprehend why one place seems to appear with regularity in Wong's films—the home. As the well-known Hong Kong film critic Shi Qi (Sek Kei) comments: "Wong Kar-wai's films are characterized by a basic structure. . . . Apart from the bond between men, there is also a tenacity expressed toward old, decrepit homes, which serve as a refuge from the wild and dangerous jungle outside, and as the only kind of place belonging to oneself and one's loved ones. . . . Few directors have made use of the home as frequently as he . . . whether it is Mongkok, the Central District in Hong Kong, the wilderness, or Argentina, the home [in Wong's films] looks more or less the same, providing a personalized space in the midst of a foreign land."[13]

As in the case of *Temptress Moon*, the significance placed on the home in *Happy Together* obliges us to ask: what exactly *is* the home? Why is there such an obsession with the home and with homelessness in so many modern and contemporary works, East and West? (The current academic interest in the themes of diaspora, exile, travel, migration, and their like is, properly speaking, part and parcel of this obsession as well.) Is it possible to argue that, much like happiness, the home is, from a modernist perspective at least, the sign of a primary unitariness, of an origin that is perceived to be under the threat of human conflict? Home in this modernist construction is not only a matter of family or kinship ties (as it often is in other films discussed in this book), and, even though it may be personalized (as Shi Qi's remarks suggest), its significance is much more than that of a personal residence and refuge. As an ideal form of togetherness, the home also carries the transcendental meaning of an interiority, demarcating the boundary between myself or ourselves (as one unit) and the hostile world outside.

To this extent, the partners involved in an erotic relationship, insofar as they can be considered as a single unit, may be regarded as insiders of a certain kind of home, marked off from the rest of the world. The relationship between Fai and Bo-wing can be thought of as a home in these terms, a home that, despite its many breakups, both attempt to keep. Ironically, it is the unfaithful one, the one who is always leaving, who most frequently desires to "start over again" and rebuild the broken home. By consenting, however reluctantly, to beginning anew each time, Fai is in effect repeatedly submitting to Bo-wing's demand that the *two* of them *remain one*, that, rather than existing as two distinct individuals, they indefinitely perpetuate the dream—and the interiority—of the home as the merging of two people into a single entity. And yet, as things never quite work out, this home remains no more than the occasion for a certain longing. As unitariness eludes the two lovers, eros gives rise to a profound homesickness.

To complicate things a bit more, it is pertinent to recall at this juncture one of the most imaginative theories about the home in the twentieth century: Sigmund Freud's argument about the uncanny (1919).[14] Freud's thesis, we remember, is that the feeling of uncanniness is not necessarily the result of what is strange and frightening but rather the result of some emotionally charged occurrence (from an earlier time) that one has repressed yet somehow continues, inexplicably, to run into. For Freud, the uncanny is thus associated with an inner repetition-compulsion, an involuntary return to some familiar, or homely, place. (Zhongliang's experiences in *Temptress Moon* may thus be described as perfectly Freudian.) In the case of *Happy Together*, this compulsion to repeat can easily be identified in Bo-wing's frequent request that he and his lover "start over again." But there is still the question of what exactly it is that demands repetition. What is the beginning from which he wants to begin again?

In a theoretical move that was to make his essay controversial, Freud would go on to suggest that, for his male patients at least, the uncanny par excellence is the female genitals, which stand as reminders of "intra-uter-ine existence," of the former home where "everyone dwelt once upon a time and in the beginning."[15] The wish to start over again, for Freud, would be the wish to return to this maternal origin, a wish that, tragically, can only be fulfilled through conscious or unconscious substitutes (of the mother). What this means is that, by virtue of its intense intimacy, an erotic re-lationship—even when it is an erotic relationship between two men—is inevitably haunted by an uncanny, because repressed, memory of the pri-mary bond with the mother. In this regard, it would be possible to see the scene of erotic indifferentiation staged at the beginning of *Happy Together* in terms of a mother-child dyad and to interpret Bo-wing's constant plea to "start over again" accordingly as a wish to revisit *this* familiar home. Should this line of reasoning that is so powerfully delineated by Freud be followed, the biological mother-child bond would by necessity become the ultimate figure of the union to which all erotic relationships, be they homosexual or heterosexual, seek to return. At the same time, for the simple fact that being-one-with-the-mother is an irretrievable loss (as Freud repeatedly re-minds us), this line of reasoning and the longing that accompanies it re-main largely fantastical—and trapped within a definite metaphysics.

ANOTHER SENSE OF HOME:
THE BANALITY OF DOMESTICITY AND ACCOMMODATION

In retrospect, what seems redeemable about Freud's argument is not his masculinist musings about the female genitals per se (as the home to which we all seek to return) but rather his imaginative introduction of the figure of woman in a discussion about the home. By equating the homely and the familiar not just with anything or any place but specifically with the mother, Freud had unwittingly provided us with a means of deflecting the age-old trajectory of nostalgia and of shifting the discussion from a metaphysical into a social frame. (To be exact, he did not volunteer to do this himself, but his argument, if only because it is so noticeably simpleminded about the mother—namely, that she equals her uterus—forces us to rewrite the terms of the discussion fundamentally.) Rather than thinking of the mother simply as the child-bearing biological organ (and hence as the site of the ultimate origin and union), then, it is also necessary to think of the mother as a worker, a caretaker, and a custodian of the home in the sociological sense. This theoretical shift, which deconstructs the metaphysics attached to the womb at the same time that it places "woman" at the center of thinking about the home, opens up a crucial alternative dimension to intimacy and happiness.

Importantly, in *Happy Together*, the shift from the metaphysical to the sociological understanding of the maternal is enacted in a relationship between men, which further validates my point that the maternal as such need not be essentialized and tied to the biologically female body but should instead be considered as the outcome of specific social configurations, of preferred arrangements of intimate bonds across or within biological groups (that is, among men and women, among women and women, or among men and men). From this perspective, the numerous details in the film that elaborate the mundane experience of domesticity become highly revelatory. What is the status of such details in relation to the erotic, on the one hand, and the quest for happiness and togetherness, on the other? Here are a few examples.

When the two lovers try looking for the waterfall, their car breaks down; there is the usual petty, bitter quarrel and another separation. The waterfall is nowhere to be seen. After this incident, Fai works at a tango bar in Buenos Aires and lives a rather boring life; Bo-wing, meanwhile, continues his promiscuous adventures and is seen going in and out of the bar with different partners. Although they often see each other, they do not talk. One day, Bo-wing is badly beaten up and comes begging to be reunited with Fai, who, though reluctant, once again allows him to stay.

Later, Fai tells us that the period when Bo-wing is recovering from his injuries is the happiest time they have spent together. (This is also the time when the film changes steadily from black-and-white into color.) This

recovery period may thus, arguably, be considered as the heart of the matter of Wong's intelligently ambivalent portrayal of happiness. Noticeably,
this portrayal is from the perspective of the faithful partner, the one who
is repeatedly betrayed and stuck at home and who is moreover forced to
assume the traditionally maternal role of caretaker when the promiscuous
partner comes stumbling back. Certainly, nothing groundbreaking happens
during Bo-wing's recuperation. Only the most trivial, indeed oppressive, of
domestic routines transpire in the apartment—with Fai, in the manner of
an exploited but loyal wife/mother/servant, cooking for and spoon-feed-
ing Bo-wing (while Bo-wing remains bossy and contemptuous in attitude),
cleaning and dressing Bo-wing's wounds, spraying insecticide around the
bed because Bo-wing complains of fleas, and going out in the middle of the
night to get Bo-wing some cigarettes. These chores that Fai feels obliged
to perform for his beloved come across as unmistakably tedious, but, to
Fai, they also bring about a sense of rhythm and security, which makes it
possible to endure even acts of cruelty from Bo-wing. For instance, one bitterly cold morning, Bo-wing forces Fai to go jogging with him. Fai catches a
cold and falls into a feverish sleep. In his typically selfish manner, Bo-wing
feels no compunction about waking Fai up simply because he is hungry and
wants to eat. Although he finds it madly annoying, Fai not only does not resist but gets up immediately; in the next scene, we see him standing by the
stove, shivering under his blanket, cooking. This remarkable scene is not at
all visually glamorous. In its plainness, however, it communicates a compelling message about love in all its messiness, its lack of a clear distinction
between domination and abuse, between submission and enslavement.

As Bo-wing is confined to the apartment, he becomes for the time being
Fai's captive, and Fai takes this opportunity to hide his passport. This detail, needless to say, is once again ordinary, but at the same time precise,
in its reflection of the confused and contradictory mind-set in which Fai
finds himself: the man he loves happens to be a jerk, who fucks around,
and comes and goes as he pleases. Apart from literally taking advantage
of his temporarily vulnerable condition and treating him like a domesti-
cated animal, what else can Fai do to ensure that Bo-wing will not again
leave? Clearly, confiscating Bo-wing's passport is by no means a reasonable
or even practical move, yet its silliness also embodies a kind of groping, a
desperate attempt to safeguard whatever stability there is in the midst of a
destructive relationship.

Describing Wong's subtle use of details, Pan Liqiong (Poon Lai-king) comments: "The profundity of the film *Happy Together* lies precisely in its 'shallowness'—different kinds of bric-a-brac, sounds, fragments of life all help to expose the difficulty of two lovers living together." Pan's view, a perceptive one, is that such trivia are what typically spoil romance—in other words, that there is a certain incompatibility, indeed incommensurability, between erotic love and domestic life as such; that romance, being the precious phenomenon that it is, cannot be made to coexist with the banal.[16] By thus preserving a kind of aura around the notion of romance (and eros)—namely, that this is something so delicate that it is susceptible to being ruined by vulgar everyday realities—Pan's reading, it seems to me, also unwittingly falls prey to a kind of essentialist or metaphysical thinking about origins (in this case, a love relationship), whereby origins are sacred, pristine, and untouchable.

Wong Kar-wai, on the other hand, is careful to balance the flamboyant romanticism seductively personified by Bo-wing with an equally powerful handling of Fai. As the ever-compromised but ever-accommodating partner, who holds on to his home (that is, his relationship with Bo-wing) even when it has become uninhabitable, Fai may (arguably) be considered the preeminent sentimental figure among Wong's memorable characters. Seen from Fai's perspective, the rather boring and repetitive details do not indicate, as Pan holds, that domestic life destroys love but rather that domesticity in all its banality is an indispensable part of a love relationship, in which even petty quarreling must be understood as a way of communicating and sharing. The metaphysical meanings of the home, the origin, and happiness are, from this perspective, punctured and deflated into quotidian, almost ritualistic, practices, which bring about a different kind of illumination and equilibrium. For Fai, happiness and togetherness need not be tumescent ideals in the form of a heroic beyond or a mythical other time. Instead, they have to do with the little, "insignificant" things that he can do for his beloved in the here and now.[17]

Interestingly, it is during the period of Bo-wing's recovery, when the two lovers reestablish their intimacy, that another male character enters the story. While working at a Chinese restaurant, Fai becomes friends with Chang, a young fellow from Taiwan who seems more interested in men than in women. Perhaps more so than his relationship with Bo-wing, Fai's relationship with Chang is conducted almost exclusively around the mundane—they get to know each other in the kitchen, amid the menial labor of food preparation—without the punctuation of a dramatic sexual encounter. In the rest of the film, while his character remains largely underdeveloped, Chang's presence nonetheless provides the intriguing suggestion of an alternative kind of relationship, in which Fai's maternal and domestic way of loving would, it seems, become a mutual, reciprocated practice and in which Fai, too, could experience being taken care of.

Rather than becoming one with Bo-wing, then, Fai's character and the affective possibilities that he embodies—tolerance, considerateness, self-sacrifice, and steadfastness—stand in effect as an irreducible alterity in the structure of eros, as the 1+ that dissolves the aura of erotic unitariness, revealing the latter to be a kind of tyranny—and a fragile one at that. In contrast to Fai's nurturance, we see for the first time that romantic love, as allegorized by the dazzle of Bo-wing, may be no more than an act of self-aggrandizement, the point of which is not to sustain a relationship with another but rather to overcome, to destroy the other's resistance. For the romantic, the other is desirable only insofar as he functions as an impediment to be conquered. Once this conquest is made—once the other gives up resisting and succumbs—he will no longer be valuable and must be abandoned for a different target. Even so, as the romantic repeatedly takes flight toward ever-newer objects of desire, his seemingly carefree loitering is forever structured by a parasitical dependency on the other's seeming conventionality and domesticity—hence his pathological compulsion to ask to "start over again." Fai's definition and expectation of love and happiness, based as they are on the attentiveness to and a need for sustained intimacy with the other, are decidedly different in kind and in quality.

Through the lackluster details of the interior that is the home (understood both as a domestic space and as a nurturing relationship), a home that is almost single-handedly maintained by Fai's caretaking efforts, Wong has, one may say, introduced an important difference to the nostalgic yearning for oneness that his film otherwise projects. Without fanfare, Fai's approach to happiness stands as a force—what in the context of this book may be called the force of sentimental accommodation—that has the potential of displacing or dismantling the habits of romanticist and metaphysical ideals. How successful is this force? To answer this question, it is necessary to turn to another aspect of Wong's filmmaking: the images, produced and assembled by cinematographer Christopher Doyle.

FROM THE CASUAL PICKUP BACK TO ETERNAL NATURE:
THE ORDER AND FUNCTION OF IMAGES

At the most basic level, Wong's visual style—with its trademark experimentalism, such as a bold deployment of speed and color, and its technically sophisticated, yet often improvisatory, methods of shooting and editing—is indeed what has already been widely acknowledged as "new wave" and "avant-garde." In the case of *Happy Together*, however, these labels do not tell us very much. To get at the manner in which Wong's images signify, it is vital to move beyond such labeling.

Many shots, made with a handheld camera, are in the style of the documentary. Recall, for instance, the multiple scenes around Fai's living quarters: the cold long corridor leading to the public bathroom, the shabby-looking kitchen shared by all the tenants, the interior of Fai's apartment, which is neither tidy nor clean. There are also the cold and deserted streets near the bar where Fai works; the kitchen of the Chinese restaurant where Fai calls home to Bo-wing every day during the recovery period; the abattoir where Fai later takes another job; the small alley where Fai, Chang, and their friends play soccer in the shadows cast by the afternoon sun; and finally the crowded commercial district in Taipei where Fai looks for Chang. None of these scenes is, strictly speaking, visually spectacular. On the contrary, they often convey the impression of things and people being captured in a drab, matter-of-fact manner. Like the ordinary and fragmented nature of the two lovers' life together, the reality displayed by these images appears unobtrusive and unremarkable.

In the midst of this unremarkable reality, meanwhile, some memorable visual moments surface and linger, such as when Bo-wing tries to teach Fai to tango, first in the apartment and then in the shabby kitchen. Between Bo-wing's skilled movements and Fai's awkward gestures, the dance becomes a unique image of love (fig. 2.1).[18] There is also the cheap lampshade printed with the waterfall the lovers want to see but never manage to see together. Placed in Fai's sparse, impoverished apartment, the incandescent tones of the lampshade bring to life a kind of otherworldly picture basked in warmth and light. These visually striking images seem to imbue the love story with a kind of magic, inserting in the modest moments of the documentarylike fragments a dreamlike world.

I would therefore suggest that the images of this film are a structural corollary to the erotic and emotional entanglement between Fai and

Bo-wing. While a logical comparison, however, working by the assumption of correspondence between image and content, might want to associate the drab, documentary images with the banality of domesticity (understood from Fai's perspective) and the brilliant, magical images with the colorfulness of romance (as embodied by Bo-wing), let me offer a somewhat different kind of reading, one in which visuality functions in a more ample manner than simply being a mimeticist reflection of the content. Conceptually speaking, it would perhaps be more productive to think homologically (rather than analogically) and argue that the coordination between the documentary-style images and their dreamlike counterpart is not unlike the relationship between a promiscuous lover and his faithful partner. On the one hand, like the promiscuous lover, the documentary-style images pick up things and people ubiquitously and indiscriminately, including even the basest kind of everyday sights such as a slipper, a rag on the floor, a public bathroom, or animal blood from an abattoir draining into the gutter. By simply making them visible, this documentary style establishes a casual, flirtatious liaison with each of these phenomena, a liaison that is replete with ambiguities about the actual significance of such arbitrary encounters. (How important is a rag on the floor? Why does it have to be included? Why does it have to be captured and shown?) On the other hand, there are the images that, like the faithful partner, simply keep being there because they are deeply ingrained in memory—and in fantasy—so deeply ingrained as to defy verbal articulation. These other images, such as the lampshade, the waterfall, the tango, and so forth, intimate that in the midst of a messy, degenerate relationship there are some tender moments, moments that have become forever for the simple reason that they have not been casually dropped for something more novel or glamorous.

These two complicit orders of images slide from one into the other and back, creating a visual ambience in which the audience must adapt to two different yet complementary emotional perspectives, which are, in the end, indistinguishable from and interchangeable with each other. After the final breakup, for instance, we see Fai having sex with a stranger in a movie theater, and he tells us in the voice-over that, to his own surprise, he is much more like Bo-wing than he previously imagined. As Fai plans on returning to Hong Kong, we also hear him speaking exactly like Bo-wing, wondering whether he can "start over again" in his relationship with his own father. Last but not least, there is the astonishing scene in which Bo-wing, returning again to Fai's now empty apartment, begins to scrub and clean the apartment's floor in a manner that literally makes him resemble Fai.

At the metanarrative level of the film as a whole, what is conjured by these at first alternating but ultimately amalgamating image orders is, I propose, a kind of superhuman agency. In the case of the lovers, this superhuman agency lies precisely in its ability to yoke together—to render as one unity—entirely incompatible or incommensurate domains (such as promiscuity and fidelity, flanerie and domesticity), so that what begins as difference eventually turns into sameness. By the end of the film, precisely the kinds of (visual) details that used to distinguish the two men—having casual sex with strangers and performing tedious domestic chores—have become instead the means of visually conflating them. Each man has, it seems, internalized the other to the point of changing places with him.

Alongside the integration of the characters, the superhuman agency of the metanarrative can also be detected in a kind of childlike wishful thinking embedded in the use of certain images, a thinking that says: "If I want something to happen, it will happen." Consider when Fai mentions how much he misses Hong Kong: remembering that Hong Kong and Argentina are at two different ends of the globe, he wonders aloud what Hong Kong would look like if it could be glimpsed upside down. Following the infantile logic of Fai's stream of associations, the camera immediately gives us scenes from the streets of Hong Kong turned upside down, as if this animistically willed, inverted order of things were indeed what the city would look like from the far end of Argentina. At a moment like this, the screen (and behind it, the director's hand/gaze) has, in effect, taken on the status of a magic wand that can, with a mere flick, make something appear as soon as that something has been fantasized and named, in complete freedom from the constraints of the empirical world. In this omnipotence, this fairy-tale fluidity in which they can instantaneously become whatever they want to become, the images materialize—to use the language of poststructuralism—as sites of logocentrism, of pure, unmediated presence.

As Shi Qi comments, "Fai keeps searching for stability in the midst of his losses. Whenever he fails, he throws himself into work and play. However, he cannot forget the romance associated with the waterfall."[19] Before departing for Hong Kong, Fai once again heads for the waterfall. As we watch the swelling torrents fill the entire screen,[20] we are reminded that this is the dream that first inspired Fai and Bo-wing to take their trip together. Now the lovers are separated, presumably for good, but the dream stands there in its abundance, seemingly unperturbed by what has transpired in the human world. The visual fullness of the waterfall brings the animistic logic of the image to its crux: it is as if the screen image, artifact though it is, has in these final moments physically merged with and become one with the origin that is the natural universe.

To this extent, one may argue that the "romance" mentioned by Shi Qi has extended considerably beyond the romance between two men to become the romance of man losing himself in nature. From the perspective of this latter union, the human stories seem paltry. When Fai stands by himself next to the surging waterfall, no viewer knows what will happen to the human stories going on around him. What will become of his friendship with Chang? Will Fai find Chang again? Will Chang, after depositing his unhappiness at the end of the world, return to his former life situation in the boisterous streets of Taipei?[21] What will happen after Fai returns to Hong Kong—how will he relate to his father, who is silent when Fai calls him long distance from Buenos Aires? What about Bo-wing, who does not appear to have family and who is grief-stricken by Fai's departure?[22] All these questions remain loose ends, but none seems particularly important. Against the changefulness of the human stories, the image itself has apparently reached a sublime eternity.

Despite the attention he compellingly bestows on the details of domestic life so as to render the metaphysics of an originary union untenable and unnecessary, by the end of the film, Wong has, to my mind, doubled back to an affirmation of the romanticist ideal of happiness and togetherness *precisely through the omnipotence he attaches to the image*. In the tumescent form of the waterfall, which Wong associates with sexual energy in none-too-subtle, heterosexist terms,[23] image has now become All, exuding an overpowering feeling of oneness that seemingly transcends the interminable, volatile human narratives around it. Is not this return to, and integration with, majestic nature—the divine home—the ultimate symbol of a lost plenitude and the final meaning of nostalgia in Wong's film? Does not the throbbing presence of the nature image foreclose the sociological alternatives and affective possibilities that the film has otherwise opened up? As the almighty waterfall leaves the indelible impression of its discharge on our memory, these are the questions that reverberate with the sappy musical refrain, "Happy together . . ."

FIGURE 3.1 Zhao Di running, *Wo de fuqin muqin / The Road Home* (Copyright Guangxi Film Studio / Columbia Pictures Film Production Asia, 1999)

FIGURE 3.2 Su Lizhen and Zhou Muyun walking, *Huayang nianhua / In the Mood for Love* (Copyright Block 2 Pictures / Jet Tone Production / Paradis Films, 2000)

3 The Everyday in *The Road Home* and *In the Mood for Love*

From the Legacy of Socialism to the Potency of *Yuan*

> In reality there is no tree—there is, however, the pear tree, and apple tree, the elder tree, the cactus—but there is no tree. Thus cinema will not be able to "reproduce" (write) a tree: it will reproduce a pear tree, an apple tree, an elder tree, a cactus—but not a tree. Exactly as in the primitive cuneiform languages. Therefore, does the language of cinema, which is the product of a technology which has come to determine a human epoch, precisely because it is a technology, perhaps have some points of contact with the empiricism of the primitives?
>
> —PIER PAOLO PASOLINI, "Quips on the Cinema"

To the extent that contemporary Chinese cinema seems repeatedly concerned with various imagined interiorities such the home, domestic life, romantic oneness, and familial relationships, its sentimentalism is in many respects the sentimentalism of nostalgia or homesickness. Although, as argued in the previous two chapters, nostalgia often tends to border on a kind of intangible transcendental longing (as is clearest perhaps in the images of nature at the end of *Happy Together* but also detectable in the idealization of children's gazes at the end of *Temptress Moon*), it can, as well, attach itself to entirely perceptible daily things. As it does so, however, it tends to run into a paradox of the everyday, for no matter how concrete it may seem, the everyday—insofar as it allows critics to fill it with different critical agendas, claiming it alternately as the bedrock of reality, the ground zero of cultural representation, or a misleading set of appearances concealing ideological exploitation—stands in essence as an open and empty category (therein, perhaps, lies its attraction). For this reason, it would be less interesting simply to unravel the pros and cons of the everyday as a philosophical question than to consider specific representations of it. To this end, I will discuss two more examples of nostalgic films, this time with a focus on the prominence they give to everyday phenomena. As a way to highlight the conceptual issues involved, let me begin by turning briefly to the Italian filmmaker and writer Pier Paolo Pasolini's well-known theorization of cinematic signification.

THE EVERYDAY AS A PROBLEMATIC IN FILM

In his attempt to distinguish the specificity of cinema from language (and hence from the type of semiotic analysis derived from structural linguistics), Pasolini reminds us that film exists first and foremost on the basis of a system of "visual communication."[1] With this latter concept, he emphasizes the communal and social character of film, a character that cannot simply be assimilated to the Saussurean notion of "differences *without positive terms*,"[2] yet that is clearly not primal nature either. This, I believe, is the juncture at which his definition of film may provide us with a viable means of thinking about the everyday in representation. The viewer of film, Pasolini explains, is already accustomed to "reading" reality visually; such a reality, suffused with a vast collectivity of actions, gestures, movements, and habits, constitutes what he calls a "brute" speech, on which cinema then constructs its (secondary) level of signification. In the essay "The Written Language of Reality," he gives elements of this brute speech the name "kinemes," whose presence he describes as infinite, obligatory, and untranslatable (*HE* 201–2). Filmmaking, in other words, is a matter of organizing the kinemes into image signs (or im-signs), without the kinemes ever completely disappearing. Because of this, the viewer of film is simultaneously engaged with two levels of signification, whereby the kinemes, the preexisting order of brute "visual communication," are copresent with the cinematic im-signs, in such ways as to give the film audience an experience similar to memory and dreams. As Pasolini notes in another, oft-quoted piece, "The 'Cinema of Poetry'":

> The intended audience of the cinematographic product is also accustomed to "read" reality visually, that is, to have an instrumental conversation with the surrounding reality inasmuch as it is the environment of a collectivity, which also expresses itself with the pure and simple optical presence of its actions and habits. A solitary walk in the street, even with stopped up ears, is a continual conver-

sation between us and an environment which expresses itself through the images that compose it: the faces of people who pass by, their gestures, their signs,
their actions, their silences, their expressions, their arguments, their collective
reactions (groups of people waiting at traffic lights, crowding around a traffic
accident or around the fish-woman at Porta Capuana); and more—billboards,
signposts, traffic circles, and, in short, objects and things that appear charged
with multiple meanings and thus "speak" brutally with their very presence.

(HE 168)

In the context of contemporary Chinese cinema's fondness for invoking
specific eras of the past as its collective imaginary, Pasolini's remarks are
germane in that they offer a way of conceptualizing the historically prec-
edent—what is supposedly already seen before the film experience—without reducing it to a naturalistic reality. The brute speech in his account is
another semiotic system/language, one whose integration into cinema
does not completely strip it of this earlier identity. The questions this then
leaves us are, what kinds of value do filmmakers and audiences alike invest
in this brute prehistory, and how can this other plane of communication be
charged with current significance even as its previously experienced quality continues to be present? The interplay, in the medium of film (with its
literal, obvious modes of signification, its accessible visuality), between
this empirical or indexical "always already" and its contemporary screen
cathexes is where the problematic of the everyday can, I believe, be fruitfully located.

To be sure, in the reading of Chinese films, the everyday can easily become equated with a crude materialism, which can in turn be equated with
history, culture, specific time periods, and so forth, against whose "reality"
the present (of film watching) is positioned. In order to grasp the intriguing relationship between the cinematic and the quotidian, however, it is
necessary to defer these commonly accepted but little examined assumptions about the everyday (at times coming from directors themselves) and
instead contemplate in some detail *how* exactly the everyday emerges in a
network of filmic elements (visual, auditory, narrative). Only then would it
be possible to chart the aesthetic and emotional effects produced by a film
and to speculate on the larger ideological issues at stake. If the everyday is,
in and of itself, always already a semiotically coded set of phenomena, as
Pasolini's writing suggests, any cinematic rendering of the everyday would
suggest compounded levels of (trans)coding, whereby signs of different or-

ders are superimposed upon and interact with one another in a hybrid—
and what may also be called synergized—fashion.

In Zhang Yimou's *Wo de fuqin muqin* (My father and mother)/*The Road Home* (1999) and Wong Kar-wai's *Huayang nianhua* (When flowers were in bloom)/*In the Mood for Love* (2000), it is possible to identify a number of resonant elements that in their transcultural cinematic contexts confirm once again the predominantly nostalgic drift in contemporary Chinese films since the mid-1980s.[3] As in the case of many nostalgic explorations, both films take the form of a journey in time, one that returns us to a specific point in the past.

Zhang, who made his film soon after his own father had passed away, tells the story of a son's (Luo Yusheng) visit home upon his father's death.[4] This visit becomes the occasion for a replay of how his mother and father's relationship began in the 1950s, when the father (Luo Changyu) was sent as a teacher to the village in which the mother (Zhao Di) lived. This trip to the past reveals in particular the mother's devotion to the father; it is she who now insists that his dead body be brought home on foot, in honor of the traditional belief that a body returned this way will never forget the road home. The narrative return to the 1950s is hence concluded with an actual trip taken in the present by the father's many former students, who carry his body back to the village, where the new school he had begun building will, we are told, be completed in memory of his life's achievements. Wong, on his part, takes us to the early 1960s in Hong Kong, when Su Lizhen and Zhou Muyun, the lead characters, happen to rent rooms in adjacent apartments in a district inhabited by immigrants from Shanghai. The film is also a return journey in the sense of an exploration of a relationship that ended as elusively as it had begun, an affair whose meanings seem far from having been exhausted and invite revisiting. To this extent, the two films' titles may be interchangeable: "in the mood for love" (or "the time when flowers were in bloom") can be used to describe the colorful recollections of Luo Changyu and Zhao Di falling in love; while "the road home" can be used to describe the cinematic (re)visitation of the scene of Su and Zhou's involvement. If we take Wong Kar-wai's whimsical suggestion that the little boy in Su's apartment at the end could be the offspring of her relationship with Zhou some years before,[5] then his film, too, may be called "my father and mother."

Apart from the comparable notions in the two works of a journey in time, both directors also draw on a memorable collection of daily phenomena, including objects, practices, activities, social interactions, and verbal exchanges, to furnish the environments of their respective stories. Both make use of extraordinary visual and aural effects to construct the ordinary, and the everyday is given to us through some of the most breathtaking maneuvers of the cinematic apparatus. What semiotic and affective implications do such maneuvers entail? What do these films by two of the most widely acclaimed contemporary filmmakers tell us about the everyday in film, and how?

THE ROAD HOME

As recalled by the son, Luo Yusheng, the father and the mother in *The Road Home* meet when the father was sent to teach at the village where the mother, then a girl of eighteen, and her blind mother live. As in Wong's film, we witness one of the most ordinary everyday happenings: a chance encounter between a male and a female that develops into a relationship.[6] Unlike other everyday practices, a chance encounter is not an entirely passive or entirely active event; it typically occurs when one is engaged in something else and is thus, strictly speaking, an accidental by-product of some other activity. Such serendipity gives it the fatefulness of the unconscious, of the dream in which one runs into things or people in ways that are not planned in advance. Unlike even a simple act such as walking, it is not entirely certain that there is a subject in command, a subject whose body and mind are knowingly engaged. Yet, in Zhang's film, we soon see a conscious attempt to steer this chance encounter and what follows in a purposeful direction.

Interestingly, this attempt to take control comes from Zhao Di, the pretty peasant girl, who has so far remained unpersuaded by proposals for an arranged marriage. As she catches sight of Luo Changyu, she becomes interested in him and begins a series of efforts to have further contact. She waits, for instance, by the road where she knows he will pass with his students. She brings water up from the well facing the school where he teaches, so she can see him. She walks by the school in order to listen to him reading texts to his students even though, being illiterate, she does not really understand the full meanings of the scholarly words. She cooks special items and puts them in a large bowl with indigo patterns (a *qinghua wan*), in the hope that he will select the right bowl and be able to taste her cooking amid all the lunch items prepared by fellow village girls for the working men. When he comes to her house for a meal, she takes special care to prepare the dishes, pointing out to him the significance of the bowl. When he is recalled to the city for interrogation by the authorities, she waits by the road for his return in the midst of a snowstorm, almost losing her life to a fever afterward.[7] We are told that eventually, when her beloved comes back to the village and they are able to get married, he will never again leave her until his death. Finally, it is she, now an old widow, who instructs that his body be carried home and who donates the family's savings to the village in order to have the school completed.

Zhao Di recalls the series of stubborn, persistent female characters in Zhang's other films—Jiu'er in *Red Sorghum*, Judou in *Judou*, Yan'er in *Raise the Red Lantern*, Qiuju in *The Story of Qiuju*, Wei Minzhi, the girl teacher, in *Not One Less*, the blind girl in *Happy Times*, and Feixue/Snow in *Hero*—who would risk (and in some cases lose) their lives in order to remain faithful to a personal goal or collective cause and who typically refuse to give up until they have completed the task they set themselves. In *The Road Home*, this characteristic determination places the woman not merely in the role of the cinematic fetish but also of the fetishist, who actively seeks ways of catching a glimpse of her love interest—who literally fetishizes his voice as he reads texts to schoolchildren, for instance. (Contrary to convention, the male here becomes an object, with little subjectivity of his own.)[8] As this willpower is firmly vested with the woman, what begins as a mere chance encounter quickly loses its chance quality and turns into a deliberate production of meaning and value. Narratively speaking, there is thus a clear telos organizing the unfolding of the events not only in individual sexual terms (a happy marriage, which leads to the birth of a son) but also in terms of the village's future as a social unit. The woman's decisions result in her union with the man of her choice, while procuring for the village a pedagogical father figure and, in the long run, a revered site of learning. By the end of the film, the recollections and the present time blend into each other, with the son helping to complete his mother's and his father's wishes.

Visually speaking, this production of meaning and value is most evident in Zhang's manner of capturing plain daily objects. Unlike Wong's film, in which the crowded conditions of urban living are reflected in households filled with fashionable but disposable commodified belongings, Zhang's picture shows a rural environment in which material possessions are scarce. Instead of the glamour of purchased things, Zhang focuses on the activity of the people involved: Zhao Di chopping vegetables, steaming dumplings, or frying pancakes; Zhao Di putting on the red padded jacket that Changyu likes; Zhao Di putting on the hairpin that Changyu gives her as a gift; Zhao Di sitting at the loom weaving; Zhao Di running on the road numerous times to catch a glimpse of Changyu or to greet him returning; and so forth. When the bowl with the indigo patterns that Zhao Di uses to hold the food breaks (as she falls while running to catch up with Changyu), her mother has it repaired by a traveling craftsman, whose patient, meticulous handiwork is captured in detail on the screen, reminding us of a primitive kind of livelihood and technology, passed on from generation to generation by the peasant classes yet fast becoming extinct.

Be it portrayed in the form of rustic utensils, activities, or behaviors, the everyday is associated by Zhang with human labor—in such ways as to connote the old-fashioned values of perseverance, endurance, and redeeming power. Keeping in mind the brute speech mentioned by Pasolini, one may say that the everyday is invoked in this film precisely as a once-experienced communal form of life, one that, despite its material impoverishment, has the ability to survive the hardship imposed by a politically repressive climate (specifically, the Anti-Rightist campaign of 1957) and the death of individual leaders. This sense of collectivity, which Zhang attaches to the countryside in the early years of the People's Republic, can be understood as that "pregrammatical history" in all its intensity, with the kinemes drawn from this history, in the form of recognizable rural habitats, objects, gestures, movements, exchanges, and so forth, being configured into the cinematic im-signs playing in front of us. In this manner, the everyday takes on the import of an allegorical, indeed symbolic, correspondence between human activity and the natural environment. The latter, shown alternately in paintinglike autumnal hues and in the prohibitive severity of wintry grays and blues, becomes a background from which human beings emerge with distinctive profiles, courageously carving out their destinies. It is tempting to conclude that cinematic allure in this instance is still part of the logic of a socialist ideal of bringing people together through work, of forging a coherent bond between human beings and the world around them.[9]

The road home, then, is the return to the father and the mother, elders and ancestors of a community who are earlier versions of "us." More important, it is a return, now possible only in remembrance, to the utopian possibilities of determination, meaningful action, communal purpose, and happiness—the constituents of a sociality that has since, to all appearances, become lost. As if to emphasize this, the story of the mother and father as young lovers is retold in color, whereas the present, the time of the narration, is shot in documentary black-and-white.

WHEN FLOWERS WERE IN BLOOM

If the chance encounter gives way structurally to sexual fulfillment and social cohesion in The Road Home, in Wong Kar-wai's hands it never transcends the arbitrary and the unpredictable, the aura of "it just so happens . . ." that characterizes most of his film narratives to date. In the Mood for Love begins with a series of unremarkable coincidences. In Hong Kong in 1962, Su Lizhen and Zhou Muyun both happen to be looking for a room to rent in a district inhabited by Shanghai immigrants.[10] They find their rooms in adjacent apartments and move in on the same day. Their chance encounter continues in the form of casual chatting as the movers keep misplacing their belongings in each other's units. After settling in, they keep brushing past each other in the company of their spouses and neighbors, at the mah-jongg table, and on the stairway leading up to their apartments. One day, over coffee at a restaurant, they confirm each other's suspicions that their spouses may be having an affair. At this point, the two, perhaps from despondency, actively turn what has so far been a series of haphazard events into a conscious exploration: asking themselves how their spouses might have begun their affair, they start seeing each other on a regular basis, enacting by turns imagined scenes of seduction, confrontation, and breaking-up as though they were rehearsing performances on a stage set.[11]

Su and Zhou's relationship is, strictly speaking, a double one. As Wong describes it, they must simultaneously be themselves and the other couple, jointly engaged in a conspiracy of keeping a secret they have discovered together.[12] In contrast to Zhao Di and Luo Changyu, who transform their chance encounter into a long-term relationship by overcoming various obstacles, Su and Zhou perpetuate the chance element of their encounter by improvising other people's lives, assuming identities that are at once their own and not their own. In this process of playacting, Zhou eventually notices that he has fallen in love with Su. This discovery of his own emotions—and of the fact that he is, after all, not so different from the adulterous others that he is trying vicariously to understand[13]—prompts him to leave for Singapore and put an end to their relationship. Su looks for Zhou by arriving in Singapore herself, but strangely, as she succeeds in locating him by phone at his workplace and is on the verge of reuniting with him, she hangs up. Back in Hong Kong in 1966, Su has rented (or bought) her old apartment, where she now lives with her child and a servant, and Zhou shows up next-door one day to visit his old landlord, who has moved. Although they are literally within a few steps of each other, Su and Zhou narrowly miss each other. The encounter of the chance encounter fails to happen this time. Zhou is next shown visiting the Angkor Wat in Cambodia, confessing his secret to a hole on a wall, around the time of Cambodia's independence from France.

Like Zhang, Wong inserts various daily objects in his picture, but while the objects in *The Road Home* are imbued with a rural, primitive, and timeless quality, Wong's objects are much more specific to the chronological referent he evokes. From the coiffures, makeup styles, *qipaos*, shoes, and slippers worn by Su; to household items such as the electric rice cooker, the thermos for carrying hot noodles, the radio set (broadcasting song request programs), Chinese-language newspapers (with serialized fiction columns); to public spaces such as offices and restaurants with their 1960s decor, deserted street corners with peeling wall advertisements, and the darkish, upholstered interiors of taxicabs at night, Wong offers tantalizing glimpses of a Hong Kong that, we are given to understand, no longer exists. (The film was shot on location in Thailand.) Reportedly, he was so intent on re-creating the ambience of the 1960s that he "hired a chef to cook Shanghai dishes for the cast and crew," "engaged retired Hong Kong radio announcers, now in their 70's, to record radio programs for the soundtrack featuring bits of Mandarin pop and Chinese opera,"[14] and used quotations from a popular newspaper columnist and novelist to frame his story.[15] Are not these objective reminders of a bygone era again a compelling instance of that brute speech alluded to by Pasolini? Especially for audiences acquainted with the Hong Kong of the 1960s, these ethnographic details constitute a kind of already-read text, one that revives, through the contemporary filmic rendering, a sense of the community that was once but is no longer.

Nonetheless, even as these everyday details, like the melodious refrains of the popular songs by Nat King Cole, Zhou Xuan, and others that punctuate them, are repeated, their repetition functions for an effect that is quite clearly in excess of simple ethnographic empiricism. Instead, these everyday details are deployed simultaneously to conjure a subjective, albeit pervasive, mood of loss and melancholy. To see this, it is instructive to compare a few details in Wong's film with categorically similar ones in Zhang's.

Body movement. In Zhang's film, the many shots of Zhao Di moving— walking slowly or briskly, running, tripping and falling, and getting up again—are examples of a capacity for and an aspiration toward a certain goal, the young girl's goal of seeing and being with her beloved male (see, for instance, fig. 3.1). Body movements in their everyday simplicity become expressive actions toward that goal, and mere treading on earth is never an aimless peregrination. In Wong's film, body movements, even when they pertain to two people meeting (such as when Su and Zhou meet on the stairway leading up to their apartments or when they brush past each other at the mah-jongg table), are a means rather of dramatizing the ephemerality of the encounter (as in the Chinese expression, *ca shen er guo*, literally, "brushing past each other's bodies"). The technique of slow motion, used by Zhang to pictorialize and externalize the young girl's subjectivity (her delight at the prospect of seeing the young man), becomes in Wong's hands a way of extending the duration and thus magnifying the granularity of an otherwise automatized, because transitory, set of motions. Whereas Zhang uses movements to unify body and mind, Wong, like some of the French New Wave directors whose techniques he often borrows, turns such movements into occasions for an alternative experience—that of defamiliarizing, and thus aestheticizing, the nature of (repetitive, habitual) motion through a manipulation of its cinematic texture and of viewing time (see, for instance, fig. 3.2).[16]

Eating. In Zhang's film, the various aspects of eating, including the preparation and consumption of meals, are shown with a straightforward gusto. Food is the communal service provided by one group of workers to another group in the village, as well as the means of bonding between the girl and the young man. In Wong's film, food, or, more accurately, the routine of eating, is rather a sign of ennui and forlornness (Su repeatedly turns down her landlady's invitation to dinner and insists on getting noodles by herself). Alternatively, it is the occasion for rendering visible the nuances of an extramarital relationship: think of the scenes of Su and Zhou munching their Hong Kong–style Western pork chop or beefsteak with mustard sauce at the restaurant and sharing noodles from a thermos when they are stuck in his apartment room; of them rehearsing Su's confrontation of her husband over a meal; or of Su talking about making sesame porridge for everyone but really in order to please Zhou, who has fallen sick. Food consumption is linked to the minutiae of labor in one case and to the finesse of languor in the other. (And just as physical labor seldom signifies in Wong's universe, so, too, does languor—together with loneliness—remain resolutely foreign to Zhang's.)

Clothing. In Zhang's film, Zhao Di has only a couple of padded jackets, but she makes a point of always putting on the bright red one that Changyu likes. Again, the simple act of dressing is filled with a purpose—that of pleasure giving—that is redirected into the story, as part of the motivation that propels the plot. In Wong's film, on the contrary, one of the unforgettable things is the large number of expertly tailored, splendid-looking *qipao*s worn by Su, whose pristine figure remains unperturbed even in pouring rain.[17] The gorgeous shapes, colors, and patterns as embodied by Su, meanwhile, are not exactly necessary to the action of the story. In their invariable perfection, in their almost mechanical (because impeccable) appearances, they are rather directed at some other gaze, for which the figure of Su stands like an uncanny, doll-like fetish (in the Freudian sense) for some unexpressed or inarticulate emotion—one, moreover, that seems to belong not to any individual character within the story but rather to some force outside the diegesis, structuring it.

Despite the film's suggestion of a historically and geographically specific setting, therefore, the audience does not get a realistic account about the 1960s in Hong Kong. Instead, it is a Hong Kong remembered—or reinvented—in oneiric images: households are shown at partial angles (through windows, doorways, and corridors); streets are dimly lit with restricted views; routes of taxi rides are shadowy and unidentifiable; food stalls are signified simply by trails of steam from cooking; a hotel counter is glimpsed only through its framed reflection in a mirror.[18] At once objective (that is, available for all to see) and subjective (that is, mediated by a particular consciousness—but whose?), these visual details raise questions about the exact relationship between the everyday as such and the historical referent that supposedly lies behind it. Whereas in Zhang, that relationship can be traced, with reasonable certainty, to a residual socialist sentimentalism with its nostalgia for, or hope in, the import of human action, in Wong, the everyday points rather to a familiar cliché, namely, the fundamentally unfulfilled—and unfulfillable—nature of human desire, to which history itself, even when it appears in the form of recognizable everyday phenomena, becomes subject and subordinate.

The concreteness of the many everyday details of the 1960s notwithstanding, what gives Wong's film its unique imprint of nostalgia is not exactly the portrayal of a vanished, 1960s Hong Kong but rather, as in the case of his other works and as I argued in the previous chapter, the elusiveness of communication and missed communication among human beings.[19] If Su and Zhou begin communicating because of a series of coincidences (both begin by renting a room; both are married to partners who seem often absent; both discover that their partners may be having an affair with each other; both are plunged into a condition of anxiety and disillusionment), the perceptible symmetry of their situations (much like the consistent parallelisms of the four-character arrangements of all Wong's film titles in Chinese)[20] does not exactly promise orderliness or guarantee harmony. The symmetry simply leads, rather matter-of-factly, to the improvisations that become the very basis of their entanglement. But improvisations are a matter of hits and misses, so to speak: as in the case of Wong's famous impromptu method of directing,[21] an improvised plot does not know where it is going until it has run its course. Even though the improvised version may be the only version there is—and it may be a remarkable one at that—the volatile relationships it projects and the atmosphere of loss that surrounds them are strong indications of a kind of searching and longing, one that can be detected in various ways in Wong's films despite their generic variations.[22] Ultimately, his work as a whole seems to say: even the most unforgettable human relationships are only a matter of fortuitous rather than deliberate performances—and perhaps not so much by human beings as by chance or fate.

If the valorization of togetherness is the epitome of Chinese sentimentalism (as I think it is), the manifestation of such sentimentalism in *In the Mood for Love* needs to be identified not merely positivistically, at the level of the nostalgic re-creation of old-fashioned objects and interiors from the 1960s, but also dialectically, in the impermanence of human togetherness, a theme to which Wong obsessively returns. And just as such impermanence is deemed melancholic (as is conveyed most readily by the soundtrack of moody tunes, inserted at crucial moments to guide the audience's emotions), so, too, does the accidental coming-together, the chance meeting or connectivity signified by the delicate touch—between gazes, between bodies, between fabrics, between thoughts, between personalities, between lives, and between happenings—become the most cherished, eroticized, and sentimentalized event.

This sense of touch, moreover, is not only physical but also metaphysical: sentimentalism in this case is specifically a matter of accepting the

potency of *yuan* 緣, the Buddhist notion of fateful affinity or higher determination that Wong, in a popular Chinese fashion, names as the rationale
for all things: "Wo juede shenme shiqing dou jiang yige 'yuan' zi. Yi lu yi lu
dui qilai, jieguo shenme dongxi douyou guanlian, dianying yeshi"/ "我覺
得什麼事情都講一個緣字。 一路一路堆起來, 結果什麼東西都有關聯,
電影也是。 " (I feel that all events are about the word *yuan*. Gradually and
steadily piling up, all things become related in the end. It's the same with
film).[23] As much as the avant-gardism of his New Wave screen designs, this
submission to a much older cultural logic (replete with its folk wisdom and
superstitions) should, I believe, be made part of any serious appraisal of
Wong's work, so that the improvisations that seem to be such an eccentric
(and to the actors exasperating) method of directing, for instance, can be
properly understood as his way of putting into practice the belief, often
invoked idiomatically among Chinese speakers, in *suiyuan* 隨緣 (following
or in accordance with *yuan*).

To this extent, the spectacular, indeed visually extravagant, images of
Wong's film are offered as a paradox: the more colorful and beautiful they
are—and the more locally concrete they seem to be—the more they serve
as an index to the capricious (that is, impermanent) nature of the human
universe that revolves around/behind them. The luxurious images become
in this manner a screen for a fundamental void. Cinematic allure, existential angst: this disjuncture, or perhaps synergy, between sensuous plenitude and spiritual longing thus stands as the hallmark of a transsocial,
transcultural film drama, for which the everyday functions as artifice, as
stage props.

In the Mood for Love ends with scenes from the ancient ruins of the
Angkor Wat in Cambodia, which the camera captures in a steady pace
against the somber music of Umebayashi Shigeru (originally part of his
score for Suzuki Seiji's film *Yumeji*). These ruins remind one of the scenes
of the magnificent Iguazu Falls in *Happy Together*, suggesting a type
of perseverance and endurance that far transcends the bounds of the
human world. Whereas, for Zhang, it is the perseverance and endurance
of the human will that triumphs over impediments imposed by nature
(be they snowstorms, a harsh landscape, or sheer physical distance), for
Wong, the ruins of an exotic land, ravaged through the ages by the elements yet standing still erect in the midst of political turmoil, offer the
final solace.

THE EVERYDAY:
A THEORETICAL CONUNDRUM OF OUR TIME?

However differently it is brought forth in the two films, the everyday seems to have become something of a privileged convention among some contemporary Chinese filmmakers. While this by itself is not a novel revelation and perhaps not peculiar to cinema, it is still of interest to explore why the everyday—in the form of casual happenings such as chance encounters or in the form of the inorganic, the trivia that make up mundane environments—has surfaced at the turn of the twenty-first century as a viable and forceful vehicle for telling stories on the screen. Where exactly is this vehicle heading?

This question brings us back to Pasolini's approach to the everyday in cinema. Among his many reflections, what I have found the most thought-provoking is not simply the possible association of the "pregrammatical" history of brute objects with history and reality; it is also his insistence that such bruteness has the ability to alter—indeed, to adulterate—the metaphorical nature of cinematic signification itself by constraining the latter's flight toward pure abstraction, by directing such tendency toward abstraction back toward a conventional objectivity. In other words, the everyday, by virtue of being brutely or readily apprehensible, serves the semiotic function of impeding the potential drift of filmic language toward pure subjectivity and metaphoricity. As Pasolini writes (in the passage cited in the epigraph to the present chapter), cinema "will not be able to 'reproduce' (write) a tree: it will reproduce a pear tree, an apple tree, an elder tree, a cactus—but not a tree." He puts the same argument in this manner in "The 'Cinema of Poetry'":

> [The filmmaker] chooses a series of objects, or things, or landscapes, or persons as syntagmas (signs of a symbolic language) which, *while they have a grammatical history invented in that moment*—as in a sort of happening dominated by the idea of selection and montage—*do, however, have an already lengthy and intense pregrammatical history.*   (HE 171; emphases in the original)

> Cinema, lacking a conceptual, abstract vocabulary, is powerfully metaphoric; as a matter of fact, *a fortiori* it operates immediately on the metaphoric level. Particular, deliberately generated metaphors, however, always have some quality that is inevitably crude and conventional. Think of the frenzied or joyous flights

of doves which are meant to express metaphorically the state of anxiety or joy in the mind of the character. In short, the nuanced, barely perceptible metaphor, the poetic halo one millimeter thick . . . would not seem possible in cinema. Whatever part of the poetically metaphoric which is sensationalistically possible in film, it is always in close osmosis with its other nature, the strictly communicative one of prose.   (HE 174)

For Pasolini, these coexisting propensities toward the metaphoric and the prosaic mean that cinema has a double nature: even as the lack of a conceptual, abstract vocabulary renders cinema's images immediately open to (the drifts and flights of) allegorization, a "crude and conventional," "strictly communicative" kind of "prose" always remains in the picture. As Pasolini comments, cinema is thus "both extremely subjective and extremely objective (to such an extent that it reaches an unsurpassable and awkward naturalistic fate). The two moments of the above-mentioned nature are closely intertwined and are not separable even in the laboratory" (HE 173).

This double nature may be the major reason cinema lends itself so appropriately to the sentimentalism of nostalgia as it centers on the everyday. In the two films under discussion, the everyday phenomena we observe in their immediacy constitute what in each case may be perceived as a subjectively composed visual representation (signifying Zhang's utopian vision or Wong's fateful perspective), each with the potential to take off on its own metaphoric (or allegorical) flight. Yet despite such subjective and metaphoric dimensions, which endow the films with their poetic or lyrical qualities, the visual elements, precisely because of their brute recognizability, come across simultaneously as literal, communal, already seen by other people, in ways that recall that pregrammatical intensity, that obligatory sociality of the everyday we perceive with our senses before it is selected and organized (by a particular auteur) into a particular audiovisual filmic work. The subjective or metaphorical crafting of the everyday relationships, practices, and objects notwithstanding, this other, prosaic, and communicative aspect of cinematic visuality casts such relationships, practices, and objects in the light of an empirical place and time, evoking a collective way of living that seems to have—or so we are led to believe, with chronological markers such as the 1950s and 1960s—existed once before. What Pasolini describes as the double nature of filmic signification, in short, becomes in Zhang's and Wong's films a special kind of mediation, in which subjective affect and objective phenomena are welded together as if they were one.

And in such welding, which seems to occur most felicitously through the representation of the everyday, sentimentalism is made palpably visible: indeed, *visibility itself is produced and offered to us as a sentimental affair.*

At the same time, as most of us watch movies increasingly in the form of portable technologies such as VCDs and DVDs, the sentimentalism generated by these filmic accounts of the past has taken on a life of rapid distribution and circulation. Rather than being opposed, sentimentalism's affective tenacity and market versatility together form a kind of capital-in-flux in global circuits, turning the most locally specific, everyday elements simultaneously into the most fabulous, because infinitely transmissible, phantasmagorias. From this perspective, it would seem that the "brute" speech and "pregrammatical history" Pasolini theorizes—and that I have been associating with the everyday in Zhang's and Wong's films—may require yet another level of articulation. For, in the age of rampant visual consumerism, has not the everyday become part and parcel of what Fredric Jameson has argued as a postmodern reification of (ethnic) culture,[24] a reification whose typicality is most evident, ironically, when directors make their most subjective (and metaphoric) attempts to recall, indeed to arrest, a historical time and place with all its cultural particulars?

In other words, precisely when directors like Zhang and Wong try to communicate "literally" by using concrete daily elements (such as the feminine fashions and household items in the two films), in a global environment in which audiences scan or surf cinematic images without necessarily having knowledge about the historical specifics behind them, the so-called abstract side of film tends to take over, transcoding even the most local details into vague generalities. Instead of the pear tree, apple tree, elder tree, or cactus, they will, most likely, simply understand "some" tree. Instead of Chinese history or Hong Kong history, they will, most likely, simply understand "some instance" of human drama, romance, loss, or the like. In a manner that challenges, perhaps supersedes, Pasolini's formulations, therefore, it seems increasingly the case that it is the abstract (rather than "brute" speech) that allows for transmissibility and enables "communication" at a transcultural level—though one should also specify that, under these circumstances, the abstract no longer operates in the old-fashioned, literary-philosophical sense of poetic-metaphorical drifts (as Pasolini still understood it) but rather in the late-capitalist and postmodern sense of reified, commodified spectacles—or, better still, of worldwide virtual networks.

To that end, the apparent polarity between Zhang's and Wong's aesthetic and political approaches—and the difference between their respective sentimentalisms—may simply be symptomatic of the *range* of a larger ideological predicament that confronts all those engaged in one way or another with the study of transnational culture at the turn of the twenty-first century. Prasenjit Duara describes this predicament succinctly from the perspective of critical historiography: "Critical historiography which had found its inspiration in Marxist and other radical social theory encounters a world in which the possibilities of non-capitalist emancipation have receded and one where the revolutionary states have been discredited. At the same time, capitalist globalization continues to widen the gap between the powerful and the powerless while the erosion of a national society itself unleashes a reaction which results in still more violent and exclusive reifications of nation, race or culture."[25]

Insofar as Zhang remains committed to the vestiges of a socialist humanism, the low-budget works from his more recent period, such as *Happy Times* and *Not One Less* (see my discussion in chapter 7) as well as *The Road Home*, are marked by a distinctive nationalist quality. Chineseness in Zhang is a residual structure of feeling that results from the specifics of a country's political history. However aesthetically controlled, a film such as *A Road Home* would not have made sense without the messiness of that history and the burden of hope Zhang continues to try to salvage therein. This attempt at redemption, incidentally, is quite different from Zhang's early works, in which the criticism of history is much more bleak and harsh and the everyday, such as is associated with oppressive wedding rituals, household customs, and various folk practices and objects, tends to be a matter of fabrication.[26]

In the case of Wong, ethnicity is at once more local and more fluid. Rather than being concerned with the Chinese nation, people, or culture as such, his interest is focused on the Shanghai community in the Hong Kong of the 1960s. This attachment to a group already in diaspora prefigures his film's much more casual, tenuous relation to Chineseness as a geopolitical issue, and *In the Mood for Love*, despite its recall of a specific place and time period, stages an essentially human drama. This other humanism, bound not to the fraught legacy of the nation's (failed) political aspirations the way Zhang's is but rather to an image-proliferating nostalgia in which history tends always already to have transmuted into pastiche and simulacra, travels with great felicity and effectiveness the world over, its structure of feeling appealing to diverse audiences in Moscow, Tokyo, New York, Paris, Buenos Aires, and Beijing alike. Precisely because Wong's film does not consciously re-collect itself as Chinese even as it uses a small Chinese migrant enclave as its site of visibility, it achieves a relevance that is, arguably, transethnic and portable. Chineseness, now displaced and dispersed in such ways as never again to form any cohesive continuum, has become an exotic, globally interchangeable part object, whose defining character is no longer simply history but also, increasingly, image, artifice, and commodity.

Between the aestheticized spectacle of a socialist humanism that has become politically bankrupt and the aestheticized spectacle of a metaphysics of human desire that has acquired global currency, these sentimental journeys through time present us with new problems in critical practice. Should we hold on to the utopic, however untimely, as part of an aesthetics of redemption—of what was or could have been? Should we merge with the global flow of chance affinities in the spirit of a seasoned and resigned "human understanding"—of the way things are and will always be? The everyday, considered in the light of these larger questions, may yet be the paradigmatic case of the theoretical conundrum we face in our time, and any filmic representation of it, in particular, will likely demand some hard critical thinking.

Part II

MIGRANTS' LORE, WOMEN'S OPTIONS

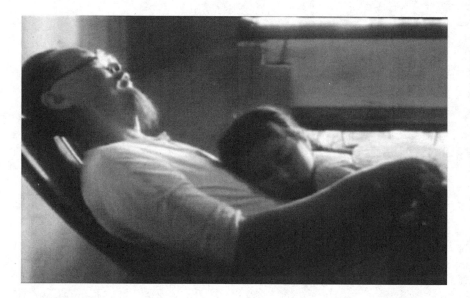

FIGURE 4.1 Little Hueyin and her grandfather taking a nap together in a flashback in *Ke tu qiu hen / Song of the Exile* (Copyright Cos Group / Central Motion Pictures, 1990)

Autumn Hearts

Filming Feminine "Psychic Interiority" in *Song of the Exile*

Few preoccupations are as banal or as popular as the exploration of the individual self. If this cultural thematic of the self continues to hold a certain fascination for us, it is probably less because of its theoretical inexhaustibility than because of its associative open-endedness, the fact that it can be inserted into virtually any type of representational situation without any perceived loss of relevance. The self, as such, has often been discussed in modern and contemporary Chinese literature and culture, which in the twentieth century alone have witnessed multifarious examples of autobiography in fictional as well as nonfictional writings. In a world still largely dominated by the interests of heterosexual kinship bonds and thus, ultimately, by male supremacy, the emergence of the self as a problematic is often closely affined with cultural experiences of marginalization and subordination such as those of women.[1] In this chapter, as part of a reading of Hong Kong director Ann Hui's film *Ke tu qiu hen* (*Song of the Exile*, 1990), I'd like to approach the question of exploring the self—clichéd as it may indeed seem to be—from several perspectives.

First, returning to an early moment of modern Chinese women's writing, I will show how processes of self-reflection are culturally specific phenomena, often constructed with recurrent formal codes—that is, fundamental features of presentation that allow a text to become intelligible in a certain way. The history of the gradual visibility and agency accorded women in modernity, then, is in many ways a history of the progressive molding and remolding of the abstraction I will call "psychic interiority." Second, it would be interesting to see how the formal codes and their variables are adapted and elaborated in different media—in film, for instance, as opposed to writing. How does film at once enrich and transform the terms in which this interiority is imagined? Finally, it is necessary to evaluate, however speculatively, the continued relation between the presentation of such feminine psychic interiority and the social strictures they are intended to counter.

INVENTING "PSYCHIC INTERIORITY": SOME BASIC CODES

In a short fictional piece, "Xifeng" (West wind), first published in 1936, the well-known author Bing Xin tells the story of a middle-aged woman's chance reunion with the intimate male friend she rejected ten years before in order to pursue her career.[2] An accomplished educator, Qiuxin is on her way to deliver a lecture entitled "The Two Major Issues for Women: Career and Marriage." Recalling her youthful decision to turn down the offer of marriage from Yuan, Qiuxin notices, with a mild sadness, that it is late autumn. This allusion to the season is a suggestion both of her age and of her state of mind, which is clearly fatigued and lonely.[3] Unexpectedly, Qiuxin runs into Yuan, who happens to be traveling to the same destination. The two renew their friendship and keep each other company on the rest of their journey, first on the train and then on a boat.

We are soon introduced into a process of quiet observation and self-reflection. Qiuxin thinks that, unlike herself, Yuan, now married with two children, does not seem to have changed. He looks as handsome as ever and seems content with his life. This wonderfully positive ability to remain untouched by time, readily attributed to the other, turns simultaneously into a negative and inferior self-concept, one that is then reprojected outward onto her own aging appearance: "Looking into the mirror under the light, she saw the dust in her hair, the black circles around her eyes, and the fatigue and pallor on her face. 'I'm not what I used to be anymore.' She stood numbly for a while. The bell for dinner startled her. She quickly changed and washed her face, and for the first time in years, put on a little rouge" ("Xifeng" 300).

The hypersensitivity to the passing of time and her own physical deterioration is accompanied by a mounting sense of regret: did she make a mistake those many years ago? Qiuxin cannot help being filled with self-loathing, which she extends to women in general: "What happened today happened too abruptly, too unexpectedly, and too much like a dream. She was so confused she did not know where to begin to think. She hated the ten busy years that made her feel she wanted to cry before Yuan yet could not. 'This is woman!' she cursed herself" ("Xifeng" 302–3).

Although Qiuxin still has tender feelings for Yuan, and although she realizes through his conversation that he cares for her and intends to remain a loyal friend, the consideration of extramarital sexual propriety means that it is unlikely they will continue in a normal relationship. Once again, we realize this through Qiuxin's painfully self-conscious ponderings: "Qiuxin . . . began hating herself again. The conversation of the past hour was not what she had wanted. Why did she reveal her vulnerability to Yuan after not seeing him for ten years? What's more, wouldn't it be harmful to Yuan's obligations to his family?" ("Xifeng," 309–10).

In this confused and self-blaming frame of mind, Qiuxin arrives at her destination. Coming to greet Yuan at the pier are his young wife and two children. After they depart in the mood of a happily reunited family, Qiuxin disembarks by herself, as "a breath of west wind brushed across her expressionless face, sweeping up scattered pieces of paper and twirling them on the ground" ("Xifeng" 313).

If the theme of this story is loneliness, loneliness needs to be further specified—less as a mere human condition, as is commonly assumed, than as a new cultural condition, the condition of being a woman in early twentieth-century China who has opted to abandon the well-trodden and relatively secure path of wifehood and motherhood. The perplexity of Qiuxin's newfound freedom lies in the heavy price she *feels* she has had to pay. To her thinking, freedom has only materialized in the rigid form of a mutual exclusion: either career or marriage but not both. Although Qiuxin can discuss this choice rationally and authoritatively (as the title of her lecture suggests), she nonetheless feels emotionally trapped while at the same time obligated to move on as though she has no choice, *as though she is the one who has been excluded and left behind*. This contradictory psychological condition—brought into sharp focus in this case by the chance reappearance of the former male friend—in which physical and social emancipation is somehow lived and experienced as paralysis, points to modern Chinese women's continued bondage to a social contract based, predominantly, on heterosexual, reproductive domesticity. Qiuxin, we might say, is the personification of an incomplete revolution: she can consciously opt against traditional womanhood, but she remains imprisoned in its affective shadow by way of a deep sense of personal dejection. Nowhere is this sense of dejection more directly expressed than in her name, "autumn heart," two characters that, when combined, form the character *chou*, meaning sadness.

Without a doubt, Bing Xin's story, like much of her work, is a piece of sentimentalism. From a technical point of view, however, what it highlights with economical means (within the space of just a few pages) is the formal congealment of—and at that time still a novel experimentation with—what we would nowadays call psychic interiority. As a progressive woman writer, responsive to the tensions of modernity in early twentieth-century China, Bing Xin rightly understood that, to portray feminine agency in a cultural context in which women, even highly educated ones like herself, had long been subordinated, one needed to present that agency with special narrative methods. What makes her infrequently read short story formally remarkable, then, are precisely the codes that remain crucial to this day to the exploration of the self as the self is sutured with modernized femininity.

The first such code is the modern woman's physical mobility: Qiuxin, for instance, is a traveler, with the freedom to move from place to place that comes with education and relative social standing. Second, physical mobility leads logically to hitherto unavailable opportunities for observation—as one is constantly in the company of strangers—and thus for self-examination and introspection. As she reminisces about events of the past, Qiuxin literally looks at herself in the mirror. Third, this "inward" turn toward the self (as seen by other people, as an objectified image), albeit stemming from freedom, is ironically accompanied by a sense of entrapment and degradation as well as by low self-esteem. Fourth, the insights of introspection are revealed to be a belated illumination—of time and relationships that have receded and/or progressed beyond one's grasp. Fifth, a predominant feeling of melancholy pervades the character(s) involved, a feeling that is then semiotically reexternalized or metaphorized as nature, in the form of the elements and the seasons, such as the west wind, late autumn, and so forth. (In this regard, the writing of feminine sorrow borrows conveniently from the rich rhetorical repertoires of classical Chinese and European romantic poetry, in which nature has often been anthropomorphized with human affect and cultural meaning.)

Ultimately, there is a lingering sense of loss. What exactly is lost? Beyond all the unpretentious signs of a mournful psychic reality, Bing Xin's story compels us to ask: how does a free and highly educated woman come to think of herself in terms of loss, of having missed out on something, when to all appearances she has achieved a degree of autonomy that few in early twentieth-century Chinese society, including men, ever enjoyed? In no uncertain terms, the story suggests that Qiuxin's emotional disorientation is caused by her skepticism and insecurity about her own choice (to forsake the rewards of the kinship family). We thus arrive at the final presentation code familiar to sentimental introspection: whereas Yuan (the other) has reached *home*, Qiuxin (the self) must, as it were, continue her journey in the form of an abject, self-imposed *exile*.

The legacy of "Xifeng" is historical as well as formal. It brings to the fore the question of how to deal, in writing, with women's agency at a time when the constraints on that agency remained, as ever, unrelenting, especially in the form of popular conceptions. To this question, Bing Xin supplied the experimental answer of constructing a feminine psychic interiority, in which it is the woman character's act of self-examination that may be seen as the beginning of an alternative form of empowerment. Yet what remains unresolved in this legacy is precisely the self-contradictory form taken by this empowerment. In the midst of action and mobility, and professional achievement, pangs of self-doubt, self-denigration, and self-beratement slowly thicken into a kind of subjecthood with unmitigated—and seemingly unmitigable—feelings of sadness. It is not the unfree woman but the free woman who feels herself trapped. Is this affective overdetermination, which occupies such a central place in the narrative, also an ideological overdetermination? The implications of this question are rich and weighty, and far from having been exhaustively scrutinized. Perhaps because of this, several if not all of the (coded) features of Bing Xin's little piece continue to reappear in different versions even in contemporary cultural representations of modern Chinese women.

PSYCHIC INTERIORITIES IN THE FORM OF CINEMATIC FLASHBACKS: MULTIPLICITIES IN MOTION

We may now turn to Ann Hui's film *Song of the Exile*, an autobiographical screen drama about the coming-of-age of a young woman, Hueyin Cheung, whose life events span the 1950s to 1970s in Portuguese Macao, British Hong Kong, England, Japan, and mainland China.[4] (Notably, the screenplay was written by Wu Nianzhen, the famous collaborator with Taiwan director Hou Hsiao-hsien and an actor in films such as Hou's *City of Sadness* and Edward Yang's *Yi Yi*.) At the heart of this drama is Hueyin's difficult relationship with her mother since young childhood. Before discussing the multiple dimensions of this relationship, let me first recapitulate the main events and the order in which they appear in the film.

Chronologically, the main events revolving around the various characters are as follows:

1. Early 1940s: Aiko (Hueyin's mother), while a young woman in Beppu, her hometown, has an episode of unrequited love. She soon leaves Japan to join her elder brother and his family in Manchuria, a Japanese colony at that time.

2. 1945: After Japan loses the war, Aiko and her family are in hiding in Manchuria. Her brother's baby has fallen seriously ill, and, in an attempt to save him, she risks her own life by running out onto the main road to seek help. Hueyin's father, a young translator for the military with a family background in Chinese herbal medicine, saves the baby's life and becomes friends with the Japanese family. When the family members, like other Japanese residents in Manchuria, are being repatriated to Japan, the young man asks Aiko to stay with him in China. ·

3. The period from the late 1940s to 1963: Hueyin's parents are married, and Hueyin is born in Manchuria in 1948. With his wife and child, Hueyin's father rejoins his parents in Macao but then leaves them behind as he goes alone to work in Hong Kong. Eventually, Aiko rejoins her husband in Hong Kong, but little Hueyin refuses to leave Macao with her parents. She remains in the care of her grandparents until 1963, when the latter decide to go back to Guangdong (south China) to join their younger son. At the age of about fifteen, Hueyin is finally reunited with her parents and younger sister in Hong Kong.

4. The period from 1963 to the early 1970s: At her parents' home in Hong Kong, Hueyin feels increasingly alienated from and critical of her mother. For the first time, she learns (from her father and to her surprise) that her mother is Japanese and that much of her mother's seemingly unacceptable behavior is the result of having to cope with living a foreign culture.[5] Despite this discovery, Hueyin decides to move out and live by herself.

5. 1973: Hueyin completes a master's degree in communications/film studies in London. (Her father is dead by this point.) She is turned down for a job at the BBC, and, despite being scheduled for an interview with another television station, she returns to Hong Kong to attend her sister's wedding. Her sister and brother-in-law then emigrate to Canada.

6. 1973: Hueyin stays in Hong Kong in her mother's flat, watching television news reports on the Cultural Revolution that is raging in China, especially in the Guangdong area.

7. Hueyin accompanies her mother on a visit to Beppu. This is the first visit home to Japan that Aiko has made in three decades. It is an eye-opening experience for Hueyin, who begins discovering things about her mother's past and comes to a new and sympathetic understanding of the older woman.

8. Back in Hong Kong, news of Hueyin's grandfather's having had a stroke arrives. Hueyin visits her grandparents in Guangzhou, bringing gifts of groceries and merchandise that her mother has packed for her in-laws. The elders are living in rather modest conditions and taking care of a young child with Down syndrome left in their care by Hueyin's uncle. As Hueyin sits by her grandfather's bed watching him fall asleep, she recalls her childhood years in Macao and tears roll down her cheeks.

As pointed out by critics, the use of flashbacks—commonly understood as a literary or cinematic device in which an earlier event is inserted into the chronological order of a narrative—is a regular feature in Ann Hui's films.[6] Does this have something to do with Hui's interest in women's issues and in devising ways to portray a nonsynchronous but not nonexistent frame of action/agency from within the minds of female characters? (As Elaine Yee-lin Ho points out, "her films centralize and individualize women subjects in ways that the earlier Cantonese cinema had rarely attempted.")[7] While the answer to this will have to remain conjectural, it seems fair to say that, in the context of modern Chinese culture, cinematic flashbacks have provided one of the most productive methods for elaborating women's psychic interiority, a method that can be traced to early twentieth-century writers such as Bing Xin.[8] Flashbacks allow for a specific kind of cognitive and epistemic shift, whereby the world becomes comprehensible not so much through direct sensory-motor movements as through temporally mediated events such as memories, retellings, and juxtapositions of disparate images. As a filmmaker, Hui's investment in flashbacks is thus historically in step with what Gilles Deleuze has discussed as the emergence of the time image in post–Second World War (European, American, and Japanese) cinema, wherein human agency itself, or so Deleuze argues, has undergone a mutation from being rational action to being a "seeing function, at once fantasy and report, criticism and compassion"[9]—a mutation in which, in other words, action (in all its spontaneity) has become irreversibly supplanted by and subordinated to time (with its inassimilable complexities). Hui's own academic work on the French *nouveau roman* author Alain Robbe-Grillet—the subject of her master of philosophy thesis at the University of Hong Kong in the 1970s—was, in this light, an early indication of her ongoing attraction to avant-garde experimentation with narrative time in contemporary literature as well as film.

Although Deleuze himself, notably, expressed reservation about flashbacks—his reason being that they tend to require external justification[10]—I nonetheless believe that flashbacks can offer a highly interesting kind of narrative mediation, one that has extensive implications for the construction of psychic interiority. In representational terms, cinematic flashbacks are nothing short of a palpable link at which the otherwise imperceptible processes of mental transition and transfer involving temporal differences can be visibly displayed and observed.[11] But therein lies the paradox, in ways that remind us of Pasolini's point about the double nature of cinema (as discussed in the previous chapter): once displayed on the screen, such flashbacks ineluctably confront us with the question of whether they can always be rerouted back to some originating consciousness. And even where such rerouting is made explicit (as, for instance, by voice-over narration or by visual focalization on a particular character), the projectile, objectlike nature of cinematic images, with their appearance of ontological self-sufficiency, tends to leave something ambiguous about their supposedly obvious (re)connectability to a clearly demarcated psychic interiority. Whereas in Bing Xin's story, psychic interiority is consigned to a single woman character in such a manner as to leave little doubt that she is the subject of the thoughts, memories, and reflections being described, the cinematic flashbacks in Hui's film seem to push beyond the demarcations of such subjecthood and beyond a simple or direct correspondence between individual characters and (the objectified images of) memory/interiority.

On the screen, through the interweaving of different characters' perspectives, the events in Hui's film actually unfold in the following order:

$$5, 3, 6, 3, 5/6, 3, 4, 6, 7, 1, 2, 8$$

One can tell by this drastically altered sequencing the constitutive role played by the flashbacks (and, by implication, memories). Even this sequencing, moreover, is not an absolutely precise rendition of the images appearing on the screen because there are occasionally memories/flashbacks inserted within memories/flashbacks. For this reason, a reading of the film cannot, to my mind, proceed by simply reestablishing the chronology of the events. Rather, it is necessary to consider how the film's materiality resides in these temporal reversals and dispersions, which are seldom straightforward.

In other words, rather than using chronology as the ultimate rationale for (re)organizing the events, the question to consider is how the disjointedness in which the events literally appear signifies. What kind of status should the flashbacks be given? Should they be treated as reality, the way the nonflashback scenes are?[12] But strictly speaking, are there nonflashback scenes in this film? After all, the film begins, continues, and concludes explicitly with Hueyin's voice-over narration recounting events of the past.[13] Even what seems to be the present or chronologically the most recent moment—1973—is rendered as a set of memories, to which Hueyin's voice-over refers, significantly, as "that year" in the latter part of the film. Is the entire film a collection of flashbacks then? If so, how are we to determine the relative or differential function of one flashback against another? Should we suppose that each flashback simply gives way to another and so on, ad infinitum, or is there some final, stable referent that transcends them and gives them coherence from the outside, in an extradiegetic fashion?[14]

To begin to approach these questions, let me note that there are at least three types of flashbacks in play in *Song of the Exile*. The most accessible type is the flashback with a voice-over. For instance, on her return to Hong Kong at the beginning of the film, Hueyin and her mother get into an argument over what she should wear at her sister's wedding. As Hueyin stands by the window with her back to the camera, we hear her voice-over—"In my memory, mother wasn't like that. . . . She used to be a silent and reserved woman"—and we are then shown the flashback to the Macao period. Or, when, toward the end of their trip to Japan, Aiko recalls (for her daughter) how she met her husband in Manchuria, her voice gives clear indications that we are reentering the past. In these scenes, a character's voice serves as the narrative consciousness guiding us back to the past, and the flashback in the form of images becomes subordinated to the voice, which provides a supporting frame.

The second type of flashback is the flashback without any voice-over. In this case, the audience is shown one set of images and then another without being explicitly told who is doing the remembering. We see this, for instance, when the unpleasant haircut scene of 1973 (in preparation for the sister's wedding) shifts (back) to the unpleasant haircut scene of the 1950s in Macao or when Hueyin's somewhat awkward experience of being surrounded and talked about by curious strangers in Japan shifts (back) to her mother's experience of being surrounded and talked about by unfriendly strangers in the Macao household. Although Hui tends in such cases to refocalize on a character's face as a way to signal to the audience "this is what *this* person is remembering," the perspectival polysemia embedded in each set of flashbacks makes it difficult to accept such refocalization as the only possible or exclusive meaning available. Instead of simply (re)matching the flashback with a character's face/consciousness (in what is sometimes called "point of view"), I believe this second type of flashback raises a more tricky issue, namely: how do we evaluate the juxtaposition of images without ultimately falling back on the logic of omniscient narration?[15] If the point is not simply to trace the images back to a definite someone, not even an omniscient storyteller or seer, how do we begin to process imagistic transitions and transfers? Are they to be grasped as connections, mutual reflections, unexpected crossings, or infinite becomings (whereby one set of images mysteriously transforms into another)?

Third, there are the flashbacks within flashbacks—the best example being Aiko's story of her past (in Manchuria and, before that, in Japan) within Hueyin's narration/memory of their trip to Japan. There is also the example of Hueyin's flashback to herself (as a child in Macao) watching her grandfather picking up a papaya at a Macao market stall, within the flashback of her (as a secondary-school pupil in uniform in Hong Kong) watching an older man (who resembles her grandfather) picking up some lotus root at a Hong Kong market stall. In this type of flashback, the act of remembering has become its own referent, so that behind one memory is not simply another memory but, strictly speaking, another act of remembering, with no clear-cut or ultimate beginning to be ascertained. At this juncture, the fact that the entire film is offered as an account of past events can, arguably, be used to advance the point that every scene we see is always already a flashback (a past self's act of remembering) within a flashback (a present self's act of remembering).

Whether it serves to unify two or more temporally segregated events, raise questions about the subject or agent of memory (and, with that, the ontological status of adjacent images—and of imagistic adjacency), or demonstrate the mise-en-abîme inscribed in the act of remembering, flashbacks in Hui's work are without question a provocative way of articulating boundaries—not just spatial and geographical but also temporal and mental—and their malleability. To this extent, the actual unfolding of events in Song of the Exile is not, and should not be, understood simply as a secondary arrangement that stands in a dualist relationship with the original, linear chronological order. Rather, it is more fruitful to see in the alternative sequencing the emergence of a temporal crisscrossing that, in the process of multiplying perspectives, also challenges a simple bifurcation of time (into, for instance, story and plot or chronology and narration). That is to say, once flashbacks are in use, what is of interest is not so much pinpointing a polarized structural relation between clock/calendar time and artificial/fictive time, as apprehending a proliferation of cognitive and epistemic potentialities beyond what is allowed by such a polarity. The meaning of successive time—of time as succession—whether in the form of linear chronology or even in the form of a jumbled sequence—is no longer the most crucial concern here.[16]

Accordingly, in Hui's hands, "psychic interiority" as a narrative technique has mutated (and advanced) to the point of being an open, because endlessly expandable and extendable, time and space, quite distinct from the claustrophobic introspective recoiling of the self that we encounter in Bing Xin. Interiority is now not so distinguishable from exteriority, if only because it has to be conveyed through objectlike images, images that are accessibly out there for all to see. In this respect, even the most simple flashback does not exactly invite a straightforward restoration of connections; rather, it makes visible what I would call multiplicities in motion (multiplicities in terms of characters, times, actions, and memories)—a specifically filmic process, perhaps, that signals at once the pluralizing and inevitable dividing—and fissuring—of mental and affective circuits.[17]

The absolute centrality of flashbacks in Song of the Exile suggests both Hui's affinity with older modern Chinese women intellectuals such as Bing Xin (insofar as she has continued to remold "psychic interiority" by borrowing some of the familiar formal codes of presentation) and her arrival, through the cinematographic interspersing of temporalities, at a considerably more dynamic working model than the single woman character's perspective. Multiplicities in motion, engendered in Hui's film by cinematic flashbacks, indicate that the exploration of "psychic interiority" has reached a stage at which a cohesive reassembling of meanings is, at the level of technique, unnecessary if not altogether impossible. Instead, it is precisely the disintegration of such cohesive reassembling that lends such exploration an energy that implodes and splinters the notion of "psychic interiority" as a neatly bounded self.

THE CHINESE KINSHIP FAMILY: ETHNOSOCIAL STRONGHOLD AND . . . RECUPERATIVE CLOSURE?

Although Hueyin is aware that her mother is Japanese, it is not until she accompanies Aiko to Japan that she finally achieves her personal enlightenment, her coming-of-age, as it were. This journey to Japan enables Hueyin to appreciate for the first time how her mother has lived in the Cheung family as a foreigner, slighted and discriminated against during her years in Macao by her in-laws and their house guests and condemned to a life of loneliness when her husband was away for long periods of time. In the figure of the emotionally remote mother with whom the daughter could not communicate, Hui offers an outsider's perspective on the Chinese kinship family, which thrives as an ethnosocial stronghold with entrenched customs and practices. These include a condoned belit.'ement of women, demand for filial piety, indulgence of young children, and, most important of all, xenophobia toward those who happen not to be familial or ethnic insiders. Because, even under the most benevolent of circumstances, a daughter-in-law traditionally occupies the suspect position of someone from the outside, Aiko's status is triply exterior—as a daughter-in-law; as a representative of the disdained, though by the latter part of 1945 defeated, national enemy; and, most crucially, as non-Chinese.

In a story that explicitly alludes to exile in its title, the boundaries governing people's cultural identities, with their modes of inclusion and exclusion, logically constitute a major source of the human drama,[18] but how is a director supposed to depict such boundaries on film? Hui's method is ingenious: I am thinking of the incidents that feature the mundane and almost unnoticeable details of food consumption and food sharing. Whereas in The Road Home and In the Mood for Love food is associated in different nostalgic manners with labor or with languor, in Song of the Exile food is perceptively presented as the place where ethnocultural boundaries are most intimately—and obstinately—drawn.

In London, as a foreign student, Hueyin leads her fellow students to purchase a Chinese takeout meal of spring rolls. Why spring rolls—why not fish and chips, for instance? Are these spring rolls, marking Hueyin as an East Asian, an outsider (a colonial subject, in fact) to England despite her fluent English, a means of prefiguring the kind of cultural conflict that is to be enacted repeatedly over food in the rest of the film? Among Hueyin's memories of her childhood and adolescence are several having to do with eating—in Macao, of buying bread from a hawker who is passing by her grandparents' house, of her grandmother taking her to school with treats of Chinese snacks (pieces of sweetened winter melon and beef jerky), and of having dim sum with her grandparents at a traditional teahouse; in Hong Kong, of being ordered by her father to cook dinner when her mother neglects her housewifely duties by playing mah-jongg all day. Food in these memories is associated with Hueyin's estrangement from and resentment of her mother, but the ethnocultural import of their fraught relationship will only be understood later (by the audience), when Hueyin learns that her mother is Japanese.

Nowhere is the phenomenon of ethnoculture as aggressive boundary setting more acutely portrayed than in the grandparents' treatment of their Japanese daughter-in-law in the Macao household. Dismissing the food prepared by Aiko as unacceptably "raw" and "cold" (*shengsheng leng-leng*)—in ways that bring to mind Claude Lévi-Strauss's analysis of culinary significations in *The Raw and the Cooked*[19]—and hence bad for the stomach, the elders are shown gathering in their own bedroom with a portable stove, cooking and sharing dishes that are more agreeable to their southern Chinese taste. "Raw" and "cold" is, of course, also the way Hueyin's mother comes across to her own child. By contrast, the camera shows the grandfather beckoning affectionately to his granddaughter to join them in their insiders' properly cooked feast, while Aiko is banished outside their door like a savage, left to eat her deplored, because uncooked and uncivilized, meal all by herself. In the name of procuring culinary satisfaction ("things taste better when cooked this way"), the grandparents have de facto used their eating habits as a way to mark their territory. By stigmatizing and excluding Aiko, what they consume and incorporate—we might also say internalize—is none other than the violence of a rigidly enforced cultural border, with "us" on this side and "them" on the other.

While the early part of the film concentrates on Hueyin's recollection of her mother's alienation (a condition that she, as a child, was unwittingly complicit in aggravating), the second half of the film reverses the roles of daughter and mother as cultural insider and outsider as they travel to Japan. Now it is Hueyin who feels she is the foreigner, observing the local customs and festivities, the reunions with family and friends, and the visit to her mother's home (including her maternal grandparents' graves) with a sense of fascination, intensified in part by her inability to speak and understand the Japanese language. Interestingly, this episode of exoticism, suggesting a brief symmetry between mother and daughter, produces a new sense of reflexivity on Hueyin's part. It is as though the inconvenience of being stuck in a foreign country where she is deaf and mute—a multi-faceted obstacle in narratological terms—becomes in the end a rewarding homecoming experience. For the first time, Hueyin feels reconciled with and able to return home to the mother from whom she has been exiled all these years. With the interruptions caused by the lack of understanding finally smoothed away, she can forge ahead in the course of her own personal growth.

From the mother's perspective, things are quite different, and the positive change and self-development that we witness taking place in Hueyin cannot be said to be evident in Aiko. Aiko thus stands out in the film as an enigma, a character who remains only partially discernible and whose perpetual cultural liminality punctures the illusion of a continuum between mother's and daughter's perspectives. For Aiko, the trip to Japan is a journey to a past—her familial and national origin—that has become distant and emotionally demanding; it is a return to a home that is fast disappearing. Not only is she confronted with her own unresolved feelings about the people and events of her youth (she repeatedly praises Japanese things when talking to Hueyin yet never forgets, while they are with her Japanese family and friends, to show off her daughter as a trophy of her time abroad and a sign of her social enviability); she also has to cope with and concede to her brothers' intent to sell their parental home, the only stable reference point she has left in Japan.[20]

More critically, how has Aiko managed to survive in a foreign land, among people who have marginalized and rejected her with such hostility? What are the revealing traces of her survival tactics among the Chinese—and of her permanent dislocation from her own culture? From the beginning of the film, we notice that she is (or has become) a quite typical Cantonese maternal figure, who dresses not only herself but also her daughters for ceremonious occasions in gaudy Cantonese styles (with overkills of deep red and gold colors and glittery jewels) and who keeps stressing the importance of their looking like one family. To be sure, Aiko's efforts to make herself look the same as the people around her have been evident since the early days in Macao, when she is always seen wearing a *cheongsam/qipao*, but, again, nowhere are such efforts more striking than in the rituals of cooking and eating.

After the wedding banquet is over, Aiko brings home the leftovers with the intention of making a "hot pot" the same way her in-laws used to do in Macao. On her return to Japan, she is at first delighted to sample again the authentic Japanese dishes she misses such as soba noodles with tempura, shrimp, and tofu. Once they have stayed for a while, however, she begins to express exactly the same critical attitude toward Japanese cooking that was expressed by her in-laws years earlier—that it is "not right" because it is raw and cold, that it makes her stomach feel uncomfortable, and that she much prefers—is homesick for—Cantonese food, especially the hot home-made soups. Having more or less completely assimilated to her husband's culture over the decades, Aiko discovers that her former home has receded to the margins of the civilized—so much so that it has become distasteful, inedible, indeed uninhabitable. Eventually, back in Hong Kong, when news of Hueyin's grandfather's stroke reaches them, it is Aiko who, like a dutiful Chinese daughter-in-law, instructs her own daughter that, no matter how busy she is, she must visit her grandparents in Guangdong. As she informs Hueyin, she has spent the afternoon shopping for and packing what she imagines are basic necessities for the elders, including, remarkably (as we find out when Hueyin's luggage is unpacked on arrival), some *caigan* (dried bok choy), a traditional Cantonese soup ingredient.

If the ending of the film shows a homecoming for the daughter, whose attitude toward her mother has become much more compassionate, it marks Aiko's future trajectory rather differently, with much more uncertainty. In the manner of Qiuxin, Bing Xin's heroine, a sense of loss and melancholy haunts the older woman's story as she faces the consequences of the life choices she made years ago when she was a courageously independent young woman. (Hueyin observes that Aiko seems to have become "much more quiet and reserved" and "turned much older" since their trip to Japan.) Although she has followed the rules of the heterosexual social contract by getting married and having children, she has, it seems, paid a heavy price in terms of what she has had to abandon along the way, namely, her ties to her own country and family. (For instance, her own younger brother has never forgiven her for having been disloyal to Japan by marrying a Chinese man.) Just when Hueyin seems to have refound her home in Aiko, then, Aiko has bade farewell to hers, not knowing if she will ever return. Because of Aiko's story, the flashbacks of the trip to Japan loom as a set of fractured passages, with profoundly divergent directions and implications for the two women, who seem to have been briefly brought together in one dimension yet otherwise go in separate ways.

Like Bing Xin, Ann Hui names her story with a purposeful evocation of autumn. "Ke tu qiu hen," literally "Autumn melancholy on a sojourn away from home," is the title of a well-known Cantonese song (based on the musical form *nanyin*, or "the southern tune") in which a poor scholar, on a trip under the autumn moon, laments his lost love, a faithful courtesan who, unlike others in her profession, did not mind his poverty and gave him her heart. Performed to great renown by the Cantonese opera actor and singer Bai Jurong during the 1910s and 1920s, the song, still heard from time to time in contemporary Hong Kong, exists now as a nostalgic reminder of bygone eras for older Cantonese-speaking populations.[21] In *Song of the Exile*, the song is introduced in flashbacks to Hueyin's childhood in Macao: her grandmother is taking a nap while the song is being played on the radio, and Hueyin (in the manner of young Chinese children who are coached by elders during their early years) is reciting Tang Dynasty poems for her grandfather, who rewards her with some candy and coaxes her how not to "forget [her] origins" (*wangben*), before the two of them fall asleep together, with the little girl lying prone on top of the old man (fig. 4.1). The leisurely daytime rest, the sweet intimacy between the generations (with the grandfather gently telling the grandchild to study medicine when she grows up so she can serve China), and the mildly sad tune of Bai Jurong's singing blend together to compose an unforgettable picture of a previous life moment. The song is heard again at the film's closing, with flashbacks to a scene of grandchild and grandparents sauntering past a pond of lotuses in bloom. Just as the lyrics speak of a lost romantic love and just as the tune recalls a musical form that has long since declined, so do Grandfather and Grandmother loom in Hueyin's mind as loved ones whose times on earth are about to end. Her own independence and freedom—as a cosmopolitan traveler, journalist, daughter, grandchild, and urban woman—hence becomes finally tinged, as the title of the song suggests, with the autumnal melancholy of the brooding exile, her mind saturated with the awareness of the passing of time.

As in Bing Xin's story, we see the prominence of a chain of imaginary associations: the well-educated woman, whose physical mobility becomes the backdrop to a series of introspective processes. In Bing Xin's story, the exploration of the feminine self is contained within one character's life and over one journey; in Hui's film, the effort is a complex one involving two women characters from two generations, over a number of decades, cultural locations, and political situations. Importantly, however, even when it is continually challenged by modern capitalist society, in which women are gaining various degrees of social and professional autonomy, the Chinese kinship family is able to reassert its demands with deep-rooted force. Just as Qiuxin's sorrow seems to confirm and revalidate the virtue of what she has forsaken (husband and children), so, too, does Aiko's voluntary conversion into a Cantonese daughter-in-law and mother seem to confirm the unyielding domination of Chinese family life, notwithstanding the imminent mortality of the elders.

In this regard, the individualization and empowerment of women in Hui's films, albeit generically and genealogically tied to the release of "psychic interiorities" into multiplicities in motion (as I suggested in the previous section), need to be assessed not only in and by themselves but also against a recurrent feature in Hui's work: the patriotic patriarch figures in whom she seems consistently and positively invested. Consider the spectrum of older men in her films: not just Hueyin's grandfather, who even on his sickbed urges Hueyin not to "lose hope in China" (literally, "not to be disappointed with China" in the Cantonese dialogue) but also the grandfather who holds on to Chinese values against the onslaught of youthful American culture in *Shanghai jiaqi* (*My American Grandson*, 1991) and the old man with Alzheimer's disease who continues to believe he is a fighter pilot flying a warplane for the Chinese Nationalist government in *Nüren sishi* (*Summer Snow*, 1995). No matter how xenophobic, prejudiced, or literally amnesic, these patriarchs are in the end shown to be worth loving and tolerating. By contrast, the women characters, in whom Hui places her vision for change, are often shown to be sympathetic only insofar as they seem capable of learning to accommodate these father figures, together with the values they embody, exactly as they are. In a nutshell, the women—and the women alone—are asked to be versatile and flexible: they must actively adapt and adjust even as the old men are adored for remaining themselves.

I am therefore tempted to read in the conclusion of *Song of the Exile* a recuperative attitude toward the Chinese kinship family. Elaine Yee-lin Ho's remarks offer a fair summation of Hui's work here: "The exploration of agency is heavily circumscribed by a continued investment in what inherited strictures will both allow and afford and increasingly reincorporated into an ethnocultural determinism that is, by history and definition, patriarchal in its social exemplifications. As such, her films tread the narrow path between the critique and reinvention of tradition and estrange it even while affirming its continued power to structure, coopt, and exclude women's subjects."[22]

Whether in early twentieth-century fiction or in late twentieth-century film, the feminine dramas I have discussed suggest that what Ho aptly refers to as "ethnocultural determinism" has survived with tenacity, condemning those who dare oppose or resist it to a life of isolation and forlornness. Autumn hearts, with their heavy sense of melancholy and loss, are thus ideologically overdetermined and seem to persist in spite of the novelization and avant-gardism that writers and directors alike have achieved at the level of technique. In Hui's case, one may go so far as to say that, where there is dispersion and disintegration at the level of the cinematic flashbacks, there is also assimilation, patriarchization, and sinification at the level of communal belonging. For Hui as for Bing Xin, if the engagement with "psychic interiority" has delivered possibilities for imagining an insuppressible feminine agency, ultimately it is also in women's social lives that the emotional strictures imposed by the Chinese kinship family seem the least escapable. Where boundaries have been made more fluid by means of avant-garde experimentalism, boundaries also seem to be reinforced—sentimentally—in terms of kinship bondage. To that extent, *Song of the Exile* is a powerful reminder of the ethnoculturally specific *and* imperialist excesses of the Chinese family tradition, which is as treacherous as it can be life-sustaining and which continues to command submission like a kind of nature. Autumn hearts are the recurrent symptoms of enduring this "natural" environment.

FIGURE 5.1 Li Qiao checking her ATM account, *Tian mi mi / Comrades, Almost a Love Story* (Copyright Golden Harvest / United Filmmakers Organization [UFO], 1996)

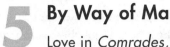

By Way of Mass Commodities
Love in *Comrades, Almost a Love Story*

Although, with the rapid modernization efforts ongoing since the early 1980s, conditions of life in many parts of the People's Republic of China have been steadily improving, for many Chinese mainlanders Hong Kong remains a symbol of material plenitude and progress.[1] Director Peter Ho-sun Chan's film *Tian mi mi* (*Comrades, Almost a Love Story*, 1996) is a story about two young mainlanders who arrive in Hong Kong on March 1, 1986, in search of a better life. Like many Chinese men who leave home to seek work abroad, Li Xiaojun, who is from Tianjin, hopes to earn enough money so that he can go home and marry his fiancée, Xiaoting. Li Qiao, from Guangdong Province, is by herself, with her family back home. For both, Hong Kong stands primarily as an opportunity for economic advancement, even though the film takes pains to portray a major difference between them: while Xiaojun seems earnest and more uncertain about things in general, Li Qiao is quick, smooth, and efficient in setting and following her goals. This difference in personal traits also corresponds to the contrast in the types of wage-earning activities they each assume as new immigrants. Xiaojun relies on family connections: to start his life in Hong Kong, he looks up an aunt, Rosie, and gets referred for a job as a deliveryman transporting slaughtered chickens to Chinese restaurants on a bicycle. Li Qiao, with no apparent kin in the colony, serves as a counter clerk at McDonald's while moonlighting as a recruiter working on commission for a commercial English language school. Whereas Xiaojun's job ties him to the local Chinese community of poultry sellers and restaurateurs, Li Qiao's professional choices are more enterprising and shrewd. Like Xiaojun's job, her job at McDonald's is about providing food, but, unlike his, it also provides an opportunity to move into the lower middle class through a foreign name-brand franchise. As well, like Xiaojun's job, her recruitment job is about delivery, but, unlike his, what she delivers are people: as a go-between, she earns her keep not by her own labor but by receiving kick-backs for recommending students who are, in the end, customers.

From the standpoint of film language, how can the activity of wage earning translate into the rather abstract process of self-fashioning? Among the high-tech symbols that greet us as the two protagonists establish themselves in Hong Kong, one stands out as a marker of Li Qiao's growing independence and self-assurance: the automatic teller machine (ATM). More than once and often with Xiaojun as a bystander, we see her checking her account balance at the ATM with anticipation and excitement (fig. 5.1). This process of specularization, performed in public in front of an impersonal electronic screen, provides a memorable encapsulation of Li Qiao's life trajectory at this point. By implementing a capitalist work ethic and by thriftily putting money away, she is able to look regularly into this special mirror, which, by enumerating her savings, also offers her the desired image of herself as an increasingly successful Hong Konger. However small those savings may be, this particular reflection, mediated explicitly through money, makes it possible for her to see herself repeatedly as she would like to be seen, in what amount to moments of narcissistic self-congratulation: "Hey, that's me. Look how I've made it!"

The ATM as mirror thus stands as an important thematic and narrative connection in this first part of the story, underscoring a process of subjectivization that occurs not through romance but through a rationalization of wage labor, frugality, and the steady accumulation of personal wealth. Indeed, Li Qiao strikes us as the stereotypical poor immigrant with a dream of assimilation and upward social mobility. For her, speculating on stocks is simply putting to use Hong Kong's own "native product," which she compares to the "oil in Arabia" and "durians in Thailand." If there is a love story here, it is first and foremost that of Li Qiao's fetishism for Hong Kong, its aggressive commercialism, and the seemingly boundless moneymaking opportunities it offers. As Michael Curtin writes, the visits to the ATM "convey an almost erotic relationship that seems to displace all other forms of interpersonal connection," so much so that, even when Xiaojun is with her, Li Qiao "seems either completely oblivious as to his presence, or she seems irritated by his intrusion upon this moment of private pleasure."[2] In narratological terms, therefore, it is the various unexpected twists and turns she encounters along the way that serve to delay, impede, and redirect the course of this narcissistic eroticism and flesh out the complexity of her story.

This perceptive association of the ATM with the process of existential self-affirmation suggests that the film's approach to the forces of capitalism—the market economy, consumerism, and various forms of commodification—is decidedly more liberal and permissive than is required by, say, an orthodox Marxist conceptual framework. In the latter, as we know, commodities are typically regarded as material manifestations of a profound human alienation in modern industrialized society. Marx's argument in *Capital*, made so famous by subsequent generations of scholars, is that commodities' mystifying appearances of ontological self-sufficiency veil and belie the fact of the human labor that has gone into their making. While such labor remains unacknowledged and often undercompensated, the surplus generated by the sale of commodities lines the pockets of the capitalists. Accordingly, in this classic political-economic analysis, commodities are the external indicators of an erroneous social process, and to desire them as such would be tantamount to a kind of misrecognition—one that is deemed complicit with the systemic ideological manipulation and injustice behind their beguiling surfaces. Instead, it is often said, we need to become conscious, vigilant, and ready to turn such deceptive practices on their heads, aiming for a righteous restoration of the agency of the worker and the proletariat.

By taking as its center of interest lower-class immigrants' struggles for survival in a ruthless transnational economic system, which has no qualms about exploiting them (first in Hong Kong, then in the United States), Chan's film, I contend, fully understands this classic ethical imperative and its stringent critique of commodification (as the core dysfunction or pathology of late capitalism). Nevertheless, it does not follow the imperative's logic to its end by assuming a straightforwardly negative, denunciatory attitude toward commodities. This deviation from Marx—even while holding the point of Marx's teaching in sympathy—constitutes, I believe, the most remarkable *thinking* that emanates from this story. In the life of the woman who seems single-mindedly driven to become rich—who, in other words, is intent on only one kind of narcissistic mirroring, namely, seeing herself empowered through money—the commodity itself, as I will go on to argue, undergoes a process of semiotic rupturing to become at once the narrative telos (the goal of socially successful self-fashioning) *and* the figure of this very telos's repeated interruption and transformation.[3] For this reason—namely, that the film is, arguably, a story about irrational linkages and potentialities brought to life by mass commodities—I tend not to agree entirely with critics who read this film primarily as an allegory, however ambivalent, of Hong Kong before 1997 or as a story about collective cultural identity.[4] In its attempt to harness the film to Hong Kong's recent history and political development, this type of reading seems to me (as I pointed out in my readings of Wong Kar-wai's work) to run the risk of foreclosing certain possibilities of analysis that may not be reducible to the demands of conventional geopolitical realism.[5] Instead, because, as Kwai-cheung Lo argues, the so-called identity of Hong Kong as a "local" culture is fluid and porous—in Lo's words, "the transnational itself in its becoming"[6]—it is essential to shift the terms of analysis to a different plane so as not simply to repeat inadvertently the ritual of placing Hong Kong in the position of a resistive native (be it in the form of history, population, culture, or something else) with a clearly defined boundary (or specificity) all its own.

Before moving on, let me recapitulate the main events of the rest of the film. Although Xiaojun and Li Qiao have become lovers and realize they have strong feelings for each other, they break off their relationship. Soon, Xiaojun's fiancée, Xiaoting, joins him from Tianjin, and they are married. Having lost all her savings in the stock market crash of 1987, Li Qiao is heavily in debt. She starts working as a masseuse, eventually becoming the mistress of one of her clients, Bao, a ruthless hoodlum who is nevertheless exceedingly kind and gentle with her. In ways she did not consciously plan, she finally finds herself living a comfortable life and making money as a versatile businesswoman, owning a florist's shop, a wedding photography studio,[7] and a small real estate development company. (Her filial wish to give her mother a new house back home on the mainland, however, is unfulfilled as the latter dies too soon.) At Xiaojun's wedding banquet in 1990, the old lovers meet again, and Li Qiao subsequently helps Xiaoting get a job as a dance teacher. Shortly afterward, Li Qiao and Xiaojun realize that their relationship remains unresolved, and, after renewing their physical intimacy, they decide to leave their partners. But just as Li Qiao is about to break the news to Bao, she discovers that Bao has become the target of a criminal investigation by the Hong Kong police. Unable to abandon Bao under such circumstances, Li Qiao ends up accompanying him on his escape from Hong Kong.

A couple of years later, in the autumn of 1993, Bao and Li Qiao find themselves in New York City's Chinatown, living the life of an anonymous, ordinary couple. During the same period, Xiaojun, now divorced, has also moved to New York City, where he makes a living as a cook at a Chinese restaurant, at times delivering takeout on a bicycle. As Li Qiao and Bao think they can finally settle down (they have been chatting about buying a house and having children), Bao, while waiting for Li Qiao to collect some laundry around the corner, is gunned down by a gang of black teenagers. Bao's death leads the authorities to notice that Li Qiao's visa has expired. While sitting in the police car and about to be deported by Immigration and Naturalization Service officers, she catches sight of Xiaojun cycling down the street. Despite a frantic chase through the hectic traffic of Manhattan, she misses him but in the process also successfully dodges the INS officers.[8] She is thus able to start a new life on her own, this time as a tour guide. On May 8, 1995, with her application for a green card finally approved, she makes plans to return to China for a visit. As she comes out of the travel agency in Chinatown, news of the death of pop singer Teresa Teng (Deng Lijun) is announced on the radio. After strolling around aimlessly for a while, Li Qiao stops outside an electronics shop where TV monitors are showing retrospective accounts and images of Teng's life and works. As she turns her head, she is greeted by the unbelievable: Xiaojun happens to be standing right next to her, also watching the broadcast. They have finally found each other—again!

SWEET TERESA

If we follow its Chinese title, *Tian mi mi*, the film may be seen simply as the romantic saga of the two protagonists.[9] "Tian mi mi," which means "sweetness," is the title of a Mandarin hit song originally performed by Teresa Teng, a superstar singer who was extremely popular in Taiwan, Hong Kong, Japan, and Southeast Asia during the 1970s and 1980s. The lyrics of the song, like many of its kind, are trite:

甜蜜蜜你笑得甜蜜蜜   好像花兒開在春風裏
開在春風裏
在哪裏在哪裏見過你   你的笑容這樣熟悉
我一時想不起
啊 。。。在夢裏

夢裏夢裏見過你   甜蜜笑得多甜蜜
是你是你夢見的就是你
在哪裏在哪裏見過你   你的笑容這樣熟悉
我一時想不起
啊 。 。 。在夢裏

A rough, literal translation (with added punctuation) goes something like this:

> Sweetly, you smile sweetly, like flowers blooming in the spring breeze—
> blooming in the spring breeze.
> Where have I seen you before? Your smile seems so familiar.
> I can't think of it—
> Oh . . . in dreams!
>
> In dreams I have seen you, smiling so sweetly.
> It's you, it's you, it's you I've seen in dreams.
> Where have I seen you before? Your smile seems so familiar.
> I can't think of it—
> Oh . . . in dreams!

Because mainland China did not open itself to the massive influx of capitalist cultural influences until well into the 1980s, Teng's success there—or at least as this film presents it—was something of a belated phenomenon. Her songs that became favorites of the mainlanders in the mid-1980s were already somewhat passé to audiences in Hong Kong.[10] In the film, this time lag in mass culture trends is the reason Li Qiao's attempt to reap a profit from Teng's cassette tapes and records fails miserably at the 1987 Chinese New Year's Eve market. Thinking that she is now a Hong Konger and that the songs *she* loves are going to be hot sale items, Li Qiao dreams of making a small fortune with Teng's recordings (as she had the previous Chinese New Year back in Guangzhou), only to reveal inadvertently that she, too, is just a new arrival from the mainland (like Xiaojun) and that despite all her pretenses she has not yet caught up with Hong Kong.

As Lo points out, the repeated appearances of Teng and her music constitute a key function in the film, helping the audience "notice structural unity and narrative coherence."[11] It remains to be argued how such structural unity and narrative coherence is achieved, however.

"Teresa Teng" introduces the predominant impact of the mass commodity both as consumerist object and as social process. This is evident, first of all, from the way music is consciously deployed in the film, in noticeable distinction from the convention whereby music is mere background accompaniment. We recall how Xiaojun's beginning ventures as a deliveryman are orchestrated by a particular tune—"Yiyongjun jinxing qu" (Tune of the righteous and courageous soldiers' march), the national anthem of the PRC, as though this country bumpkin's new life activities in capitalist British Hong Kong can somehow be choreographed and made harmonious with the Chinese national spirit. By contrast, the trajectory chosen by Li Qiao is decidedly that of commodity fetishism, as is suggested by Teng's song "Tian mi mi," which she starts humming while riding on the back of Xiaojun's bike one day (thus unwittingly confessing her origins as a mainlander, something she has wanted to hide). Even though she has to learn the painful lesson that she is, despite her efforts, out of date in her entrepreneurial endeavor to sell the cassette tapes and records, Li Qiao's activities continue to follow the lead of money rather than that of the nation or even romance.[12]

But what is it about Teng's music that makes it so popular and well liked? This is a more difficult question than it seems. At one level, one could, of course, mention the obvious positive qualities of Teng's voice—that it is soft, throaty, and feminine—and of her songs—that they are balladlike, pleasant to the ears, and easy to repeat with their catchy refrains, and so forth. It would also be possible, as is demonstrated by some critics as well as by director Chan, to ascribe to Teng's music a seemingly self-evident sentimental value derived from China and Chineseness.[13] However, this latter tendency to explain Teng's appeal by naming China or Chineseness as the ultimate reason (and referent), while certainly reasonable, seems also to foreclose the possibilities and trajectories of the form of attachment conveyed distinctly by the semiotic logic of the film—a form of attachment that is other than simple ethnic unity or ethnic communal bonding. As Lo argues:

As new immigrants suffering from culture shock, poverty, and discrimination, the protagonists have achieved a transcendent unity and a community of one not by any traditional folk-cultural forms but, ironically, through an "alien" commercial Taiwanese song. . . . The style and cultural connotations of Teng's love songs allow the viewer to easily attribute a particular emotional cast to the musical accompaniment of various scenes in the film. But what is telling about the film's score is that the identification of the musical expression involves transnational cultural codes and differences under a seemingly unified national representation. The romantic desire for unity is overdetermined and structured by a transnationalized musical mode rather than by any indigenous folk songs.[14]

Insofar as these songs are part of a mass culture phenomenon, "Teresa Teng" should, I believe, be treated less as a real person than as a type of sign that is characteristic of the modes of social relations based on consumerist desires and habits. "Consumption," as Jean Baudrillard writes, "is not a passive mode of assimilation (*absorption*) and appropriation which we can oppose to an active mode of production. . . . Consumption is an active mode of relations (not only to objects, but to the collectivity and to the world), a systematic mode of activity and a global response on which our whole cultural system is founded."[15] In this light, the positive qualities of Teng's music that are easily identifiable—qualities that, to all appearances, account for her appeal as a mass idol—should perhaps be approached in a more imaginative way. Rather than being taken as a concrete truth that can be rationally accounted for, the so-called sweetness of Teng should, I contend, be regarded as an inexplicable something that, in fact, serves to veil a certain void, the void of a fundamental triviality and nonsense. Strictly speaking, no one really knows why Teng's music gives so much pleasure (purportedly even to Chinese Communist Party cadres), yet this nonsense, this no-thing-ness, this lack (of substance) is precisely what energizes the circulation and consumption of her music. As Baudrillard puts it: "Consumption is a system which assures the regulation of signs and the integration of the group: it is simultaneously a morality (a system of ideological values) and a system of communication, a structure of exchange."[16] Paradoxically, then, Teng's music is desirable because everyone else desires it (even if only in secret, as in the case of the party cadres). As a sign that is, in and of itself, empty, "Teresa Teng" enables the formation not of any individualist or solipsistic pleasure as such but rather of sociality through consumption.

This capacity of the reified mass commodity to mediate, indeed to create, interpersonal bonds is an insight that consistently distinguishes *Tian mi mi* from many of its contemporaries.

When Li Qiao and Xiaojun meet again in 1990 and discover that they are still in love with each other, "Teresa Teng" once again turns up at a fateful moment. One day, as the two of them happen to drive down the street together, one of Teng's songs ("Goodbye My Love") comes on the car radio, and Teng the singer actually happens to be on the street, surrounded by fans, whereupon Xiaojun jumps out of the car and obtains an autograph from her. The reappearance of "Teresa Teng" at this point serves not only to rekindle the feelings of attachment but also to seal the bond between the two former lovers. It is as if their love, never completely fulfilled, has been left behind and preserved outside their consciousnesses, in the saccharin melodies of a mass idol, melodies that now return in the impersonal time and space of a public broadcast to captivate them anew, reinserting them into the loop of an intimacy they have tried in vain to escape. Finally, in New York's Chinatown, it is once again sweet "Teresa Teng," now in the form of posthumous televised images displayed inside shop windows, who brings about a reunion of the separated lovers in the most mundane, yet extraordinary, manner.

Unlike the song "Ke tu qiu hen" in *Song of the Exile*, which is introduced consciously to help establish an interpretative frame for understanding the film, "Tian mi mi" and other songs by Teng are often heard by chance by the characters within the diegesis (as well as being played, on some occasions, extradiegetically). Above all, these songs serve the purpose of acting as a metacomment on the events through their emotional intensity, which is less an effect of the songs' formulaic lyrics (or contents) than an effect of the powerful modes of externalization and objectification they provide, repeatedly, for intersubjective relations. Giving these relations a palpable shape and continuity, "Teresa Teng" invokes the sense of an inexplicable affinity—what in the discussion of Wong Kar-wai in chapter 3 I referred to as *yuan*—between the two protagonists that seems to have been prescripted somewhere else. Contrary to traditional Buddhist beliefs, however, this somewhere else is not to be located in the realm of the spiritual or the metaphysical (such as a former incarnation) but rather in the realm of the profane, the marketable, and the consumable. If, as I suggested in the previous chapter, *Song of the Exile* is an experiment in the construction of psychic interiorities through filmic flashbacks, in *Tian mi mi*, it is rather mass commodities that have taken over the function of producing such interiorities. Even the deepest human attachments, it seems, are now conjured and lived—that is, become real—through these commodities.[17]

Li Qiao and Xiaojun, we might say, love and find each other again *in* "Teresa Teng." Theirs is a special kind of love story: their hearts are connected not so much on their own as through the fetishized commodity, through their lingering mutual devotion to (and consumption of) a celebrity performer's lowbrow pop songs. The last series of scenes outside the shop window in Chinatown—preceded by Teng's "Yueliang daibiao wo de xin" (The moon represents my heart), which then gives way once again to "Tian mi mi"—shows them both transfixed on another kind of electronic screen. This time, it is not an ATM but the images of their dead idol staring back at them through television, enlivening them yet once more with the never-quite-satisfied but therefore irrepressible mutuality of their identities and destinies.

To the extent that it exhibits a clear understanding of how concrete human actions, beliefs, and relations in contemporary society are inextricable from a consumerist relation based on reified commodification, especially in the form of showbiz glamour, *Tian mi mi* is resonant with director Chan's previous works, such as the 1993–94 blockbusters *Jinzhi yuye* (*He's a Woman, She's a Man*), a comedy about the sexual identity confusions triggered by a crazed music fan's entry into her singing idols' world, and *Xin nan xiong nan di* (*He Ain't Heavy, He's My Father*, coproduced and codirected with Lee Chi-ngai), a comedy in which hit songs such as "Tell Laura I Love Her," the household names and faces of Hong Kong Cantonese film stars of the 1950s and 1960s, their personalities as reported in the tabloids, and the clichéd roles they used to play on screen are all part of the unraveling of a story about a son's changing attitudes toward his father.

ALMOST A LOVE STORY

What, then, is the epistemic status of the mass commodity ultimately projected by this film? In the case of "Teresa Teng," the mass commodity is, as I have suggested, a narrative hinge, a motif mobilized both thematically and structurally to bring coherence to the story of romance between the two protagonists. But it would be insufficient to stop at Xiaojun and Li

Qiao's relationship. Given the common tendency to demonize commodities as loci of error, deception, and injustice, is the film not implying something at once bolder and more subversive, perhaps going so far as to offer a fundamentally deviant way of thinking about this chain of standard moral associations? And how does this explicitly staged prominence of reification and consumerism, refreshingly unperturbed by the usual Marxist qualms, bring supplemental dimensions to the main story line? To begin to answer these questions, it would be necessary to move (as, unfortunately, few critics bother to do) beyond the story of Li Qiao and Xiaojun and see how commodification works as well in the events surrounding other characters and their life stories. In this regard, what is noteworthy is that this film is made up not of one but of multiple stories of love and attachment.

Consider, for instance, the case of Xiaojun's Aunt Rosie and her dedication to the Hollywood movie star William Holden. A former call girl who now manages her flat as a brothel, Rosie is in the habit of telling people the story of how she once went out with "Wei Leem," as she calls Holden, and how he took her (purportedly while he was shooting *Love Is a Many-Splendored Thing* in Hong Kong during the 1950s) to dinner at the Peninsula Hotel, a historic colonial landmark on the Kowloon Peninsula. Common sense tells us that this was most probably a one-time transaction between a white male celebrity tourist and a local prostitute, a transaction whose pulp-fiction makings call to mind the well-known orientalist tale *The World of Suzie Wong* (the Hollywood adaptation of which also starred Holden, with Irene Tsu, the Chinese American actress who plays Rosie, cast as one of the Wanchai prostitutes). For Rosie, nonetheless, who has for decades kept the silverware, napkin, and menu from the Peninsula as well as photographs of "Wei Leem" as souvenirs, this is the story of the love of her life. It is virtually impossible to disentangle the reality of these obsolete commercial objects from the tenacity of the feelings she has for so long attached to them. (She even owns a man's suit that was supposedly left behind by "Wei Leem" and that she lends to Xiaojun to wear for a job interview.) Are these objects not much closer to her than the actor ever was? Did it all really happen as Rosie claims, or are these stories just fragments of her deluded mind? Does it matter? As she tells Xiaojun in a letter she writes before her death, "He [Wei Leem] probably forgot all about me a long time ago. But never mind—as long as I remember, that's enough."

As if to support the possibility that Rosie might indeed be telling a kind of truth, the film shows us another couple—a Thai prostitute, Cabbage, and Jeremy, her client-turned-boyfriend (played with good humor by cinematographer Christopher Doyle) who teaches English in Hong Kong. Although Cabbage has AIDS, her white male lover is selflessly dedicated to her. He is taking her back to Thailand because she is homesick. As in the case of Rosie and "Wei Leem," love in this instance also begins in a commodified relationship—and why not?—with a pretty Asian woman selling her body to a white customer. Cabbage and her lover are hence the living proof that the romance that Rosie dreams of having but never completely experienced with "Wei Leem" is, perhaps, not just the fantasy of a crazy old whore. Rather, the couple with AIDS has helped vindicate Rosie by showing that her fantasy can actually come true.

Finally, there is the story of Li Qiao and Bao, a typical story of the hoodlum and his loyal gal. The question of romance hardly arises in this case: the two meet in the massage parlor and become cohabitants even though they do not seem at all romantically involved in the conventional sense. Instead, Bao displays the magnanimous indulgence of an older man toward a younger woman.[18] (On meeting Xiaojun for the first time at his wedding banquet, for instance, Bao correctly senses that Li Qiao and Xiaojun must have been involved before and that she still has feelings for the younger man, but he does not express any resentment or jealousy.) What they share is a mutual commitment based on affection and trust—hence Li Qiao's inability to bring herself to tell Bao the truth or to leave him when he is on the run from the police, even when it means reneging on her promise to reunite with Xiaojun.[19] By the time they arrive in New York's Chinatown, the two have already been to a number of other places and are making plans to settle down. This relationship, incidentally, is the closest Li Qiao has had to a home since she left the PRC, yet with Bao's untimely death this home is destroyed in an instant.

The scene in which a completely distraught Li Qiao is asked to identify Bao's body in the hospital may well be the most moving of the entire film. As Bao's face is probably disfigured by the gunshots, she asks that his corpse be turned over on the gurney. Once she sees his back, Li Qiao knows without a doubt that this is Bao: grinning at her on his back is a tattoo of Mickey Mouse, a token he had made specifically for her amusement simply because she once told him that she was scared of mice. (Earlier, while in Hong Kong, there is a Mickey figurine, presumably also a gift from Bao, dangling from the rearview mirror in Li Qiao's car.) As we can tell by the involuntarily contorted expressions on Li Qiao's face, which move from smiling to violent sobbing while she calls out his name, the sight of this skin inscription of a thoroughly childish, commercial icon has turned at this moment into a shattering experience, reminding her, in a cold hospital room in a foreign land, of the depth of Bao's devotion, a devotion he never directly verbalized.[20]

In all these relationships, the idea of the love story itself is explored as a cliché and a formula, with well-recognized roles, ingredients, and twists and turns. Following the English title of the film, each of these relationships is, we might say, *almost* a love story: not quite, not complete, not the real thing. Is not Rosie's love for "Wei Leem" just her side of the story? Are not Cabbage and her lover soon to run out of time? Is not Li Qiao and Bao's relationship merely a relationship of convenience after all? These questions reveal the problematic negatives—the holes or voids—in these affairs, but precisely in the places where something seems amiss or missing appear magical substitutes and stand-ins—the black-and-white pictures of "Wei Leem" and the yesteryear items stolen from the Peninsula Hotel; the bona fide, life-and-death bond between an oriental prostitute and her white knight; the tattooed image of Mickey—which provide ways of suturing and holding things together and thus of authenticating the relationships. Rather than being embodiments of falsehood and alienation, these substitutes and stand-ins, these partial objects that are far from classy fare, have become unique gifts of commitment, creating, enacting, and commemorating the loves that *almost* are.

The crowning instance of such a gift of commitment is, of course, none other than "Teresa Teng," through whom the two protagonists rediscover each other in 1995. That they are fated to be together is now, at the end of the film, shown through a reprise of the opening scene: unbeknownst to each other, Xiaojun and Li Qiao were napping back to back on the train that brought them to Hong Kong in 1986, their heads touching as though they were conjoined twins—an image that suggests that they have long been sharing the same dream. They missed each other then, as they keep missing each other in subsequent happenings through the years, but they are, at long last, reunited.

THE COMRADES' DREAM

The English title of the film also contains the word "comrades," a form of appellation that, until recent years, was in daily use in the People's Republic of China. Whereas the precommunist Chinese system of interpersonal address (the one that continues to be in use among Chinese communities everywhere, including those in the PRC) follows the hierarchical distinctions specified in kinship and other social relations, the term "comrade" (*tongzhi*) introduced a level of equality, uniformity, and comparability that was meant to eliminate such feudalist class differences. Since the modernization campaign of the 1980s and 1990s, "comrade" has become an anachronism, a reminder of a political past whose idealism is now laughably irrelevant. The word "comrades" in the film title therefore marks the two young protagonists' former identity, one that they are supposed to shed in order to become Hong Kongers. Time and again, we hear Li Qiao addressing Xiaojun teasingly as "Comrade Li Xiaojun," always at moments when she wants to remind him that things work differently in Hong Kong and that they are no longer in China. By 1990 Li Qiao can proudly tell Xiaojun that people in five-star hotels in Hong Kong now greet her in English, that the clerks in upscale department stores no longer look down on her, and that even the villagers back home in Guangdong no longer recognize her: she has finally become a real Hong Konger.

These overt references to the contrast between Hong Kong and China further this discussion about commodities and love stories with the significance of migration. This migration should be understood not simply in geographical terms (as a migration from a rural to an urban environment, for instance) but also in political-economic terms, as a migration from communism to capitalism. As will become even more pronounced in films such as Zhang Yimou's *Happy Times* and *Not One Less*, this kind of migration, often a practical consequence of the despotic economic order that Guy Debord has famously called "the society of the spectacle,"[21] in which human relations are increasingly (re)configured as images, commercial objects, and monetary transactions, may well take place within the same geographical area (for instance, in rural as well as urban areas of contemporary mainland China).

As a film, *Comrades* self-consciously engages with such a migration by repeatedly focusing on technological mediation: people meet and brush past one another on trains; move through high-speed immigration cameras, close-circuit television screens, and escalators; use ATMs; communicate via large glass barriers, grates, pagers, and so on—all this, in implicit distinction from the more leisurely, bicycle-riding world the "comrades" have left behind. In Hong Kong, people do not address or relate to one another as comrades; more often than not, they are strangers jostling for security, power, influence, or a simple foothold in a metropolis in which political ideals are inseparable from economic aspirations. (Soon after arrival, Xiaojun discovers that his monthly salary and bonus as a deliveryman in Hong Kong add up to more than what the mayor of Tianjin makes.) Migrating into this world means moving at the same speed as everyone else, as Li Qiao quickly learns to do at the beginning of the film. Her keen sense of economic opportunism and longing for assimilation may, in this regard, be described as symptomatic of a transindividual drive toward capitalism, toward precisely the kind of world that is established on the basis of commodified and reified human relations.

Interestingly, then, it is when Li Qiao stumbles—most notably in her lack of success in marketing the Teresa Teng tapes and records but also in her losses on the stock market in 1987—that this drive is interrupted. (Her ATM shows a negative balance at this point, and her self-identification as a Hong Konger is abruptly aborted.) Remarkably, however, this interruption does not assume the form of a nostalgic return to the values of communism and socialism, or of a condemnation and rejection of consumerist society itself. Instead, the film shows us, another path opens—a detour, a form of agency that does not so much oppose and abandon the mass commodity as it forges a substitute track from within it, whereupon an alternative, perverse process of subjectivization emerges alongside the recognizably rationalist, progressivist march toward capitalist gains and achievements.

Rather than being pure or pristine emblems of an indomitable economic triumphalism (as they are commonly perceived to be), mass commodities, in the debased forms of trite sentimental songs, faded pictures of a foreign movie star, a silly tattoo of a Disney cartoon character, and so forth, have now taken on the status of affective anchors, motivating circuits of connectivity in the midst of relocation, separation, flight, sickness, and death—even though this is quite distinct from the uppity understanding of the commodified world with which the "comrades" first migrated to Hong Kong. As Li Qiao says to Xiaojun at the point of their first breakup, in an attempt to set the record straight: "Comrade, I did not come to Hong Kong because of you; nor did you come to Hong Kong because of me." Yet, despite their efforts to stick with their original goals, the mass commodity keeps taking them by surprise, delivering them where they do not expect to be. Is not these comrades' resolute yearning for the capitalist way of life the ultimate love story?[22] And, given the unexpected passages prized open—and the lifelines made possible—by the mass commodity, is not this love story, too, in the end only an "almost"—not quite the simple encounter with capitalism and happiness that they once naively dreamt of, their heads touching, on that train to colonial Hong Kong?

FIGURE 6.1 A picture of the happy family reunion in California at the end of *Eat a Bowl of Tea* (Copyright Columbia Pictures, 1988)

FIGURE 6.2 The three young people arriving at a solution to their problems, *Xiyan / The Wedding Banquet* (Copyright Central Motion Pictures / Good Machine, 1993)

All Chinese Families Are Alike

Biopolitics in *Eat a Bowl of Tea* and
The Wedding Banquet

In his classic *Three Essays on the Theory of Sexuality*, Freud made
what was then a novel but has since become a well-known argument that
human sexuality is traceable to infancy and childhood and that it is mani-
fest in the numerous forms of what are considered sexual aberrations: "A
disposition to perversions is an original and universal disposition of the
human sexual instinct," he writes.[1] By displacing human sexuality onto the
realm of the perverse, Freud's point was to distinguish it from the straightforward animal instinct of procreation and thus, epistemically, from the
telos of a practical end (in this case, continued biological survival). For
Freud, this characteristic of being at once polymorphous and purposeless
was what made human sexuality fascinating as an object of study. He went
on to give this object a specialized name—the unconscious—on which he
founded the institution of psychoanalysis.

Freud's bold and imaginative conceptualization may be considered an act
of aestheticizing human sexuality. By "aestheticizing," I do not, of course,
mean that he made sexuality pretty to look at but rather that his work has
methodically carved out a space in which an entire (counter)logic—replete
with plots, characters, obstacles, tragedies, and partial resolutions—can
be elaborated in distinction from the reproductive purposefulness of non-
human animals. Central to Freud's aestheticization was a groundbreaking,
and to many readers sympathetic, rendering of human sexuality as a fugi-

tive and fragile figure: being, as he asserts, "the weak spot" in the process of human cultural development,[2] sexuality can never be fully compliant with the constraints of civilization and must thus be regularly repressed in order for individual persons to attain social acceptance.

Insofar as it is presented as an intractable arrangement in which sexuality always gets punished, restrained, diverted, and sublimated, sociality appears in Freud's work as a source of oppression. Human sexuality and human society are permanently in conflict, so much so that even when human beings seem to conform to the rules of nature and seek biologically to reproduce themselves, it is already the result of social adaptation. Biological reproduction as it manifests itself among humans is anything but a natural phenomenon. Jean Laplanche summarizes Freud's insights into human sexuality in a remarkable phrase—as "'instincts lost' and 'instincts regained'":

> The whole theme of *The Three Essays on the Theory of Sexuality* (Freud, 1905) could be summarized as "instincts lost" and "instincts regained". The whole point is to show that human beings have lost their instincts, especially their sexual instinct and, more specifically still, their instinct to reproduce. The thesis of the first two sections of the *Three Essays* at least is that human instincts have no fixed or definite object, and no goal, and that they follow no one, stereotypical path. . . . The "instincts regained" aspect of the *Three Essays* can be seen in its account of the transformations of puberty [*die Umgestaltungen der Pubetät*]. This theme might be termed "instincts mimicked" or "instincts replaced". . . . Although it is apparently natural, the genesis of a wish to have a baby is, in Freud's description, far from simple. A woman has to struggle through a veritable labyrinth before she learns to *wish* for something that any living creative instinctively *wants*.[3]

Nonetheless, despite its understanding of (even) biological reproduction as a mimicked—that is, socially acquired—instinct, Freudian psychoanalysis tends by and large to focus on the so-called aberrations and perversions as the proper realm of human sexuality and as a result has left the problematic of human procreation conceptually oversimplified and, relatively speaking, unexplored. In Freud's terms, when it does happen, human procreation can only be the result of social coercion: women can only "wish" to have a baby after they have learned and internalized the painful reality of what is expected of "normal" womanhood. By pitting the individual and his/her sexuality against the social collective in a more or less opposed fashion, his aestheticized and segregated notion of human sexuality, though illuminating in many respects, seems increasingly inadequate in dealing with the evolving complications of human reproduction, especially as reproduction is enmeshed in cultural and intercultural contexts in which meanings are conferred on it in ways that go well beyond a simple biological end.

THE ENTRY OF LIFE INTO HISTORY

This is the juncture at which Freud's framework needs to be read against Michel Foucault's critique of the widespread, post-Freudian attitude toward sexuality. As is well known, Foucault gave this attitude a name—the repressive hypothesis. Whereas Freud specialized in arguing the vicissitudes of a human sexuality struggling against the forces of repression, Foucault's aim was rather to ask a definitively different type of question: how did we come to believe that we are repressed in the first place? Foucault's oft-cited remarks are worth quoting again if only because they relativize, rather than essentialize, repression by foregrounding the discursive process involved: "The question I would like to pose is not, Why are we repressed? But rather, Why do we say, with so much passion and so much resentment against our most recent past, against our present, and against ourselves, that we are repressed? By what spiral did we come to affirm that sex is negated? What led us to show, ostentatiously, that sex is something we hide, to say it is something we silence?"[4]

For Foucault, accordingly, sexuality could no longer be thought of, as it was in Freud, as "a stubborn drive, by nature alien and of necessity disobedient to a power which exhausts itself trying to subdue it and often fails to control it entirely." Instead, he argued that sexuality needs to be theorized as "an especially dense transfer point for relations of power"—one, moreover, that is "endowed with the greatest instrumentality."[5] If it succeeded in challenging the paradigm of lack and castration that is lodged firmly in the narrative of sexual repression, Foucault's critique of Freudian psychoanalysis at the same time acknowledged that it is an extraordinarily effective mode of discourse. Indeed, Foucault's own notion of discursive power was based in part on his understanding of how *talk* about sexual repression (as instigated by Freudian psychoanalysis) had activated an unprecedented proliferation of practices and discourses, leading henceforth to more obsessions with the topic, ad infinitum. Foucault's own engagement with the

Freudian legacy, however, introduced an important difference: it explored sexuality on explicitly social and historical grounds.

Unlike Freud, Foucault argued that sexuality is not the opposite but rather a vehicle and an effect of power. The aberrations and perversions Freud discussed as variants of a polymorphous and purposeless sexuality, Foucault rewrote as part of a totalized outcome of Western society's control of populations, since the eighteenth century, through the implementation of specific mechanisms of power-as-knowledge.[6] Foucault's interest in the social regimentations and penalizations of sexual behaviors meant that, while his work proceeded fully in accordance with Freud's basic argument that the sexual instinct is nonessentialist in character, he had chosen to sidestep that argument per se in order to focus, instead, on the complex rationalizations of human sexuality in modern times through steady institutional surveillance. Rather than a matter of "instincts and their vicissitudes," which require ever more efforts of differentiation and categorization (as they did for Freud), sexuality in Foucault's work is a vast, heterogeneous apparatus that includes legal, moral, scientific, architectural, philosophical, and administrative discourses, all of which are linked to the production of knowledge with ever-shifting boundaries and effects of inclusion and exclusion.

Between Freud's and Foucault's analyses, one can discern two methods of conceptualizing human sexuality as an object of inquiry: one treats human sexuality as an oppressed figure and attempts to chart its paths of attempted rebellion and escape—the infinite mutations, variations, and transformations—*within itself*; the other treats human sexuality as a historical phenomenon and seeks to investigate the numerous sociological linkages that lead to its discursive prominence, its being taken for granted as our insuppressible "nature." Between the two types of analyses, there is, one might add, also a crucial shift in epistemic emphases: if Freud's is an aestheticization of sexuality (which is portrayed as being always marginalized by and in conflict with social forces), Foucault drew attention instead to sexuality as a nexus of governmental monitoring and control, whereby even the most mundane, private, or culturally specific sexual minutiae may be traceable to an entire power apparatus at work.

Foucault's analyses of the various institutional practices devised and implemented in European society since the Enlightenment for handling human sexuality lead, in the final part of *The History of Sexuality*, volume 1, to the argument that such practices are part of a biopolitics—a calculated management of life through the administration of bodies and the systematic perpetuation of the rationale for continued human reproduction. Reconsidered from the vantage point of this latter part of Foucault's book, sexuality would perhaps need to be seen as just a component—albeit an indispensable one—in the much larger world picture of biopolitics, which Foucault also named by a remarkable phrase, "the entry of life into history."[7]

In the following, I would like to read Wayne Wang's *Eat a Bowl of Tea* (1988) and Ang Lee's *Xiyan* (*The Wedding Banquet*, 1993) as two entertaining performances of this "entry of life into history." The two films have many elements in common. Each tells the story of a Chinese family with a beloved son; each family has members on both sides of the Pacific and is preoccupied with the question of the son's marriage and reproduction. Each story involves a powerful father figure and an intelligent young female who eventually bears an offspring for the family. Both stories end on a relatively happy note with some form of geographical relocation. In the terms of the present discussion, what makes the two film texts especially interesting to contemplate together is that, in them, the problems of sexuality assume center stage against a background of diasporic life in North America, so that the biopolitical imperative to reproduce—an imperative that constitutes the real dramatic action in each case—makes its appearance, as it were, under the guise of an ethnic culture's efforts to survive domination by modern or Western (in these cases, North American) values. Apart from the actual sexual issues faced by the characters in the stories, in other words, it is now ethnicity itself, in the form of Chinese culture (together with its values), that is imagined in the "repressed" manner human sexuality was presented by Freud—as a figure that is primitive, besieged, minoritized, and/or threatened with scarcity or extinction. Be that as it may, such logics of the repressive hypothesis provide only the beginning of the tragicomic family enterprises involved.

THE MAGIC BOWL OF TEA

Based on the 1961 novel of the same name by Louis Chu and made after independent film classics of his own such as *Chan Is Missing* (1982) and *Dim Sum* (1984),[8] Wayne Wang's film (with a screenplay by Judith Rascoe) uses the background of New York's Chinatown to tell the story of a father, Wong Wah Gay, and son, Wong Ben Loy, whom we meet in 1949. When he came to work in the restaurant business, Wah Gay left behind his wife, whom he had married in 1923, in south China. (This was the period when the Chinese Exclusion Act, passed in 1882 and not amended until 1943, prohibited immigration except for a few exempted groups, and Chinese wives and daughters were not allowed to join their husbands and fathers who had come to the United States to work.) Although Wah Gay has no plans to return to China, he sends Ben Loy, a U.S. war veteran, "home" to his mother so she can arrange for him to meet Lee Mei Oi, the daughter of his Chinatown friend Lee Gong. The two young people instantly take to each other, their horoscopes are found by the matchmakers to match (auspiciously), and Mei Oi accompanies Ben Loy on his return to New York as his new bride.

The early marital bliss is dampened by an embarrassing problem: Ben Loy has become impotent. As a restaurant manager, he is immersed in his daily work and often returns home after midnight, leaving Mei Oi to spend most days by herself. In her loneliness, Mei Oi starts having an affair with Ah Song, a notorious, good-for-nothing womanizer, until her secret is exposed by word-of-mouth to the entire Chinatown community. Enraged and ashamed by the scandal, Wah Gay follows Ah Song one night and hacks off one of his ears with a cleaver. Sensing that they can no longer stay in Chinatown, Wah Gay departs for the Caribbean, and Lee Gong departs for Chicago. As Ben Loy himself is getting ready to leave town, Mei Oi and he become reconciled. She offers him a big packet of "some very special tea all the way from China" that is guaranteed to cure impotence. The two of them finally settle down in San Francisco. The film ends with a scene of them having a barbecue in their yard, with the two grandpas and a crying toddler having his first haircut—and Mei Oi is heavily pregnant again. With Caribbean music in the background, the whole family poses for a happy picture (fig. 6.1).

Conceptually speaking, *Eat A Bowl of Tea* can certainly be described as popular-Freudian—and perhaps specifically post–Second World War American—in that individual sexual gratification and fulfillment are given focalization as the secret to social cohesion. In terms of narrative design, Wang's film makes use of the repressive hypothesis in several senses. Contentwise, at the center of the story is the mystery of a sexual lack/dysfunction, Ben Loy's impotence; structurally, this lack/dysfunction is what propels the narrative and enables it to develop; finally, the viewers, in being drawn into the hermeneutics of the story, have to ask themselves *why* Ben Loy is in such an afflicted condition. This last question turns the story into

a kind of interpretative puzzle and demands that details be read allegori-
cally, in terms that go beyond the literal or purely physical.

David L. Eng, for instance, has responded thoughtfully to this last
question by drawing on Freud's and other scholars' studies of hysteria.
Decoupling hysteria from the female body and from a strictly anatomi-
cal classification, Eng argues that Ben Loy, the Asian American male from
Chinatown, inhabits a similarly resistive position to the dominant culture
as Freud's female hysteric. "What . . . does Asian American male hysteria
symptomatize socially and politically?" Eng asks.[9] After giving the pathology of male impotence ample theoretical resonance in this manner—that is,
by translating it into the already-known sexual perversion or aberration of
hysteria—Eng proceeds to diagnose it as a symptom of the repression (or
what he calls racial castration) that ethnic subjects suffer in mainstream
white America. In this context, Eng writes, "hysteria not only testifies to
a failed social interpellation but it also speaks to the production of subjects marked by particular depriviliged social positions. In other words,
it speaks to the production of a class of male subjects who are excluded by
and large from symbolic privileges."[10] By adhering to a certain logic of the
repressive hypothesis, then, Eng provides an answer to the question of why
Ben Loy is impotent. The ethnic male's penile-cum-existential struggle is,
Eng implies, a kind of U.S. national allegory:

> Ben Loy's impotence cannot be characterized as the result of an organic ailment.
> On the contrary, it must be described as an unconscious effect of his limited so-
> cial role within the segregated borders of Chinatown as well as his limited access
> to the larger space of the U.S. nation-state. . . . His hysterical impotence marks
> an unconscious protest against past exclusions and economic exploitations suf-
> fered by Chinese male immigrants in America. That is, his hysterical symptoms
> reprise a long-repressed history of institutionalized racism and disenfranchise-
> ment that subordinated the Chinese male immigrant as alien and thus exclud-
> able, while configuring him as socially emasculated and powerless.[11]

Without a doubt, Eng's reading sheds important light on a parallel relationship between masculinity and race, though I believe he may have been
overhasty in matching one type of lack (male impotence) with another
(racial degradation or castration), thus producing an analysis that seems
a little too neat and predictable. Wang's film, on the other hand, offers a
much less conclusive approach to Ben Loy's predicament.

Rather than resisting mainstream white America, Ben Loy is, to all appearances, actively invested in becoming as American as everyone else. Before being sent to China, he dates and presumably has sex with an American girl; while in China, he tells his mother that his dream wife should look like Rita Hayworth; after getting married, at his doctor's advice, he takes Mei Oi on a trip, and they visit Washington, D.C., the nation's capital, where he becomes temporarily potent again; as they relocate briefly to New Jersey, he clearly disdains his job of making Chinese fortune cookies; finally, as he gets ready to leave New York, he eagerly looks forward to a new job broadcasting a radio sports program in San Francisco, a job that, though still a Chinatown operation, will, he says, "lead someplace." If these incidents of Ben Loy's aspirations to assimilate to mainstream American culture are indications of any kind of tension, it would be tension in resistance to the Chinatown community, its assumptions and expectations, and, most of all, its practices of surveillance, as personified by his own father. In an early scene, long before Ben Loy gets married, Wah Gay is shown telling Lee Gong about his worry that he won't see his grandchildren. After Ben Loy is married, Wah Gay quickly grows impatient that his daughter-in-law is not yet pregnant. One day, while grabbing his own crotch, he admonishes his son: "This is for making babies," he declares, "not just to have fun with." As Ben Loy remarks to Mei Oi after a failed attempt at having intercourse: "I just feel like everyone is watching us." He feels so intimidated by this paternalistic communal gaze that he must turn Wah Gay's picture on the nightstand face down as he tries to resume sex with his wife.

So, instead of mainstream white America, isn't the cause of Ben Loy's problem quite simply his own old man and the Chinatown community? And wouldn't this reading be equally dependent on the repressive hypothesis, involving as it does the literal presence of a demanding father and a tightly knit social network? The answer here would definitely be "yes"— though I contend that it is the beginning rather than the conclusion to the film's mode of dramatization. Indeed, with the emphasis placed on Wah Gay and the Chinatown community, it becomes clear that Ben Loy's story is not simply that of a minority individual's struggle for sexual success in white America but also—and more pointedly—that of an ethnic male faced with the responsibility and obligation, imposed by the group, to produce heirs. Ben Loy's problem is not exactly the impotence of a private man; it is that he, as a male descendent of the Chinese community, cannot get it up with his legally married Chinese wife within the confines of

New York's Chinatown. It is with this realization—of multivalent cultural forces working concurrently, alongside and/or against one another, with a father figure who is as manipulative as he is nurturing—that the repressive hypothesis reading, which tends to focus on sexuality (together with the unconscious) as a personal or individuated event, needs to give way to a different method of conceptualizing the problems at hand.

Eng, being rightly mindful of the realpolitical stakes of anti-immigration and antimiscegenation laws, which remained in force in the United States until the mid-twentieth century, repeatedly describes the bachelor community in Chinatown as being "on the verge of biological extinction."[12] This claim is also made by Wah Gay in his brief voice-over narration at the beginning of the film, when he refers to how "Chinatown was dying" as Chinese men were, for some sixty years, not allowed to bring their wives or daughters to America. Rather than accepting this impending crisis at its face value, I'd suggest that it would be more productive to think of it as predominantly an *anxiety* about extinction. How so?

Again, Wang's film offers interesting clues. To begin with, there is no dearth of sexual potency and activity on the part of the men in Chinatown: an early scene shows Wah Gay visiting a Chinese prostitute while a long line of men waits outside the door as he finishes his transactions, and Ben Loy, as a young bachelor, dances with and presumably has sex with an American girl (who, not knowing about his marriage, shows up later at his apartment to try to resume relations). Given that these youthful women are readily available, can't the Chinese males—in theory at least—produce heirs with their likes and thus avert the grave danger of biological extinction? The fact that this is so obviously outside the realm of possibility as to be unthinkable indicates that biological reproduction is in this case imagined to be (a) exclusively reproduction with/by pure Chinese women (prostitutes and non-Chinese females are thus disqualified) and (b) exclusively the reproduction of Chinese in America (otherwise, with the staggering numbers of Chinese people on this planet, what is the problem?). Furthermore, (a) and (b) are mutually contradictory preoccupations: if it is inconceivable for the Chinese lineage to be tainted (that is, to be made impure) in the first place, why should the possible biological extinction of Chinese Americans—by definition already a suspect, because impure, category—be such a concern?

Therefore, even though it is, to all appearances, the obstacle to overcome and the enigma to resolve, male impotence is not the ultimately determinant issue in the purported crisis of biological extinction. The ultimately determinant issue is that, for the production and continuation of a community, only certain types of women—not whores, not non-Chinese females—can bring Chinese male potency to fruition: someone like Mei Oi, who is a virgin and from the real China. Rather than a Chinese male's penis (which, in the film as well as in the novel, has already found its way into other types of women's bodies), it is the chaste Chinese woman's womb—"clean," accessible, and healthily functioning—that is absolutely essential for the continuation of the family line and the ethnic heritage, that will put an end to the imagined horror of biological extinction. This womb will serve as the supreme, sentimental boundary marker between "us" and "them."

To return to Wah Gay's admonition that the penis is for "making babies," what articulates itself as an obsession with procreation is thus, when examined closely, a form of homosocial male bonding over the female body. Consider some of the small details the film offers in passing. First, Wah Gay and his male friends, as they meet at the Wang Family Association, at the barber's, and at mah-jongg gatherings, regularly gossip about other people's, especially women's, sex lives. Despite their own not exactly pristine sexual behaviors (which may, arguably, be justified by the Chinese Exclusion Act), these men morally disapprove of female infidelity (even when it is merely a rumor) as a kind of pandemonium. (For this reason, one can surmise that, although most of them, like Wah Gay, have not been back to China for decades, they expect their wives to remain sexually faithful to them. The question of these elderly women's sexual unfulfillment in China—that is, outside the United States—is clearly inadmissible into the epistemic frame of this story.)[13] With their male chauvinistic double standards regarding male and female sexuality, these gossipy exchanges amount to a form of positive social bonding, uniting the men with a sense of shared values. Second, as Mei Oi's affair becomes known, Ah Song's status changes from that of a (disliked) member of the community to that of an explicit enemy, even though this hostility directed at a male, too, must be understood as a form of social bonding, albeit a negative one. The male who violates the cardinal rule of the community—the rule that one does not touch another male's property, including his wife—must be punished and ostracized, but such punishment and ostracism need to be understood as sacrificial, and thus sanctimonious, rituals, performed for the sake of reinforcing the foundations of tribal integrity.

What comes across as a rather banal preoccupation with biological re-production—the aspect of human sexuality that Freud considers not ter-ribly interesting because it is merely animal-like and purpose-oriented—turns out therefore to be the force field of a particular form of biopolitics, a biopolitics that fantasizes the indispensability of the penis as an instru-ment for reproduction even as the men, Wah Gay himself included, direct their wishes, anxieties, furies, and vengeances exclusively at a demand for female chastity. The way these men actually talk and interact among one another implies—fantastically—that without such female chastity, "mak-ing babies" would be out of the question. The ostensible narrative suspense surrounding male impotence, in other words, functions really as a veil for something far more disturbing and beyond control. Behind the obsession with biological reproduction—with the continuation of the family line, the ethnic heritage, and so forth—is ultimately an obsession with the contain-ment of female sexuality, a task whose near impossibility must remain dis-guised and disavowed.

Contrary to Freud's attempt to distinguish human sexuality definitively from the teleological end of reproduction, the film *Eat A Bowl of Tea* demon-strates that the management and manipulation of reproductive potentiality belong squarely within the realm of human sexuality as mediated by a type of collective cultural fantasy centered on women's bodies. Freud's dichoto-mization of human sexuality and animal reproduction does not exactly work in this instance because, although sexual disturbance (such as Ben Loy's im-potence) is inextricable from the imperative of procreation as imposed by the ethnic community, what is far more thought-provoking than this sexual disturbance is the scene of its dramatization (that is, the way it is played out collectively), which points to a larger biopolitical strife in which the rise and fall of the penis is not necessarily the exclusive critical event.

Not surprisingly, then, the solution to Ben Loy's problem has to come from sources other than the father and his male cohorts. With Wah Gay temporarily out of the picture, it is Mei Oi, the adulterous wife, who deliv-ers the "very special tea" that miraculously cures Ben Loy's impotence.[14] As in all acts of gift giving, however, what is being delivered and recipro-cated—that is, exchanged—is far from straightforward.

Her silly affair with Ah Song notwithstanding, toward the end of the story, Mei Oi seems to have returned to her proper role as a good wife who helps resolve her husband's predicament. From this perspective, the end-ing is indeed a happy one: past conflicts have subsided, difficulties are overcome, the family is reunited, and everyone can live happily ever after. At the same time, the fact that the gift is "all the way from China"—rather than Chinatown—raises the question of where exactly "home, sweet home" is for Chinese Americans such as Ben Loy. Toward the beginning of the film, as Ben Loy visits his mother and extended family in south China, we are shown an idyllic picture of this "home" accompanied with sentimental music: albeit quaint and backward, China and the Chinese people seem to possess an alluring charm. That the cure for Ben Loy's genealogical block- age in the end comes from this distant homeland suggests a profundity and intimacy of connection that the United States simply cannot provide. In keeping with some popular trends in present-day Asian American iden- tity politics, whose identification with the culture and power of the United States tends paradoxically to be mediated by the fantasy of a linguistically and culturally alien Asia as the authentic and original home, the bowl of tea that heals is nothing short of a magic potion.

Yet clearly few Chinese Americans ever return home to China. Like Ben Loy and his family, they are much more likely to move from one place to another within the bounds of the United States. If America is indeed the desired home (even for someone such as Wah Gay), what about the dream of the pure Chinese lineage?[15] How are these two libidinal trajectories to be reconciled? Can they ever be reconciled?

As the miraculous gift that enables the family to live happily thereafter, therefore, the bowl of tea—that secret formula of potency, that authentic Chinese fix—simultaneously raises a new set of unsettling questions. As the bearer of the vital gift, Mei Oi also bears a child in the process, but who is the biological father of the child? Whereas, in Louis Chu's novel, the father is clearly indicated to be Ah Song, in Wang's film this remains ambiguous: it is possible that Ben Loy has fathered the child during the trip to Wash- ington, D.C. (as Ben Loy himself believes, after double-checking the dates on the stubs of the train tickets), but it is equally possible that Mei Oi is pregnant by Ah Song. In the film, there is no indication that Mei Oi herself knows for sure, either, though it is entirely plausible that being pregnant is what, in the end, prompts her to seek reconciliation with her husband.

From a liberalist perspective, the uncertainty of fatherhood can be taken to suggest a potentiality of reformed kinship rules, of a new kind of social contract by which a married pregnant woman does not have to be punished, excommunicated, or slaughtered simply because she has com- mitted adultery. Instead, whoever the biological father may be, there is no uncertainty about motherhood, and the woman, as mother, can be fully accepted by the community on the basis of her own sexual agency, while the impurity or illegitimacy she embodies (both in the sense of her adultery and of her bastard offspring) need not be deemed a violation or lead inevitably to a tragic ending.[16]

But as Wah Gay, Lee Gong, Ben Loy, Mei Oi, and the first grandchild pose for the family picture, with the second grandchild clearly on his/her way, this jolly ending may also be glossed in a radically different way. For isn't female adultery (together with its biological consequence) simply patched over by the same old patriarchal ideology with its resilient power to neutralize and normalize everything, including a fundamentally subversive gift borne by the unfaithful woman? After all, the most important preoccupation of this patriarchy is with making babies—Chinese babies in America, to be precise—so that the community will not become biologically extinct. Whoever the biological father may be, Mei Oi's child is still Chinese and male—and that, perhaps, is the most important consideration. Is that why everyone can smile happily at the end—because even Mei Oi's sexual transgression and its outcome have been safely recontained within the bounds of the sanctity of Chineseness; because after all, all Chinese belong together in one big family?

Accordingly, the most challenging issue that emerges from the ending of *Eat a Bowl of Tea*, replete with the lively tunes and rhythms of Caribbean music, is not "Whose baby is it?" but "Does it really matter?" And, if it does not matter, is it because of a triumph of American liberalism, which can accommodate murky beginnings and corrupt origins as long as they lead to material success and accomplishment—noticeably, in locations that pride themselves on cultural pluralism and diversity such as the San Francisco Bay Area, California—or is it rather because of the time-proven endurance of Chinese patriarchy, with its great assimilating powers, its magic potions for turning even aggressors and invaders into part of the continuous Chinese heritage?

THE BRAVE NEW WORLD ORDER OF
THE WEDDING BANQUET

In Ang Lee's *The Wedding Banquet*, the Chinese heritage is personified by Mr. and Mrs. Gao, an elderly couple of considerable social standing in contemporary Taiwan, whose son, Wai Tung, is a successful slumlord in New

York City. Like many Chinese parents, the Gaos are preoccupied with Wai Tung's marriage and procreative prospects. Although Wai Tung is gay and has a live-in partner, Simon, he has never informed his parents of his sexual orientation. In an attempt to put an end to their incessant pestering, he (at Simon's suggestion) persuades Wei Wei, a poor young artist from Shanghai, the People's Republic of China, who owes him rent, to marry him and move temporarily into the basement of their house. In exchange for her willingness to play this role, the two men will help Wei Wei get her green card.

Being firm believers in honoring traditional rituals and ceremonies, however, Mr. and Mrs. Gao decide that they must come for a visit to meet their new daughter-in-law. Much of the film's comedy, then, arises from the hilarious situations caused by the young people's efforts to create a fake domestic situation and by the Gaos' erroneous but insistent presumptions, which culminate in an elaborate wedding banquet for Wai Tung and Wei Wei, with Simon as the best man. By the end of the wedding day, Wai Tung and Wei Wei have become so drunk and exhausted that she ends up seducing him into having intercourse, which results in her getting pregnant. This crisis, together with Mr. Gao's ill health, finally obligates the disclosure of Wei Wei's and Simon's actual identities to Mrs. Gao, who wants to keep the news from her husband, even though Mr. Gao reveals in a private conversation with Simon that he has understood the situation all along.

If parents are stand-ins for one's original home, in this film, the rather traumatic experience of homecoming takes a reverse direction from what usually happens: instead of the son returning home to Taiwan (as Ben Loy returns to China in *Eat a Bowl of Tea*), the parents are arriving in metropolitan New York, bringing with them the classic conflicts over value that are characteristic of many homecomings. But the trans-Pacific trip Mr. and Mrs. Gao have taken signifies the difference between them and Chinatown elders of a previous generation such as Wah Gay in a more immediate and economic sense of value. Being Chinese mainlanders of a pro-Nationalist Party, high-ranked military background in Taiwan, the Gaos belong to the well-respected and materially comfortable echelons of a hierarchically stratified society. In contrast to the low-class and decrepit-looking Chinatown inhabited by the folks in *Eat a Bowl of Tea*, they come from a wealthy environment in which they are used to being pampered by the loyal, indeed obsequious, attentions of inferiors. (A male domestic, Old Chang, has been serving them for forty years in Taiwan; a former army driver, Old Chen, now the owner of a fancy Chinese restaurant in Manhattan, continues to address Mr. Gao as "*shizhang*" [commander], considers himself unworthy of sitting down [as an equal] in Mr. Gao's presence, and tells Wai Tung he must show filial piety to his parents by having a formal wedding banquet.) And, in contrast to the often vulgar subject matters and vocabularies that constitute the daily exchanges of Wah Gay and his friends, Mr. Gao is a cultivated man with sophisticated tastes in Chinese art and calligraphy. (Such tastes are part of a sense of loss—Westernized Chinese like his son no longer cultivate them—though Mr. Gao is pleasantly surprised to discover them in Wei Wei, his daughter-in-law from the mainland.)

These obvious class differences aside, the ultimate question at the center of the Gaos' reverse homecoming is, as in *Eat a Bowl of Tea*, that of biological reproduction. Ang Lee's approach to this question is quite distinct from, though no less provocative than, Wayne Wang's.

The setting of New York City enables the introduction of a supplementary issue, homosexuality, something that is much more openly accepted (by the educated and professional classes) in contemporary North America than in contemporary Chinese society. Wai Tung and Simon's relationship as a couple remains relatively unproblematic—it is recognized by their friends; they are definitely not living in isolation—until Wai Tung's parents enter the picture. Indeed, in the two young men's relationship, the stereotypes of Asian men as effeminate and American men as macho are, arguably, utopically transcended in the way they divide their labor: while Wai Tung is the manly business professional, Simon, a physical therapist, is the sensitive caretaker both at work and at home. Nor do the two fit the mainstream gay male stereotype of the young Asian "Rice Queen" in an economically dependent relationship with an ordinary-looking and much older white man.[17] Ironically, Wei Wei, despite being female, is much less adept at performing domestic chores (she cannot even fry eggs for breakfast) and much less conventionally feminine in the manner she carries herself. But the significance of these inversions of Asian and American, gay male, and heterosexual male and female stereotypes—inversions that few critics have failed to notice but that, it is important to note, are already in place before the parents' arrival—gives way to a rather different type of drama once the young people's lives are brought face to face with the elders.

The parents' arrival therefore constitutes the key to Ang Lee's narrative/dramatic design: it is the (kind of) narrative turn or dramatic entrance that animates the plot and sets the terms of what the story is all about.[18]

The seemingly liberal—one might say, contemporary "American" or "Western"—situation of two gay men of different races living together and a single, illegal, minority female immigrant fending for herself in a foreign country,[19] in other words, simply becomes the mise-en-scène for the unfolding of another kind of event—namely, the updating of a specific biopolitical script or what might be called, in the spirit of today's hegemonic financial-management-centered culture, the redesign of a specific biopolitical investment portfolio. Mr. Gao alerts us to this when he meets Wei Wei for the first time at the airport. Telling his wife, "Wo de touzi meiyou baifei!"—"My investment has not been wasted!"—he proceeds to size Wei Wei's pelvis up from behind and concludes with confidence that she will be able to bear many children.

Mrs. Gao is just the supporting cast here. In her obtuse and rather absurd reactions to the truth about her son's sexual orientation, the elderly lady is portrayed as someone who has bought into the values of patriarchal culture, period. While often a source of comedy, her character offers no real surprises. Mr. Gao, on the other hand, is given a much more sympathetic portrayal as a patriarch (as is consistent with Lee's other films *Pushing Hands* [1992] and *Eat Drink Man Woman* [1994], with which *The Wedding Banquet* is regarded to form the "Father Knows Best" trilogy).[20] Like many Chinese mainlanders of his generation who migrated to Taiwan under the leadership of Chiang Kai-shek, this quiet old man, too, has wounds from the past: he recalls to his son how he rebelled against an arranged marriage by joining the army, leaving behind his own family on the mainland.[21] He has a heart attack shortly before their trip and then a mild stroke while in New York,[22] causing a delay in their return to Taipei. Finally, in a conversation with Simon, he reveals that he has tacitly accepted his relationship with Wai Tung all along. How are we supposed to understand this startling flexibility on the part of the old man? Of all the questions raised by this film and Lee's work in general, this has been, perhaps not surprisingly, the most controversial.

Wei Ming Dariotis and Eileen Fung, reading Lee's film work positively as a series of attempts to negotiate a place for the Chinese tradition in Westernized modernity, suggest that the father's response could be read as a possible sign of a disruption of the otherwise homophobic formulation of that relationship within the film.[23] For them, Lee's work stands as a transnational, boundary-crossing cinema that offers "new methods" of coming to terms with what is Chinese in Chinese culture so as "to meet the changes and challenges" presented by contemporary global cultural economies.[24] In contrast, Shu-mei Shih sees such patriarchal flexibility as symptomatic of a suspect twin desire on the part of Lee's "Father Knows Best" trilogy, which "embodies the nationalist appeal to a Taiwan audience through resuscitated patriarchy and its craving for international fame, while embracing the exoticist requirements necessary for the approval of the American audience." Shih's analysis implies that flexibility is a clever means of smoothing over the tensions between nationalist and minoritized subjectivities (with their loyalties respectively to Taiwan and the United States) and that it is nonetheless a futile defense against Western racism.[25] For Chris Berry, the father's flexibility may be read as part and parcel of *The Wedding Banquet's* ambivalence, an ambivalence that "is itself an ideological move appropriate to the sustenance of globalised liberal capitalism."[26]

Although I do not disagree at all with the criticism of patriarchal flexibility as being complicit with globalist capitalist forces, I believe that it tends to overlook an important element, namely, the ethnically specific dimensions of Mr. Gao's open-minded attitude. His handling of the crisis at hand is nothing short of complex. It bespeaks a seasoned capacity for accommodating what seem to be incompatible prerogatives—notably, *by reconfiguring them as nonconflictual*. Chris Berry and Mary Farquhar have referred to this capacity in terms of a deep-rooted Chinese strategy of inclusion that can be traced to the ancient tribute system and is typically deployed for the purposes of minimizing or harmonizing differences presented by foreigners. In *The Wedding Banquet*, they argue, this strategy of inclusion ensures that no one character's perspective predominates and that all the characters receive some degree of empathy from the audience.[27] Still, what exactly is the rationale that enables Mr. Gao to be inclusionary in such a mellow manner? Among the well-educated upper classes in premodern China, as is historically known, homosexual practices were not necessarily understood as mutually exclusive to heterosexual practices such as marriage or concubinage.[28] From the perspective of the Chinese patriarchy, as long as the goal of perpetuating the family line is not forgotten, there is no practical reason to perceive the "perversion" and "aberration" (that is, the purposeless pleasures) of homosexuality as a threat. As Cynthia W. Liu comments, "This capaciousness suggests . . . that Chinese patriarchal lineation and male homosexuality are . . . readily compatible."[29] The father's function (at least as it is performed by Mr. Gao) is hence not to overreact to homosexuality—there is no need to—but rather to oversee the much more urgent task of procreation (even if it means acting a bit duplicitously) by ensuring that it can take place under stable and harmonious circumstances.[30]

Accordingly, as critics have noted, Simon's position is akin to that of a beloved first wife and daughter-in-law whose problem is simply that she cannot bear children.[31] As tradition would have it, however, the problem can be easily solved by having the son take more wives.[32] As long as heirs are forthcoming, everyone can continue to live together as one united family. For this reason, Mr. Gao treats Wei Wei and Simon with equal affection and beneficence. He gives them both red packets filled with cash and expresses gratitude to both. To Simon, he says: "Thanks for taking care of our son"; to Wei Wei, he says: "The Gao family will always be grateful to you."

Meanwhile, much as this patriarchal flexibility toward sexual orientation is rooted in the Chinese tradition, patriarchy cannot simply be reinstated as though it were timeless but must also be brought up-to-date, as is evident in the manner in which it goes about enforcing the mandate of procreation. And it is at this particular juncture (of the enforcement of procreation), I contend, that it would be viable to speak of collusion between Chinese patriarchy and global capitalism. In his perceptive analysis of the film, Mark Chiang draws attention to the exploitation of undocumented, transnational migrants such as Wei Wei: "The film's resolution . . . depends most intently upon disciplining Wei Wei as the figure of resistance. . . . The consolidation of a transnational patriarchy of capital is fundamentally dependent upon the subordination of women and labor, and women and labor are conflated in the film, so that woman becomes the very sign of labor." Reading in a neo-Marxist frame, however, Chiang has brought up "labor" only to leave it in a generalized category even as he alludes to labor's "sexual division."[33] Lee's film, on the other hand, is more explicit and literal as to the exact kind of labor Wei Wei can provide.

Like Li Qiao in *Comrades, Almost a Love Story*, Wei Wei is a smart, assertive immigrant from a less privileged origin (the People's Republic of China) who sees being able to reside and work in a capitalist locale as a means of upward social mobility. Indeed, insofar as the Chinese idiom "comrade" (*tongzhi*) refers both to the way people (used to) address one another in the PRC and, in popular usage, to gays, *The Wedding Banquet* could itself be named *Comrades, Almost a Love Story*. Like Li Qiao, too, Wei Wei succeeds in getting a foothold in the world she desires through partnership with a man of means, but she has gone much further in her transactions by deciding to bear a child. With this decision, what Wei Wei contributes is the reproductive labor of a surrogate mother in the contemporary global network of commodified procreation, in which, oftentimes, scientific technologies and market economics collaborate to liberate certain classes from the cumbersome and risky animalistic chore of childbearing and childbirth, while impoverished women sell their fertility and/or their offspring to those who can afford to pay. As Fran Martin comments: "The symbolic updating of Taiwanese patriarchal authority for participation in the global (American) cultural order hinges on the availability of the undervalued labour of a poor working woman from the People's Republic of China."[34] And, as Chiang points out, Wei Wei's dependence on global capital is "vividly dramatized," at the moment she decides not to abort the baby, "in the act of consuming that quintessential transnational food commodity and symbol of Americanization, the hamburger."[35] To return to Jean Laplanche's memorable phrase, what the impoverished woman in *The Wedding Banquet* "mimics" is no longer the instinct to reproduce *tout court* but rather the role assigned, around the globe, to materially underprivileged females in what Gayatri Chakravorty Spivak has called "uterine social organization"—"the arrangement of the world in terms of the reproduction of future generations, where the uterus is the chief agent and means of production."[36]

Thus, although from Mr. Gao's perspective the crisis of genealogical extension can be resolved sentimentally, through the capacious flexibility and strategic inclusionism of the Chinese family, the actual solution being collectively adopted by the characters in fact far exceeds purely ethnic bounds to become the reality of what, combining two well-known phrases, I'd call a brave new world order. As a result of the elderly Gaos' arrival and meddling, Wai Tung and Simon align themselves anew with the moneyed cosmopolitan classes under globalization—be they gay, heterosexual, transgender, single, married, or cohabiting—who can enjoy parenthood as a consumerist choice and right by selecting, appropriating, and/or adopting the product(s) of someone else's, usually a poor female's, reproductive labor. To this extent, the obsession of Chinese patriarchy with procreation, an obsession dating back to ancient times, feeds elegantly into the trends of contemporary transnational capitalism: even when one's son is gay, it turns out, continuing the family line need not be a problem because procreative possibilities (a cross-generational family investment interest) can now be accessed, made available, and fruitfully reinvested through a worldwide web of commodified sites. As Chiang suggests, "insofar as it ultimately charts the Chinese diaspora's coalescence into the global system of capital," *The Wedding Banquet* is "a transnational allegory."[37]

As in *Eat a Bowl of Tea*, the seemingly happy ending of *The Wedding Banquet* raises hitherto unasked questions about biopolitics. These questions emerge, in large part, amid the historical transition undergone by the Chinese diaspora in America from the mid- to late twentieth century, a transition that the two films together signify.[38] As the earlier moment of a depressingly ghettoized existence, shaped by nostalgia for the motherland and longing for recognition in the adoptive country, gives way to the turn-of-the-century moment of an affluent, professionalized, and jet-setting upper middle class's ascendancy on both sides of the Pacific, biopolitical urgency is met with new and creative tactics. In both films, the younger generations have shown themselves woefully incompetent in managing the family business. As the mess they have made escalates out of control, the fathers, custodians of the families' long-term trusts, literally take matters in their own hands.[39] But whereas, in Wah Gay's case, the daughter-in-law's adultery still demands a primitive resort to violence and bloodshed, in Mr. Gao's case, the son's sexual pathology is handled peacefully with civilized tact and entrepreneurial cunning (as he explains to Simon, "If I didn't pretend ignorance and let them fool me, how would I get my grandchild?"). One father raises his hand to chop off the enemy's ear to avenge his tribal honor; the other father raises his hands to signal to the airport security guard: "I am unarmed—I cross borders as an enlightened world citizen."[40]

In both cases, however, despite the temporary derailing by female adultery or male homosexuality, the endings are about implicitly or explicitly accepted alternative reproductive arrangements. In both cases, some kind of new deal has been made with parental acquiescence.

Are the updating, reconfiguration, and diversification of reproductive arrangements, historical phenomena so well analyzed by Foucault, an optimal advancement made on human sexuality's fundamental purposelessness? Or are they further proof of Freud's notion of the ever-expanding reach of human civilization—now manifesting itself through new-age kinships across sexual orientations and racial boundaries, as well as through transnational medical, technological, commercial, and legal institutions—to direct sexuality toward a socially practicable—that is, infinitely reproducible—end? Is this end—appearing in *The Wedding Banquet* in the form of a multicultural, queer ménage à trois (fig. 6.2)—an irreversible displacement of compulsory (and patriarchal) heterosexuality, with its vested interests in property ownership and social privilege as much as in biological reproduction—or is it compulsory (and patriarchal) heterosexuality's latest, coolest version? As Spivak writes, in a society still bound to the (nuclear) family and its forms of material possession, "The uterine norm of womanhood supports the phallic norm of capitalism."[41]

Like Mei Oi's return to her proper role as wife and mother, the significance of Wei Wei's decision to go through with her pregnancy remains ambiguous, indeed epistemically indeterminate: as much as it is a sign of her being actively in charge of her own destiny (by using her femininity to procure not only legal immigrant status but also a significant emotional connection and shelter and long-term financial assistance), it can also be taken as evidence of her domestication by and submission to a world still governed by patriarchal anxiety about reproductive prospects.[42] In the latter instance, the fact that Wai Tung was the sperm donor to the fetus she is carrying is what finally appeases the elders.[43] In the former instance, the fact that Wei Wei, a minority female in the United States, seems to have a modicum of personal autonomy could perhaps help validate the reasoning of an optimistically liberalist interpretation—even though such an interpretation would, precisely because of its liberalism, have to come to grips with the implications of material unevenness that so glaringly underpin "the entry of life into history," now administered ever more efficaciously, under the aegis of a progressive cultural pluralism, across all conceivable borders.

Part III

PICTURING THE LIFE TO COME . . .

FIGURE 7.1 A "client" falling asleep during a massage session at the fake massage parlor, *Xingfu shiguang / Happy Times* (Copyright Guangxi Film Studio / Xin Huamian Film / Zhuhai Zhenrong, 2000)

FIGURE 7.2 The teary image of Wei Minzhi on national television, *Yige dou buneng shao / Not One Less* (Copyright Guangxi Film Studio / Beijing New Picture Distribution / Columbia Pictures Film Production Asia, 1999)

7 The Political Economy of Vision in *Happy Times* and *Not One Less*; or, A Different Type of Migration

Following the lead of Edward Said and other critics of Western imperialism, some contemporary academic authors, whenever they encounter images of another culture, tend readily to be on the qui vive about stereotyping, exploitation, and deceit and make it their mission to correct the falsehood especially of visual representations. In my previous work on contemporary Chinese cinema, I have attempted to critique such knee-jerk antiorientalist reactions with regard to the early films of Zhang Yimou.[1] From a comparative cultural perspective, what continues to concern me is that a certain predictable attitude tends to dominate the agenda these days whenever works inhabiting the East-West divide come under scholarly scrutiny. Instead of enabling the critical potential embedded in such works to come to light, this attitude often ends up blocking and annulling that potential in the name of political rectitude.

In the study of contemporary Chinese cinema, this fashionable—and at times facile—vigilance over orientalism dovetails felicitously with a long-standing bias in modern Chinese literary studies (published in English as well as in Chinese) for realism, whereby the prerequisite of mimetic responsibility remains hegemonic.[2] This intriguing scenario, in which orientalism critique, initiated theoretically in the West, seems to have become smoothly allied with the pursuit of certain non-Western native traditions and their ideological demands on representation; in which the politics and ethics of vision, in particular, cannot be discussed in separation but must be understood as mutually imbricated paradigms—this I would highlight as the specific, thorny discursive locus for the ongoing relevance of Zhang's work.[3] In an academic climate in which iconophobia—the distrust and rebuke of the image—seems to have become a predominant way of reading cross-culturally (even as visual images proliferate and circulate across borders at unprecedented speeds), Zhang's work challenges us with the following questions: how might one approach *any* representation of the non-West as such without immediately resorting to the (by now) familiar and secure means of attacking orientalism, by nailing down a certain culprit, in the form of "What has he done and how"? Is it at all possible to conceive of a noniconophobic way of handling social and visual relations?

These questions are worth reiterating at a time when vision has become a totally open yet also totally treacherous minefield of negotiations. Precisely because anything can be instantly transformed into electronic virtuality and precisely because so many of our experiences now come to us first in the form of technologically mediated images, the status of the visual as such is likely to become increasingly polysemic, unpredictable, yet unavoidable. What kinds of processes—mechanical, electronic, and digital, as well as cultural and narrative—stand between our "natural" or spontaneous acts of seeing and the object images "out there"? How to deal with the seemingly obvious or literal appeal of the visual while being mindful of the complexities of engaging with vision? Can visuality include the possibility of not having vision or not having a visual exchange in the first place, or must it be defined exclusively within the positivistic realm of the optically available/present?

Insofar as it approaches vision as a social act as well as an objectified event or a mass spectacle and insofar as it presents the lure of the visual in bold and infinitely expandable possibilities (as light, color, sexuality, narrative, experiment, melodrama, and technical dazzle) even as it heeds the communal and nationalistic demands for mimetic responsibility, Zhang's work occupies a unique place among that of directors from the People's Republic of China. Notwithstanding the rather misleading critical consensus that his more recent films depart sharply from the early ones (*Hong gaoliang* [*Red Sorghum*, 1988], *Judou* [1990], and *Da hong denglong gaogaogua* [*Raise the Red Lantern*, 1991]) that made him internationally famous,[4] Zhang's films of the late 1990s and early 2000s—such as *You hua haohao shuo* (*Keep Cool*, 1997) and *Wo de fuqin muqin* (*The Road Home*, 1999) as well as *Yige dou buneng shao*

(*Not One Less*, 1999) and *Xingfu shiguang* (*Happy Times*, 2000)—continue to be marked by a shrewd grasp of the materiality of a medium that has traditionally been associated with transparency, clarity, and wisdom but has become, as some of his stories tell us, quite otherwise.

Among Chinese audiences, it is now often suggested that Zhang has more or less abandoned the visually striking style of his early classics, which supposedly pander to the tastes of foreign devils by portraying a mythified, backward China, for a realist cinematic style that depicts simple people's lives in contemporary Chinese society. The well-known cultural critic Zhang Yiwu, for instance, has argued that this stylistic difference, observed in films such as *Qiuju daguansi* (*The Story of Qiuju*, 1993) and the others from the late 1990s and early 2000s, as mentioned above, may be traceable to the changing trends in the mainland Chinese film industry, which has been compelled by the pressures of globalization to produce a more inward-looking approach to the issues of China today.[5] Having allegedly repositioned himself thus, Zhang has, it seems, finally been accepted and endorsed even by the Chinese authorities, once his most hostile critics, who not only consented to having him serve as the director of the unprecedented, internationally collaborative performance of Puccini's opera *Turandot* in Beijing in September 1998 (with Zubin Mehta as the conductor) but also appointed him to film the official documentary showcasing Beijing in China's bid to host the 2008 Olympics. As I write these lines in 2006, Zhang is scheduled to direct the opening and closing ceremonies of the Olympic Games in Beijing, with Steven Spielberg as one of his artistic advisers.

Without question, this saga of how a native son who was first accused of selling out to the West has subsequently been fully embraced by his state censors for purposes that are, strictly speaking, no less orientalist, no less opportunistic, and no less commodification-driven deserves an independent treatment all its own. (The latest episodes in this saga would have to include the phenomenal box office successes, inside and outside China, of Zhang's still more recent blockbuster films *Yingxiong* [*Hero*, 2002] and *Shimian maifu* [*House of Flying Daggers*, 2004] amid storms of controversy among Chinese audiences, who attack him this time for pandering to Chinese state authoritarianism and, once again, to orientalism.)[6] My point in bringing it up is simply to emphasize how the seemingly unending melodrama of alternating vilification and approval that has been following Zhang's career may itself be taken as an example of the power struggles over vision and visibility in postcolonial postmodernity, power struggles on which Zhang's work to date has provided some of the most provocative commentaries.

While the early films such as *Red Sorghum*, *Judou*, and *Raise the Red Lantern* have been frequently accused of orientalist tendencies involving ungrounded fantasies, the more recent realist ones are generally considered as a return to more authentic subject matters and down-to-earth, documentarylike shooting methods. As one critic, Shi Wenhong, points out in relation to the film *Not One Less*, however, the subject matter of present-day poverty, too, can be exotic in the eyes of some (Western) audiences.[7] (As will become clear in my discussion of the film, such subject matter is increasingly exotic to urban middle-class Chinese viewers as well.) Within the post–Second World War global framework, the valorization of realism as an ethnographically authentic/truthful manner of representation is, arguably, part and parcel of an ideological legacy that has long accompanied the objectification of non-Western peoples. (One need only think of a periodical such as *National Geographic* to see my point.)[8] Indeed, in the institution of postwar U.S. area studies, this bias toward so-called realism has been instrumental to the strategic targeting of non-Western political regimes and their cultures during the cold war period and since, and the representational politics surrounding China and Asia, we should remember, remain as ever in the grip of such targeting. Accordingly, whenever it comes to Chinese authors, even the most imaginative writings and avant-garde artworks have tended to be read for factographic value, for what in the end is empirical information retrieval. Against the backdrop of this thoroughly politicized history of cross-cultural reading and viewing, the laudatory revaluation of a director such as Zhang in the form of "Ah, he is finally becoming more realist!" is deeply ironic, especially when it comes from native Chinese audiences.

As I will argue in the following analyses of the films *Happy Times* and *Not One Less*, what is noteworthy about Zhang's work is much less its departure from or return to so-called realism than the possibility it offers for a critique of the historical import of the mediatized image—a critique that may have little to do with Zhang's personal intentions but is definitely discernible in the semiotic nuances of his handling of vision. If, in contrast to the mythical stories of his early classics, Zhang has in some of his more recent work chosen seemingly matter-of-fact locales, characters, and happenings,[9] this more recent work nonetheless continues to deliver sharp reflections on the politics of vision and cultural identity and their imbrications with the massively uneven effects of globalization.

Such reflections have to do with Zhang's fundamental conception of vision as a kind of second-order labor—labor not in the sense of physical exertion but rather in the sense of mediated (and mediatized) signification. Hence, strictly speaking, even the early films displaying China's decrepitude are not only about poor peasants struggling against the injustice of life in the countryside but also about a process in which such struggles are transcoded, through the film apparatus, into signs of a cross-cultural encounter—signs that convey an imaginary Chineseness to those watching China from the outside as well as to those watching it from the inside. Constructing these signs, building entertaining stories around them, and rendering them visually appealing are for Zhang seldom a matter of mimetic realism but always a matter of the specificities of filmmaking, of experimenting with color, sound, narrative, and time coordination and control. His critics, on the other hand, have repeatedly ignored the materiality of this filmmaking process and insisted on some other reality lying beyond it.[10] For such critics, unquestioningly, that reality is China and its people; moreover, it is a reality that (a) must direct and dictate how a film should be made; (b) will itself be exempt from any such framing considerations; and (c) must also be used as the ultimate criterion for judging a film's merits.

In the light of such hegemonic demands for realism and reflectionism in the fields of Chinese literary and film studies and in the light of the intransigent moralism of many of his critics, it is interesting to consider some of the tactical adaptations Zhang has made in his evolving work.[11] As a way perhaps to distract and elude these critics' sight, he did, from the mid-1990s to the early 2000s, make a few films that are more obviously documentarylike in their contents and settings. Often, these films are about poor rural folk or *xiaoshimin* (ordinary citizens) in big cities, whose lives are unglamorous and filled with hardships. Like *Red Sorghum*, *Judou*, and *Raise the Red Lantern*, these films are characterized by Zhang's fascination with human endurance: the female characters in *The Story of Qiuju*, *The Road Home*, and *Happy Times*, like those in the early films, stubbornly persist in their pursuit of a specific goal, but whereas Jiu'er, Judou, Songlian, and Yan'er (the servant girl in *Raise the Red Lantern*) pay for their strength of character with their lives or their sanity, the more contemporary female characters in the realist films tend to be more or less successful in getting

what they want. These young females' struggles against systemic indifference and cruelty end merely ambivalently (rather than tragically) or even
happily. And, whereas the early films stand as exhibits of a bygone cultural
system, sealed off with an exotic allure, films such as *Happy Times* and *Not
One Less* seem to offer some hope.

Is this indeed so?

In the midst of the assaults and the compliments, few, to my knowledge, have ever stopped to consider the consistent perspicacity with which
Zhang has been handling the implications of the give-and-take of visuality
or the critical statement his work as a whole has been making on this activity, event, object, commodity, and instrument called vision in postcolonial,
postmodern times. While the reception of his work lingers over issues of
cinematographic spectacularity, historical truthfulness, and state coopta-
tion and at times over a naive celebration of so-called realism, what I would
like to pinpoint instead is the refreshingly intelligent ways in which two
of his small-budget films explore the political-economic implications of vision and visuality and, in the process, produce nothing short of an aesthetic—indeed, a Brechtian—staging of the tragicomic antagonisms em-
broiled in social interaction during an era of ostensible national progress
and prosperity.[12]

ALTRUISTIC FICTIONS IN CHINA'S HAPPY TIMES

The story of *Happy Times* begins as Lao Zhao, a retired factory worker,
is proposing to a fat divorced woman who lives with her indolent teen-
age son and blind stepdaughter. The woman is agreeable but only if he
can come up with the 50,000 yuan for the wedding she requires. To make
himself seem like a good catch, Lao Zhao has told the fat woman that he
owns a hotel, but in reality he and his friend Li simply try to renovate an
abandoned bus in an overgrown area with the intention of renting it as a
place of assignation—called "Happy Times"—for young lovers with nowhere to go. Soon, as is often the case nowadays with urban development
in mainland China, the renovated bus is abruptly removed by the authorities to make space for a commercial project. In order not to lose his bride-
to-be, however, Lao Zhao must perpetuate his lies, so he offers to hire the
blind young girl as a masseuse in his fantastical hotel. In the huge, darkish spaces of the deserted state factory where they used to work, he and
his friends put together a makeshift massage room with corrugated metal

and carpet remnants and then take turns at playing customers coming for massage sessions, paying the blind girl handsomely with blank, bill-sized pieces of brown paper (for a glimpse into this farcical situation, see, for instance, fig. 7.1).

Although Lao Zhao and his friends are engaged in an ever more elaborate series of hoaxes to fool a blind person, they are motivated by kindness, and their clumsy, bumpkinish endeavors are often hilariously comical. Knowing that the girl's deepest wish is to be reunited with her father, who has gone south to Shenzhen, the boomtown near Hong Kong, Lao Zhao writes a fake letter in which the father tells his daughter how much he loves her and promises to find her a cure for her eyes as soon as he has earned enough money. The film ends with Lao Zhao reading this letter aloud, the girl and their friends listening, while the factory grounds on which they have been working together as masseuse and customers—the very stage on which they have been producing their collective performances, so to speak—are being demolished by bulldozers.[13]

Narratively speaking, the girl's sight deprivation provides the impediment around which much of the film's action revolves. The blind person, according to Naomi Schor, is conventionally given a philosophical or critical function in literature: "The blind person as *seer* is the central figure of the literature of blindness, . . . it rests on the double, oscillating meaning of seeing, as both a physical and cognitive act."[14] Although the blind girl in Zhang's film is a sympathetic character, it is important to note that he does not follow this literary convention of turning her into a transcendent seer. Given the fact that he does his work in a visual medium, his alternative approach to sight and blindness is, as I will go on to show, ingenious.

Consider the scene in which Lao Zhao makes his first visit to the fat woman's home. For the first time, we encounter the blind girl, left in the fat woman's care by her previous husband, who has moved on. In order to impress her suitor, the fat woman, who normally treats this stepdaughter with contempt, gives her some ice cream. This gesture of kindness lasts only as long as the duration of Lao Zhao's visit. As soon as he leaves, the fat lady snatches the ice cream from the blind girl and, scolding her as someone not worthy of such a luxury item, puts it back in the freezer.

Although it is possible to draw a moral lesson from this scene (for instance, by viewing it as a commentary on the lamentable condition of human cruelty and hypocrisy), what is far more interesting is the suggestive reading it offers of the semiotics and politics of seeing—indeed, of sightedness itself as a kind of material sign around which specific values are implicitly transacted.

The fat woman's opportunistic manner of handling the ice cream indicates that sight, as what renders the world accessible, is not a natural but an artificial phenomenon, one that is, moreover, eminently manipulable. The fat woman consciously performs for Lao Zhao's sight by creating an appearance of generosity, yet as soon as that sight is removed, there is no need for this performance to continue. Sight, in other words, is not a medium of revelation or a means of understanding, as we commonly think; rather, it is a prosthesis, a surveillance mechanism installed on (other) human bodies, which means that one must behave appropriately when someone else is watching but that there is otherwise no intrinsic reason to do so. What Lao Zhao sees—the sight of a kind and fair stepmother—is just that: a sight. It does not, as he assumes it does, have a deeper reality ("a real kind and fair stepmother") attached to it.

The fat woman's behavior is disturbing because, contrary to what most people believe, she has not internalized or naturalized the function of sight in such a way as to make it her own conscience, her automatized self-surveillance. Sight remains for her something of an arbitrary and external function, a kind of mechanical device to be exploited solely for her own benefit. As the film goes on to show, with the events that unfold around the blind girl in the fake hotel, sight can also be a disability, an elaborate network of mendacity devised to deceive others that ends up, ironically, trapping one more and more deeply. Having sight is not necessarily the opposite of being blind but may under some circumstances become an extension of blindness, a kind of handicap that distorts or obstructs reality as much as the physical inability to see.

At the same time, despite convention, Zhang Yimou does not attempt to idealize the *deprivation* of sight by endowing it with the lofty association of philosophical wisdom. In his hands, blindness, like poverty, remains a condition of misfortune of which anyone who is afflicted would want to be free if the means could be found, because, as the simple incident with the ice cream indicates, it is a condition that puts one at the mercy of others. Having thus broken away from the conjoined (philosophical) paths of at once privileging (the accident of most people's natural) sightedness and bestowing an otherworldly value on blindness, Zhang reorganizes sight and blindness as comparable rather than opposed events on the same plane: what those with sight see is not necessarily clarity but often distortion and

obstruction, and *sightedness, too, can be a deprived sense*. Through such re-
organization, he delivers a radically different way of coming to terms with
vision, whereby the ability to see itself does not (as is often the case in a
binary opposition) become the privileged term for judging the other term,
blindness, but rather stands close to it as a correlate, an approximation.

This subtly reorganized relation between vision and blindness in turn
brings into focus the entire problematic of lying, which seems to be the
only kind of activity in which Lao Zhao has been engaged from beginning
to end. In the scene in which she finally rejects him, the fat woman scorns
Lao Zhao as a liar. For those who want to defend him, it can be said that his
lying, especially in connection with the blind girl, is justifiable in terms of
altruism and that the lies are morally compensated for by his good intentions. But something more is going on in this scene of rejection. Just as her
ability to manipulate others' sightedness does not make her a decent person, so, too, does the fat woman's knowledge of the truth (that Lao Zhao
lies) stop short of any personal improvement on her part. Indeed, access to
the truth simply makes her more viciously self-righteous, as she uses it to
attack her suitor and rid herself of him. Like a candid camera in the hands
of the wrong people, then, her effortless ability to record and replay—and
thus to expose Lao Zhao for the liar that he has been—strangely does not
bring about any moral illumination; it simply helps her conveniently to put
an end to their relationship now that she has found herself a more lucra-
tive marriage proposition.

As the interplay between sight and blindness, truth and lies, leads toward what becomes increasingly evident as a drama of irresolvable moral
confusions, some of the prominent elements of the story paradoxically
come together. The awkward marriage proposal at the beginning, the reprehensible conditions in the fat woman's home, the construction first of
the fantastical hotel and then of the fantastical massage room with its
"clientele," and finally the ubiquitous triumph of big corporate businesses
in present-day China: all these narrative details coalesce to highlight the
emergence of a political economy in which money and money alone is the
agent—and arbiter—of reason and power. Nowhere is this more acutely
demonstrated than in the empty factory in which Lao Zhao and his friends
put on their absurd acts of altruism. These unemployed factory workers,
who at one time probably worked hard day in and day out with their hands
and were considered the backbone of the socialist "people's republic," have
now turned their abandoned workplace into a surrealist stage on which

they become at once the script writers, directors, actors, and audience of a collective fantasy, replete with its (endlessly reproducible, because fake) paper currency, with the sole purpose of cheating a blind person.

When promoting the film in the United States, Zhang Yimou is reported to have commented on this part of the story as follows: "At the end, when they are building the hotel, it becomes very symbolic. It's like the workers are building a dream in an old abandoned factory. Society has changed a lot in China lately, and everyone dreams of changing their life. Money has become very important, but in the middle of this wave of commercialization, I have started to feel the importance of real sentiments, of the caring among people. Caring is even more important than money."[15] Obviously, such uncontroversial—and, yes, sentimental—remarks should be understood in the context in which they were made—namely, as part of the publicity for the film. As the idiom "Trust the tale, not the teller" reminds us, it seems fair to surmise that, like all gifted artists, Zhang has, perhaps without being consciously aware of it, put his most acute interventions across in silence—that is, within the fictional space opened up by the work itself.

Accordingly, if workers' labor used to be a revered source of national vitality in China's communist ideology, what has become of such labor? In the fantasy acts composed and consumed by Lao Zhao and his friends, such old-fashioned labor has evidently outlived its usefulness and gone to waste. Indeed, human labor itself is no longer regarded as the origin of social relations, which are now increasingly governed by money and by the expedient transactions of exchange values. The only person who still works manually is the blind girl, but her labor, as we know, merely serves a bogus currency (as she is paid with pieces of scrap paper) in a workplace that does not really exist.

This film, in other words, invites one to read it as a kind of national allegory—not necessarily one that represents the familiar, inextricable entanglement between an individual's existential struggle and his nation's political fate but rather one in which the seemingly lighthearted story of fraudulence and debauchery at the trivial, mundane level may be parsed as a story about those in charge of the state and its economic order, engaged conscientiously as they are in the manufacture of altruistic fictions as a strategy of governance even as conditions are moving by leaps and bounds in an opposite direction. The nation, the film suggests, is no more than a bunch of well-meaning, kindhearted people who are collectively *putting on a show* to appease the downtrodden and powerless. China's astonishing feat of a rapid transition to market capitalism on the very site(s) of its former, state-owned national production: isn't *this* the spectacle of a vastly duplicitous operation, in which those who perform physical labor will increasingly be consigned to the margins, their iron rice bowls shattered, their dreams and aspirations bulldozed into the garbage heaps of modernization? Yet who are the culprits? Aren't they, too, often "nice" people—ordinary citizens, local officials, or even party cadres—who are themselves victims of the remorseless forces transforming Chinese society today? Michael Dutton's perceptive comments on urban life in contemporary China may be borrowed for a summary of the volatile situation: "The market arrives in China in what appears to be an Adornesque moment where everything is rendered 'for sale.' Yet what one quickly discovers is that saleability has chiseled away the certainty of meanings on which party propaganda relied. . . . Our antiheroes [i.e., ordinary people in China] are no pristine harbingers of any future civil society, any more than the despotic state or Communist Party is the single source of their oppression. Our antiheroes are the 'collateral damage' suffered in the globalization processes that we [the world's observers] have come to call economic reform."[16]

On the surface, then, Zhang's film offers an apparently straightforward moral tale involving a simple reversal of common sense: in spite of his tendency to tell lies, Lao Zhao ends up impressing us as a more or less benevolent person who, even after his own marriage deal has fallen through, heroically continues to assume the role of a surrogate father to the blind girl. His avuncular kindness brings a modicum of relief in the midst of a desperate environment. This, perhaps, is the story that allows Zhang's audiences to see him as having returned to cinematic realism and humanism and has won him approval even from some of his harshest critics. But the irony that quietly lurks in all the humanistic details, that, in fact, displays such details to be, politically as well as ideologically, thoroughly antagonistic to and irreconcilable with one another, is unmistakable. With the preemptive triumph of artificial vision (the kind of seeing that is not internalized or naturalized as conscience), the ensuing capacity for deception and self-deception, and the efficacious devaluation of human physical labor, what Zhang has produced here (as he has also, as I will argue, in *Not One Less*) is a stark portrayal of a migration—contemporary Chinese society's "advancement" to a new, relentless regime of power.

HOW TO ADD BACK A SUBTRACTED CHILD?
THE TRANSMUTATION AND ABJECTION OF
HUMAN LABOR IN *NOT ONE LESS*

The story of *Not One Less* can be briefly retold as follows: At the primary school of an impoverished northern Chinese village (Shuiquan Village), a group of pupils are learning under difficult conditions. Their teacher, Mr. Gao, has to go home to tend to his sick mother, and a thirteen-year-old girl from a neighboring village, Wei Minzhi, is hired as his substitute for one month. Before leaving, Mr. Gao advises Wei that quite a number of the pupils have been dropping out and instructs her to make sure that the remaining twenty-eight stay until he returns—"not one less," he says. For her substitute teaching, Wei has been promised fifty yuan by the mayor, and Mr. Gao reassures her that not only will she get paid but he will himself give her an additional ten yuan if all the students receive proper attention during his absence. As Wei starts teaching, the pupils are not exactly cooperative, and she is confronted with various obstacles, including the relative lack of chalk, which she must use sparingly. One day, a boy named Zhang Huike fails to show up: his mother is ill and in debt and can no longer afford his school fees, so the boy has been sent off to the city to look for work. Wei is determined to bring this pupil back. After a series of failed efforts at locating him, she succeeds in getting the attention of the manager of the city's television station, who arranges for her to make an appeal on a program called *Today in China*. Zhang Huike, who is washing dishes at a restaurant and sees Wei on TV, is moved to tears by Wei's appeal and turns himself in. Teacher and pupil return to the village with a crowd of reporters as well as a large supply of classroom materials and gift donations to the village from audiences who have watched the program.

If (as I mentioned in my discussion of *The Road Home* in chapter 3) stubbornness, perseverance, and endurance are qualities that frequently recur in Zhang's films, in *Not One Less* they take on the additional significance of being constituents of a humanism vis-à-vis an impersonal and inefficient official system, which is impotent in remedying the disastrous conditions of the village school. Exactly how does this humanism express itself? In contrast to the situation in *Happy Times*, in which humanism appears against a framework of general unemployment (whereupon Lao Zhao and his friends can spend their excess time fabricating lies in order to be kind to the blind girl), humanism expresses itself in *Not One Less* in a vigor-

ous spirit of productionism. A leftover, arguably, from the heyday of official socialist propaganda, such productionism is most evident in the form
of quantifiable accumulation. (We recall, for instance, the slogans of the
Great Leap Forward period, during which the campaign for national well-
being was promoted in terms of measurable units of raw materials—so
many tons of steel and iron to be manufactured, so many kilos of wheat
and vegetables to be harvested, etc.) The clearest example is the elementary method of counting and permutation adopted by Wei and her pupils to
collect her bus fare for the city. Moving one brick (in a nearby factory), they
discover, will earn them fifteen cents, so, to make fifteen yuan, they should
move one hundred bricks. Although this method of making money is based
on an exchange principle—X units of labor equals Y units of cash—its
anachronism is apparent precisely in the mechanical correspondence established between two different kinds of values involved—concrete mus-
cular/manual labor, on the one hand, and the abstract, general equivalent
of money, on the other. Persuaded by the belief that if they contribute their
labor they will indeed get the proper remuneration, the girl teacher and her
pupils put themselves to work.

Under Zhang Yimou's direction, this simple incident, what appears at
first to be a mere narrative detail, turns out to be the manifestation of an
entire political-economic rationale. As is demonstrated by the numerical
calculations Wei and her pupils perform on the blackboard, this rationale
is based not only on manual labor but also on the mathematics of simple
addition, subtraction, multiplication, and division. At the heart of this rationale is an attributed continuum, or balance, between the two sides of
the equation—a continuum whereby effort logically and proportionally
translates into reward.

The tension and, ultimately, incompatibility between this earnest, one-
on-one method of accounting, on the one hand, and the increasingly tech-
nologized, corporatized, and abstract (that is, Enronesque) method of value
generation, on the other, is staged in a series of frustrations encountered
by Wei, who is confronted each time with the futility of her own methods
of calculation. First, having earned $15 for moving one hundred bricks, she
and her pupils discover that the bus fare is actually $20.50 each way. She
attempts to solve this problem with her physical body, first by trying to
get on the bus illegally and then, reluctantly, by walking. She is finally able
to get a ride with a truck driver. On arriving in the city with $9 (having
already spent $6 on two cans of Coca-Cola for her pupils), she has to agree

to pay $2.50 to the girl who was last with Zhang Huike before this girl will
take her to the train station to look for him. The two girls end up paging
him with a loudspeaker announcement around the station—to no avail.
Wei spends the remainder of her money, $6.50, on ink, paper, and a brush
in order to write out her notices one by one, only to be told by a passerby
that such notices are useless and then to have them blown all over by the
wind and swept away by the morning street cleaners. By this time, Wei has,
at the passerby's suggestion, made her way to the television station. After
a long and persistent wait, she finally succeeds in getting the attention of
the manager.

Unlike her counterparts in Zhang's early films, women characters who
have become immobilized in their rural positions or household status, Wei
(much like Qiuju) is the heroine of a migration, one that takes her from
the countryside to the city. Even the countryside, however, is not the pure,
original, primitive locale it is often imagined to be: the bus fare and the
price tag of a can of Coke are but two examples of how a remote poor village, too, is part of the global capitalist circuit premised on commodified
exchanges. If there is a residual primitivism here, it is the ideology of accounting that Wei embodies, an ideology that has led her to assume that
the expenditure of physical effort will somehow be balanced off by due
compensation—and that, if she would try just a little harder, equivalence
will somehow occur between the two.

To this extent, the film's title, *Yige dou buneng shao*—literally, "not
even one can be allowed to be missing"—foregrounds this ideology of accounting in an unexpected manner: the ostensible goal of bringing back
the missing child becomes simultaneously the epistemic frame over which
a familiar kind of passion unfurls—one that is organized around actual,
countable bodies, in a political economy in which value is still imagined in
terms of successive, iterative units that can be physically subtracted and
added, saved, stockpiled, expended, or retrieved at will.[17] Wei's migration
to the city is thus really a migration to a drastically different mode of value
production in which, instead of the exertions of the physical body, it is the
mediatized image that arbitrates, that not only achieves her goal for her
but also has the ability to make resources multiply and proliferate beyond
her wildest dreams.

Despite her strenuous physical efforts (moving bricks, walking, writing
out notices longhand, sleeping on the street, starving, waiting for hours),
it is when Wei transforms herself into an image on metropolitan television

(fig. 7.2) that she finally and *effortlessly* accomplishes her mission. This is what leads Wang Yichuan to comment that there are two stories in Zhang's film—one is about human struggle; the other has to do with the importance of money and television and the emergence of the mediatized sign:

> Money has been playing a fundamental role throughout the entire film: it is closely linked to Wei Minzhi's job as a substitute teacher, her attempt to save chalk, the collective moving of bricks, her ride to the city, and her search [for the missing pupil] through television; what's more, money controls it all. On this basis, the film seems emphatically to be narrating or confirming a frequently forgotten "reality," namely, that television and money are playing controlling functions in people's ordinary daily life experiences. My sense is that the narrative structure of the entire film contains two stories: underneath the story about a girl as a substitute teacher lurks another story—the story about the magic of television or money. . . .
>
> When the bumpkin-ish and flustered Wei Minzhi is brought before the TV screen by the program anchor as the interviewee making her appeal to the public, her bumpkin-ness and simplicity are no longer just bumpkin-ness and simplicity but instead turned into a powerful and conquering sign.[18]

Although I concur with Wang's observations, and although it is true that Wei has originally come to Shuiquan Village to work for fifty yuan, I would add that the "magic of . . . money" is only part of the picture here. As the film progresses, what becomes increasingly clear is less the importance of money in and of itself than the transition inscribed *in the very concept of accessing resources*—the fundamentals that drive a system and make it work, the fundamentals of which money is an important but not the exclusive component. Specifically, the film reveals how resources, rather than simply being found, are to be produced and how such production is part of a whole new system of doing things.

The return to Shuiquan Village should therefore be understood as a postmigration event in this sense, whereby the system of value making has been fundamentally revamped and the fatigued, confused, and powerless figure of the girl herself has been repurposed as an image signifying "the rural population." Recall how Wei's appeal is dramatized on television: she is featured on the program *Today in China*, aimed explicitly at educating metropolitan audiences about China's rural areas. As the anchor introduces the objectives of the program, in the background appears a bucolic, bright green lawn with pretty bluish hills in the distance and a clean white tricycle with flowers in front. This landscape fiction, in stark contrast to the landscape of Shuiquan Village we have already seen, conjures the national imaginary by drawing attention to the plight of the countryside as an urgent social problem. Anonymous and unrelated TV consumers are, in this way, interpellated as "the Chinese people": although they have never met the villagers in the flesh or seen how materially impoverished they are, the effect of Wei the image is such that it forges meaningful links among this network of strangers at the speed of virtuality.[19]

Once the rural population has been beamed and disseminated as a televised image, charitable donations pour in, and the return of Wei and Zhang to the village is accompanied by a plenitude of supplies, including especially color chalk of various kinds, which allows the students to practice writing a character each on the blackboard. As well, this return is accompanied by eager reporters with cameras, intent on documenting the village and its inhabitants with a relentless, henceforth infinitely reproducible, gaze. In a public sphere made up of electronically transmitted signals, virtuality transforms exponentially into cash, in ways that would never have been achievable by the earnest logic of physical counting on which Wei and her students once sought to rely. The closing credits offer a glimpse of the positive outcomes of this migration toward the system of the image: Zhang Huike's family debt is paid off, Wei is able to return to her own village, the girl pupil who is a fast runner has gone on to join the county's track meet, and the village is now renamed Shuiquan Village of Hope. Finally, we read this important message: "One million children drop out of school because of poverty in China every year. With financial assistance from various sources, about fifteen percent of them are able to return to school."[20] To use the title of a U.S. primetime television program in the mid-2000s, what we witness in Shuiquan Village is in effect an episode of *Extreme Makeover, Home Edition*.

If what Zhang has provided in his early films is an imaginary ethnographic treatment of China—as a decrepit primitive culture—what he has accomplished in *Not One Less* is, to my mind, a similar kind of ethnographic experiment, albeit within Chinese society itself. What is often criticized as the orientalist gaze in his early films, a gaze that produces China as exotic, erotic, corrupt, patriarchally oppressive, and so forth, for the pleasurable consumption of Western audiences, is here given a thought-provoking twist to become none other than the nationalist gaze. Whereas the object of the orientalist gaze in the early films is arguably an ahistorical China, in

Not One Less, that object is more specifically China's rural population living in wretched conditions, especially children deprived of education. In the latter case, the similarly fetishistic and exploitative tendency of the media is underwritten not by the discourse of orientalism (read: depraved Western imperialist curiosity) but instead by the oft-repeated and by now cliched discourse of national self-strengthening and concern for future generations (as in Lu Xun's well-known phrase "Save the children!").[21] These two seemingly opposed discourses are affined, paradoxically, through the magic of the televised image, which not only supersedes older notions of the exchange value of labor but also eradicates the validity of manual labor and production altogether. This image asserts itself now as the indomitable way of creating resources, displacing an obsolete method such as "moving one brick equals fifteen cents" to the invisible peripheries of contemporary Chinese society.

This migration toward the dominance of the mediatized image, which Zhang explores through an apparently realist contemporary story, is therefore (in a manner contrary to his critics' judgment) in tandem with the experimental attitude expressed toward vision in his early films. The humanistic impulses that guide the narrative, leading it toward the telos of collective good, proceed side by side with a firm refusal on Zhang's part to idealize or eulogize the image, including especially that of Wei making her teary plea on the screen. Instead, the latter is consciously presented as a typical media event in the new information economy. The mediatized image works, Zhang's film suggests, by deflating—and subalternizing— the currency of (human) work.

Seen in this light, *Not One Less* rejoins the many explorations of non-urban others in the Chinese films of the 1980s (such as *Huang tudi/Yellow Earth* [Chen Kaige, dir., 1984], *Liechang zhasa/On the Hunting Ground* [Tian Zhuangzhuang, dir., 1985], *Qingchun ji/Sacrificed Youth* [Zhang Nuanxin, dir., 1985], *Dao ma zei/Horse Thief* [Tian Zhuangzhuang, dir., 1986], *Liangjia funü/A Good Woman* [Huang Jianzhong, dir., 1986], *Haizi wang/King of the Children* [Chen Kaige, dir., 1987], to mention just a handful), albeit with a different emphasis. In the 1980s, when cultural introspection took shape in the aftermath of the Cultural Revolution, film offered the Fifth Generation directors and their contemporaries the exciting possibility of experimenting with technological reproducibility and artful defamiliarization. As China's economy took off at astounding rates at the turn of the twenty-first century, the anthropological-ethnographical impulses of the 1980s films have given way to a sociological one. From an investment in, or a fascination with, China's otherness, filmmaking for Zhang—at least insofar as it is evident in a work such as *Not One Less*—has shifted to a seasoned and cautionary approach to vision as social regimentation, discipline, and surveillance but above all as benevolent coercion.

In dramatizing this transmutation of human labor—the labor performed over quantifiable, slowly cumulative time or empirically countable units (bricks, hours, days, dollars, written notices)—into an instantaneous spectacle, *Not One Less* stages a schism between two irreconcilable kinds of philosophical trajectories. There is, on the one hand, the trajectory opened in accordance with a pro-Enlightenment and promodernization telos of a better and brighter future, toward which human willpower and media capability inadvertently join forces. On the other hand, as is demonstrated by the usurpatory nature of the mediatized image and its tendency to cannibalize human labor, we are confronted with an aggressive—and in all likelihood irrevocable—radicalization of the very terms of communication, communal relations, and—increasingly in the case of the People's Republic of China—communism's own founding agenda. The image's limitless potential, in this regard, cannot be seen naively as an ally to human willpower or simply as its latest instrument. Rather, its suave and speedy superficiality announces a new collective reality to which human willpower is likely to find itself increasingly subordinated and to which human beings, especially those struggling against any kind of social inequity, will need to resort just to be seen and recognized. As the ending of the film shows, it is to the mediatized image that people will give their concern and compassion, and it is such images, rather than actual suffering human bodies, that now generate capital and, with it, social influence and political power. Instead of propelling us toward the telos of an improved future, then, this other philosophical trajectory lays bare the expanse and intensity of a new kind of oppression.

This dialectical narrative method, which is as astute in its cynicism (in the etymological sense of skepticism) about mediatized visibility as it is skilled in conveying an eminently warm and sentimental story, remains Zhang's distinctive contribution. In myriad ways, his work has been about the relationship between labor and the image, about the transit from a political economy in which humans can still make the world with their physical bodies to one in which the image has taken over that function, leaving those bodies in an exotic but also abject—because superfluous—condition, a condition in which being "real" simply means being stuck—that is, being unable to undergo transmutation into cash.

As in *Happy Times*, the (positivistic) ability to see, the (positivistic) availability of vision, and the (positivistic) possibility of becoming a spectacle that are made such palpable and topical events in contemporary Chinese life are turned in *Not One Less* into the ingredients of a fable with a certain moral. But the notion of fable is rooted in the process of fabulation, and the moral at stake in Zhang's work is often elsewhere from the place at which his detractors, often driven by their own self-righteous agenda, are determined to see it. However artificial, being and becoming visible is, his recent work says, something no one can afford not to desire; yet, as this work also shows, the ever-expanding capacities for seeing and, with them, the infinite transmigrations and transmutations of cultures—national, ethnic, rural, illiterate—into commodified electronic images are part and parcel of a dominant global regime of value making that is as utterly ruthless as it is utterly creative. With the harsh *and* flexible, inhuman *and* sentimental, materialities of this regime, most critics of Zhang's work have yet, seriously, to come to terms.

FIGURE 8.1 Yuan making a narrow escape from the mines, *Mang jing / Blind Shaft* (Copyright Tag Splendour and Films / Kino International, 2003)

8

"Human" in the Age of Disposable People

The Ambiguous Import of Kinship and Education in *Blind Shaft*

The most massive form of poverty in today's world is the one we see in *underdeveloped* countries, where the combination of the destruction of traditional activities, the domination of foreign financial institutions, the establishment of a so-called New World Order, and so on, leads to a situation . . . in which millions of human beings *are superfluous*. Nobody needs them—they are, so to speak, disposable people . . . they are facing—and we are facing once more—the prospect of an extermination whose forms are not only violent but specifically *cruel* . . .

—ÉTIENNE BALIBAR, *Politics and the Other Scene*

In China there is a shortage of everything—but no shortage of human beings!

—Owner/manager of a coal mine, *Blind Shaft*

HOMELESSNESS AS A MODERN WORLD CONDITION

In the essay "Letter on Humanism," published soon after Germany's defeat in the Second World War, Martin Heidegger referred to the condition of homelessness as "coming to be the destiny of the world."[1] By homelessness, Heidegger meant something more than not having a roof over one's head, even though the notions of dwelling and shelter were not at all excluded from his thinking. Heidegger's assertion of homelessness as the condition of the modern world—not merely for the defeated but also for the victorious—was part of a critique of the status of humanism in the West. From Roman times to the onset of Christianity, to the Hegelian phenomenology of spirit, the Marxist theory of labor, and Sartrean existentialism, Heidegger wrote, every type of humanism, understood "in general as a concern that man become free for his humanity and find his worth in it" (225), had remained erroneously preoccupied with the "throng of beings unthought in their essence" (235) and thus mired in metaphysics. In other words, despite considerable efforts by devoted thinkers, the concern with humanism had hitherto been ensnared—and limited—by a consistent failure to engage with the question of Being, that reservoir or reserve of irreducible surplus presence that sustains every human undertaking but forever exceeds rational human consciousness. Defined in these terms, humanism was seen by Heidegger to have a negative relation to Being—in the form of a forgetting, an exile, a closing off. Hence the condition of homelessness, which he specified as "the symptom of oblivion of Being" (242). "Yet Being—what is Being?" he asked. "It is It itself" (234).

My aim in this chapter is not exactly to reconsider various notions of humanism in Western history as such but rather to ask if and how the suggestive concepts proposed by Heidegger—specifically, homelessness and its implications for what it means to be human—can be brought into dialogue with the film *Mang Jing/Blind Shaft* (2003). Directed and produced by Li Yang, who wrote the screenplay by adapting it from the novella "Shen mu" (Sacred wood) by Liu Qingbang,[2] *Blind Shaft* appears in many respects to be just a Chinese story about the plight of migrant workers. (The film was released in early 2003 and won some major awards at film festivals around the world before an edited version was officially released in the People's Republic of China late that year.)[3] But the culturally specific locality of the story is paradoxically also what lends it its abstract, philosophical resonance. What can a story like this bring to the interrogation of humanism—as the corollary of homelessness—that Heidegger initiated over half a century ago? Does humanism—as a concern for human beings finding themselves and becoming free in their humanity—still remain valid for critical thinking and practice, when we are faced daily with so many tragedies affecting those who are described by Balibar as the "superfluous" and "disposable" people along the peripheries of the contemporary world? Or are such human tragedies themselves the latest symptoms, as Heidegger wrote, of the oblivion of Being that has for so long constituted humanism itself?

Heidegger's austere deconstruction of the metaphysics of Western humanism, I should note, was framed by an affirmative urging, the urging that we remember, that we think of the essence of man in terms of what he called *techne* and *poiesis*. As David Farrell Krell, the editor of Heidegger's *Basic*

Writings, points out, however, this affirmative pedagogical reminder is not without its own problems. Krell puts it succinctly: "Why, for instance, insist that there be an 'abyss of essence' separating humanity from animality? Perhaps most disturbing, can Heidegger invoke 'malignancy' and 'the rage of evil' without breaking his silence and offering some kind of reflection on the Extermination? And how can Heidegger's thought help us to think about those evils that continue to be so very much at home in *our* world?"[4]

The point about the "Extermination"—that is, the European Holocaust of the mid-twentieth century—is especially salient because, in ways that resound with echoes of contemporary global conflicts, this is a point about the politics of dealing with human beings deemed to be lacking legitimate membership in a particular group, nation, or community—the so-called foreigners. Heidegger's silence on the Holocaust is, without question, deeply troubling; at the same time, if by criticizing such silence what we intend to underscore is the urgency and ineluctability of the question of racial/ethnic violence for *any* account of humanism, it would seem salutary to move beyond an exclusive focus on the anti-Semitism of mid-twentieth-century Europe as the definitive representative event of such violence. In the twenty-first century and indeed long before then, racial/ethnic violence has far exceeded the bounds of the Holocaust, in such ways as to necessitate a rereading of Heidegger's universalist pronouncements with a much larger set of connotations. From the ethnic cleansing in Eastern Europe to the aftermath of 9/11 such as the U.S. implementation of so-called Homeland Security; from the wars led by the United States in the 2000s on Afghanistan and Iraq to the renewed reinforcement of secularism in France in reaction to the wearing of headscarves by Muslim schoolgirls, the question of the boundary between "us" and "them" continues to structure collective imaginaries and actions around the globe, from legislation and prohibition to penalization, mass resistance, and suicidal protestation and defiance. At once large and abstract *and* quotidian and intimate, this question is also a question about homelessness and what it means to be human. It is from this perspective that I would like to discuss Li Yang's film.

THE "LOCAL" TRAGEDY

Blind Shaft presents the chilling tale of two wandering coal mine workers, Tang Chaoyang and Song Jinming, engaged in the scam of making large sums of money by murdering a coworker while in the mines, claiming dam-

ages by pretending to be kinsmen of the dead person, and then moving on
to their next victim. The (privatized) mine owners/managers, who maxi-
mize profits by disregarding safety measures, are callously indifferent to
the life and death of their workers and often consent to some form of pay-
ment so as to be able to cover up an incident. After successfully performing
their mournful acts of monetary transaction and receiving their compen-
sations, Tang and Song see to it that all evidence is removed by collecting
the belongings of the dead as they depart. At the first opportunity, they
flush the cremation ashes down a toilet.

In this frame of mind, they entice a sixteen-year-old boy, Yuan Fengming, into pretending to be Song's nephew and going off with them to a
new mine. Everything happens as usual, except that this time Song is beset
with doubt because of Yuan's tender age and because he suspects, after
being shown a picture of the boy's family, that they have already killed his
father.[5] As the time approaches for the murder to take place in the mine,
Song becomes unable to act. Sensing that their conspiracy is about to dis-
solve, Tang takes matters into his own hands and whacks Song with a metal
tool before proceeding to kill Yuan. Miraculously, Song regains consciousness and musters enough strength to strike Tang down before he is able to
touch Yuan. The young boy manages to exit the mine just before a regular
session of dynamite explosion begins (fig. 8.1), while the two older men are
left behind. As Song's designated "relative," Yuan must now take charge of
his remains—but the irony is that he is also, despite his reluctance, bound
by the contract signed by the older men to accept a sum of thirty thousand
yuan as compensation for the death of his "uncle."

Obviously, this film can be interpreted as a local tragedy with an unexpected "happy" ending. As the English synopsis on the film's DVD jacket
indicates, for instance: "*Blind Shaft* presents a hugely ironic vision of the
Mainland's inexorable thrust towards 'socialist' advancement with capital-
istic characteristics. . . . The first half hour of the film is a stunning introduction into the dark side of China's industrialization programme—essentially an exposé of the country's reliance on and exploitation of migrant
labourers." The synopsis in Chinese spells out the "meaning" of the ending
more matter of factly: "The ending is contrary to expectations. Despite the
brutality and hopelessness, a sense of humanity still remains."[6]

As exemplified by the managers in charge of the mines, the major culprits here are the structural deficiencies that pervade the entire industrial
production system in China, where working in coal mines is notoriously

dangerous and where the death rate of workers is by far the highest in the world.[7] When the leaders are corrupt, greedy, and irresponsible, the film seems to say, can it be any surprise that the workers don't give a damn about moral compunctions? If socialism, as a form of modern humanism, is about honoring the contributions and rights—and thus the basic dignity—of the downtrodden classes, *Blind Shift* is first and foremost a stark portrayal of the bankruptcy of Chinese socialism at the turn of the twenty-first century, when China moves opportunistically forward, instead, in capitalist global networks of production and exchange. In one scene in which Tang and Song are entertaining themselves and prostitutes at a karaoke bar, they proceed to sing a familiar socialist song with which many Chinese mainlanders grew up, "Shehuizhuyi hao" (Socialism is good)—only to be mocked by their companions as "hicks" because the lyrics have long since been rewritten to reflect China's current procapitalist thinking and lifestyles. The old and new versions of the song go respectively as follows:

社會主義好，社會主義好
社會主義國家人民地位高
反動派被打倒
帝國主義夾着尾巴逃跑了

Socialism is good, socialism is good!
Socialist countries are high atop.
Reactionaries have been overthrown;
The imperialists have run away with their tails down!

反動派沒打倒
資本主義夾着美金回來了
全國人民大解放
掀起了社會主義性高潮，性高潮

The reactionaries were never overthrown.
The capitalists came back with their U.S. dollars,
Liberating all the people of China,
Bringing about the orgasm of socialism![8]

In light of such drastic transformation of the political-economic climate, when the two men carry out their murder schemes, they are, as Ban Wang points out, simply pushing the reifying logic of capitalism "to its grotesque extreme" by "using other human beings as a source of capital that can yield quick returns."[9] At the heart of this local story is, of course, the typical Chinese intellectuals' concern about the fate of China as a culture, as suggested in rather explicit terms by the names Tang, Song, and Yuan, which correspond to three major imperial dynasties in Chinese history.

Even as the film addresses the Chinese situation in details scarcely known to the rest of the world, however, the obvious locality of its significance quickly morphs into a much larger, even if not immediately visible, picture. No matter how enormous it is, China is simply one player in the unstoppable, transnational processes of exploiting and depleting the earth's resources to satisfy the insatiable demands of human consumption. China's unprecedented need for energy sources such as coal is, in this regard, simply part of a vicious circle of world trade in which we all participate, as is evidenced by the many goods in our possession labeled "Made in China." At the level of nature—as captured on the screen in the desolate, inhospitable landscape—a kind of violence and cruelty is thus being mutely staged even as our attention remains focused on the human story. There is a way in which the wretched lives of the migrant laborers—not only the makeshift livelihood and deplorable living conditions to which they have been reduced but also the level of depravity to which they have sunk—are a reflection of the bleak environment around them. Together, the laborers and the land form a pool of reserve energy that the world (ab)uses and abandons at will. To this extent, *Blind Shaft* can be viewed as a gritty, unsentimental documentary of the cesspool that human history has become.[10] (There is, for instance, no melodious background music from beginning to end to soften things up.) China, where there is "no shortage of human beings," as one coal mine owner/manager in the film puts it—where, in other words, the goods *we* want can always be produced dirt cheap—is simply the most extreme and egregious showcase of this universal waste dump.

But wait, some readers may object, doesn't the ending of the story give us a modicum of hope, when goodness in the form of remorse (on Song's part) provides the unexpected twist and rescues the young man, who is symbolically a stand-in for future generations? No matter how small a turn it is, would it not be possible to reinvest a sense of humanism in Song's change of hearts? Could this not be seen as the beginning of a different pathway, even if it is to things we do not yet know for certain?

In my view, all such approaches to the film, including the director's own—which see it alternately as being about local problems of abject migrant labor, global problems of capitalist avarice and environmental debilitation, or a humanistic quest for goodness—are entirely valid but inadequate in explaining the film's powerful affinities with modern world politics. While all these approaches tend to revolve around the assumption of a moral decline, of the disappearance of a viable value system that effectively monitors human behavior (toward fellow human beings and toward the earth), the film is, I believe, simultaneously performing another, much less comforting, kind of thinking that goes considerably beyond these more familiar moral concerns. Viewing *Blind Shaft* from the domain of the West, it is especially important that we recognize what this other thinking could be and resist the temptation of readily deciphering the film's message as simply an other-culture-speak (or a kind of third-world-speak), with the kind of neoliberal, egalitarian (but, in fact, discriminatory) undertone that comes across all too often in influential publications such as the *New York Times*. In this spirit, I'd like to suggest that, despite Li Yang's conscious designs, *Blind Shaft* delivers nothing short of a dramatization, albeit on a small scale, of the predicament of human community formation in general.

KINSHIP AS CONSCIENCE AND EDUCATION AS HOPE

In a strikingly philosophical manner, the activity of coal mining reminds us of the inextricable relationship that humans have with nature, of the fact that it is through the excavation and channeling of nature's energies that human developments—industrial, commercial, cultural—are possible. (The title of the original story, "Shen mu," is, from this perspective, ecologically as well as fictionally suggestive: it refers to the mythic beginnings of the discovery of coal in that area—by some villagers who mistook the inflammable quality of black graphitelike material, churned up from the riverbed after a flood, for the presence of some divine spirit.[11]) For Heidegger, this relationship between humans and nature is premised on a process of revealing, a bringing-forth (in cultural processes that he names *techne* and *poiesis*) that, importantly, never ends:

> The revealing that rules throughout modern technology has the character of a setting-upon, in the sense of a challenging-forth. That challenging happens in that the energy concealed in nature is unlocked, what is unlocked is trans-

formed, what is transformed is stored up, what is stored up is, in turn, distributed, and what is distributed is switched about ever anew. Unlocking, transforming, storing, distributing, and switching about are ways of revealing. But
the revealing never simply comes to an end. Neither does it run off into the
indeterminate. The revealing reveals to itself its own manifoldly interlocking
paths, through regulating their course. This regulating itself is, for its part, everywhere secured. Regulating and securing even become the chief characteristics of the challenging revealing.[12]

Following Heidegger's hints about revealing and bringing-forth but not
strictly complying with his famous insistence on the so-called essence
of humanity as such, we may ask: what is being unlocked, transformed,
stored, distributed, and switched about in the events of *Blind Shaft*? Other
than as a subject ordering the universe by various instrumental means,
what kind of truth about "human" is being revealed and brought forth?

On close examination, the story of *Blind Shaft* is, I contend, not so much
about good versus evil (about, for instance, the murderers versus their
latest victim or the poor miners/laborers versus the capitalist system, or
the like) as it is about the politics of human group formation. In Tang and
Song's practice of recruiting and murdering strangers, one feature repeats
itself as an indispensable melodramatic ingredient: the person they pick
must take on the fake identity of being related to one of them by blood
(as Yuan has to become Song's "nephew"), so that their eventual claim for
damages can be justified. The key to the entire scam is, in other words, the
fabrication of a particular unit of social organization—namely, the kinship
family—that appeals to others as something natural and authentic.

Insofar as the accidental death of a kinsman is deemed a major loss, one
that deserves due compensation, the kinship family stands as the inviolable basic social unit—what one might further specify as a kind of inalienable property or evidence of (self-)ownership—that rationalizes human relations. Hence, when this basic social unit is perceived to be threatened or
harmed (as in the case of a death), it is assumed that it needs, somehow, to
be redressed like a fatal injury. What enables Tang and Song's scam to function smoothly, then, is not simply that they lie but that other people—the
owners/managers of the mines in particular—are ready and willing to
credit the non-negotiable centrality of the kinship family. Tang and Song
can get away with their murderous schemes because everyone else has always already been fully interpellated into the "reality" of kinship ties.[13]

Why is kinship so important?

Ironically, throughout the film, these same men who slaughter nonkins-
men without compunction also reveal themselves as caring and respon-
sible kinsmen: we see them chatting about their sons' progress at school,
sending money home, and contacting loved ones by long-distance phone,
promising to be home for the New Year. Despite having to drift from place
to place to find work, these murderers have nonetheless not neglected their
obligations to their families. Li Yang's interesting remarks on this crucial
(because seemingly self-contradictory) dimension of the story are worth
quoting at length at this juncture, because they point to what is perhaps
most at stake in the interpretation of this film:

> When I was observing the miners, although their lives were hard, they were
> not morose or dispirited. They possessed a kind of humour, or a sort of mag-
> nanimous view of life—what the Chinese call *renming* (or an acceptance of fate).
> They want to change their lives but they can't do it. Being poor citizens they are
> concerned about how to earn money safely and go home to feed their families.

> *I adopt a sympathetic attitude [toward the two lead characters].* Because one of
> them wanted to free himself from the evil but couldn't do it. Though we are con-
> fronted with his immense evil, humanity isn't entirely obliterated and he's ca-
> pable of being touched by sentimentality or the benevolent side of humanity.

> *[These two men] have a decent side—they are thrifty* as shown by the fact that
> they are not willing to spend even five dollars watching a video, and they stay in
> cheap hotels—*the first thing they do once they have money is to send some back to
> their families.* Why are such people capable of evil? . . . Why are these two people
> on the road to destruction?

> *The family as a virtue has been passed down through thousands of years of Chinese
> civilization.* Our traditionalist culture in respect to the family, its ethical values,
> has withstood the Cultural Revolution and foreign invasion. Why has it contin-
> ued to be passed down the ages? I have constantly thought about this question.
> The family is a theme in the background, and *because of this, you can't say that
> conscience has been completely eliminated from the two characters.*[14]

Although, in terms of its documentarylike film language, Blind Shaft is
on first viewing quite different from the other films featured in this book,
Li's sympathetic reflections help clarify why the film appropriately belongs
in the company of sentimental fabulations. By attributing to the kinship

family—or, more precisely, the emotional attachment to the kinship family—the foundational import of "conscience," Li returns us to the very core
of Chinese sentimentalism, a sentimentalism whose residual pull is experienced, as it were, even by the most ruthless of murderers, who are (for
Li) themselves victims of the chaotic changes sweeping through China. Of
equal importance is the fact that these murderers express their sense of
familial attachment in the form of a concern for learning—specifically, for
making sure that their children receive good educations. Kinship bonds
matter, then, not only as an age-old cultural legacy that has "withstood the
Cultural Revolution and foreign invasion," as Li says, but also as a way to
the future: such bonds present the possibility of extending one's life—bestowing on one a kind of immortality—through the secure (social as well
as biological) survival of the next generation.

Insofar as a redeemable sense of good can be traced in the two evil men's
commitment to kinship and education, *Tang and Song are, in fact, not so
distinguishable from Yuan*: the young boy, we are told, is interested in making enough money so he can return to school. In other words, despite their
differences, the three males are ultimately subscribing to the same value
system in which it is believed that education is the best means of future
success and in which one should have no qualms about sacrificing oneself
for one's kin.[15] Moreover, this value system is thoroughly steeped in patriarchy, at least insofar as it is enacted by Tang and Song (Yuan, on his part,
is working so that his sister can stay in school). Through the coal miners,
we are introduced to a world in which women function primarily as sex objects (prostitutes are a cheap form of entertainment in the towns near the
coal mines); the males socialize by sharing cigarettes, drinks, food, baths,
sex jokes, and even a hotel room for simultaneous acts of copulation, and
a young boy like Yuan must, it is said, be given his initiation into sex (however unwilling he may be) before he can be killed off. The presence of good
strong women (such as the young prostitute who was forced on Yuan and
the older woman who sees him off at the end) notwithstanding, this is a
world in which a projection of the future is made primarily through sons.
For instance, as someone who cares about his own son's education, Song's
primary reason for hesitating to kill Yuan is that, with Yuan's father (possibly) already dead, killing the son might mean driving the Yuan family line
into extinction.

As we move our attention to the vestiges of kinship as the moral—and
ideological—backdrop of the story, the violence and cruelty that accom-

pany group formation come into much sharper focus. For instance, although Tang and Song are not related by blood, they have in effect formed a secret, bloodlike bond, which serves as the basis for their illegitimate undertakings. What makes their partnership work is none other than an implicit mutual consent to a demarcated interiority of relations, one that must remain firmly marked off from the exterior. The strict adherence to this differentiation between the inside and the outside, this boundary between "us" and "them," is precisely what coheres and sustains the aggression against the outsiders, even when the material well-being of the insiders (the family or kin group) is structurally dependent on—indeed, derived from—the labor, good will, and collaboration of these outsiders. Under this type of social organization, the survival of the insiders—the possibility for them of a future, so to speak—is contingent on the status quo, that is, the continued solicitation, exploitation, and extermination of the "foreign" bodies that are considered as excess and disposable once they have served their utilitarian purpose.

In Song's refusal to carry out the murder plot as planned, the blind and primal desire to continue an inside group's existence ad infinitum at the expense of outsiders is, notably, interrupted. In this interruption—what amounts to an unprecedented recognition of the outsider's equal right to life—lies a small but significant opening, whereby Yuan can, presumably, return home, resume his formal education, become a good citizen, and help transform his society. Following the logic of this briefly emergent, benevolent moment of tolerance, it would perhaps be possible, finally, to view education as a type of human cultural activity that occupies the status of *techne* and *poiesis*, in what Heidegger would affirm as a positive instance of the "challenging-forth" of Being. Li Yang, on his part, puts it in the form of hope: "As for the ending, vis-à-vis the boy's fate, I wanted something open. . . . A child is the hope of mankind. . . . He is also the hope of the story."[16]

Li's deliberate intentions notwithstanding, the conceptual trajectory taken by the film is, intriguingly, ambiguous as to the precise connotations and implications of education as a real solution. To begin with, the respect for education is, as I have noted, something shared by all the characters, including the irrevocably "evil" Tang (who appears to be semi-illiterate). If education is so unquestionably valuable, the film compels us to ask, how is it that some of those who so firmly believe in it can at the same time exhibit such cruelty and indifference to others, the "outsiders"? Can this simply be explained by, or blamed on, causes such as the capitalist mode of production, globalization, China's new social situation, etc., or does not the answer need to be sought elsewhere? How can a supposedly "enlightened" belief in the virtue of learning—as the hope for the future—coexist so matter-of-factly with the cold-blooded practice of extirpating those who are not "us" simply for the sake of money? Is education really the solution to the magnitude of the problems unveiled before our eyes?

Reflected on in these terms, the iterative references to education in the film are not unlike the refrains of humanistic platitudes that we encounter everywhere around the globe, from the orations of politicians to the declarations of entrepreneurs and media personalities alike, even as the new world order of inhumanity saturates international relations on a daily basis with incidents of torture, illegal detention, persecution, and numerous other forms of discrimination and brutality against helpless peoples. Exactly what are the power relations that sustain *this* alienation—not so much the existential alienation created by class or economic disparity (as is so poignantly portrayed in the film), as the disjuncture between the sign of a collective ideal (such as "education"), on the one side, and, on the other, the shockingly raw violence of actual human interactions? How do we come to terms with the copresence of these incommensurate human realities—a copresence that, to return to Heidegger's terminology, seems to be at once the symptom of a certain oblivion and a revelation/bringing-forth that is nothing short of a fracturing of the *continuum* of the "human" as such?

I am therefore inclined to seeing *Blind Shaft* as an allegory about the very mutation of the concept of "human"—that is to say, as the unconcealment of a process of species differentiation that is happening at the rupturing between a positive sign of human culture—"education" (read: humanity-as-progress, or hope)—and the ubiquitous biopolitical warfare around natural and other resources and, above all, around kinship and other types of group survival, all of which being, of course, inseparable from education. To bring our reading of Heidegger up to date, this particular unconcealment, it would seem, has to be recognized as our contemporary global condition of homelessness.

In the context of Chinese sentimentalism, the most unsettling questions posed by this film's narrative and characterization are these: Is kinship, defined as an inviolable interiority of familial/familiar relations, as I have specified, in essence the last vestige of morality (and of humanity) left in an utterly amoral world—in the sense that, except for the protection and preservation of one's kin, nothing else matters?[17] At the same time, is not such commitment to kinship bonds, so deeply rooted in Chinese societies as to be associated with, and reaffirmed as, conscience itself, precisely complicit with some of the worst xenophobic—indeed, murderous—practices in the contemporary world? What kind of conscience are we talking about when kindness is literally—and exclusively—directed at the purpose of advancing one's own kin(d)?

Ironically, then, the Chinese sentimental attachment to *home* (in the multiple senses of one's blood family, kin, house, and so forth—all those ties marked off as belonging in the inside of a particular group as opposed to the outside) stands in this analysis as an instructive case in point of the modern and contemporary world condition of homelessness. As a defense against this dangerous and depressing—yet obviously contagious—condition, our only viable choice is perhaps to give allegiance, after all, to the collective cultural ideality of education (as the last-ditch custodian of Being). Even so, we should not forget Balibar's warning about the inevitability of violence in the resort to such ideals:

> Supposing . . . that the counterpart to the experience of cruelty is always some sort of particularly demanding thirst for *ideality*—either in the sense of *non-violent* ideals, or in the sense of ideals of *justice*—how are we to deal philosophically and practically with what I consider to be a matter of incontrovertible finality: that there is no liberation from violence, no resistance to its worst excesses, especially no *collective* resistance . . . *without ideals*? However, there is no guarantee, and there can be no guarantee, concerning the "good use" and the "bad use" of ideals—or, if you prefer, there are certainly *degrees* in the amount of violence which goes along with civilizing ideals; but nothing like a *zero* degree. Therefore there is no such thing as non-violence.[18]

FIGURE 9.1 The old man trying to steady Hsiao Kang's head as they take a motorcycle ride, *Heliu / The River* (Copyright Central Motion Pictures, 1997)

The Enigma of Incest and the Staging of Kinship Family Remains in *The River*

這一次他與父親狹路相逢，他沒有殺了他，他只是和他做了愛。

This time, as he came upon his father on that fateful path, he did not kill him. He just made love with him.

—CHANG HSIAO-HUNG,
"Guaitai jiating luomanshi: *Heliu* zhong de yuwang changjing"

Once in a while, the encounter with a particular scene in a film is so challenging that it preempts one's relation to the entire film. Such a scene will be my focus of interest in this final chapter. It is from Taiwan director Tsai Ming-liang's (Cai Mingliang) *Heliu/The River* (1997), a film in which a father and a son, not recognizing each other in the dark, engage in sex in a gay men's bathhouse (what in Taiwan is known as a *san wen-nuan*, itself a local transliteration of "sauna"). Like much of Tsai's work, this scene is without musical accompaniment: the simple movements and gestures, the shadows cast by the dim light on the characters' flesh, and the occasional sounds they make constitute the totality of the diegesis of this astonishing event.

Why astonishing? The obvious answer, for some viewers, would be that this is a reprehensible depiction of incest, though this obviousness becomes questionable upon reflection. In a society in which gay and lesbian sexual relations remain on the margins of social propriety and permissibility, as is the case of contemporary Taiwan, it is difficult, if not impossible, to decide on the exact significance of this scene of two males engaged in sex. As Gayle Rubin, in her groundbreaking essay on the political economy of sex, wrote: "Hunger is hunger, but what counts as food is culturally determined and obtained. . . . Sex is sex, but what counts as sex is equally culturally determined and obtained."[1] Perhaps this is why, to avoid having to say what it really is, one critic simply recapitulated the scene in these matter-of-fact terms: "In *The River*," he wrote, "[Hsiao Kang, the son] winds up being anonymously jerked-off by and then fellating his dad in a darkened sauna room . . . until the old man switches on the light and slaps Junior across his girlish mouth."[2]

The enigma posed by this scene may be described as follows: In order to charge that what has taken place is incest, one must imply that one acknowledges the reality of same-sex sex (in this case, sex between two males); yet once that acknowledgment is made, the normativity accorded to patriarchal heterosexuality would by necessity have to become relativized, as would the purportedly nontransgressible boundary between man and woman, parent and child, mother and son, father and son that derives its status from such heterosexuality. The charge that this is a scene of incest would thus have to contain within it already the crucial (if implicit) recognition that both the categories of the kinship family (on which the norm of heterosexual marriage rests with its set relations of filiation) and the categories of heterosexuality (on which the norm of the kinship family rests with its set mechanisms of biological reproduction) are unstable cultural inventions.

Conversely, if same-sex sex is not recognized as real sex to begin with, what would be same-sex incest? Would not the latter, like the former, be a simple contradiction in terms? As has been pointed out by scholars, the taboo against incest itself has primarily been based on a heterosexual conceptualization of sexual and family relations and may at times become an instrument in the perpetuation of such conceptualization, thus helping to derealize gay and lesbian erotic and kin formations.[3] As the classical story of Oedipus indicates, convention presumes that incestuous relations are sexual relations within the same family between members of the opposite sexes. This presumption is confirmed in a leading definition offered by the *American Heritage Dictionary*, according to which incest refers to "sexual relations between persons who are so closely related that their marriage is illegal or forbidden by custom." The reference to marriage in this instance is revealing because it is marriage—invariably assumed to be between a man and a woman—that stands as the ultimate legitimation for sexual relations.[4] By this logic, as long as father and son do not want to get married/are not married to each other, can they have sex? If and when they have sex, would they be committing incest? In other words, can incest actually happen between father and son[5]—and, by implication, between mother and daughter, brother and brother, sister and sister (whether or not they are related by blood)? To the extent that these questions are fundamental to any attempt at clarifying the status of the event shown in *The River* and that the answers to them are by no means self-evident, the viewers who reacted with moral indignation to Tsai, such as the ones in Taiwan when the film was first released,[6] might have reacted overhastily. How could these viewers have been sure that what has happened in this scene can indeed be categorized unproblematically as incest, a known and well-defined taboo? When same-sex marriage became legalized, with much debate and controversy, in North America for the first time in the summer of 2003, it seemed that Tsai's film, made a number of years before, had already, with foresight, taken us a major step further by raising this scandalous supplemental question: if same-sex marriage should become socially permissible and recognizable, wouldn't it mean that same-sex incest, too, must finally become thinkable?

A CINEMA OF ENIGMAS

This scene thus offers a unique entry point into Tsai's cinema: rooted in a cosmopolitanism that is recognizably high modernist in its thematic, narrative, and aesthetic designs, this cinema is one that poses questions, puzzles, and enigmas, confronting us repeatedly with the limits of our epistemic certainties, our comfort zones. Much like the plays of Samuel Beckett and Harold Pinter, Tsai's works, which have won him critical acclaim at film festivals in Europe and North America as well as Asia, are noticeably marked by a sense of existential alienation, with loneliness being the signature obsession that runs throughout his feature films to date (*Qing shaonian nezha/Rebels of the Neon God* [1992], *Aiqing wansui/Vive l'amour* [1996], *Dong/The Hole* [1998], *Ni nabian jidian?/What Time Is It There?* [2001], *Bu san/Goodbye, Dragon Inn* [2003], and *Tianbian yi duo yun/The Wayward Cloud* [2005], as well as *The River*).[7] As in Beckett, Pinter, and, to some extent, Eugène Ionesco, the breakdown of human communication is often signified by the banality and nonsense of speech and by the absence of any intricately plotted turn of events or absorbing storytelling. What philosophers and theorists traditionally consider as the features that distinguish humans definitively from animals, that make humans human, as it were—features such as language, speech, thought, and narrative—are typically reduced to a minimum. This desubstantiation of human exchange at the abstract, verbal level is then played out in the often absurd, tragicomic situations in which characters somehow find themselves:[8] a vacant apartment in which various characters who happen to have keys to it develop transient relationships, including a scene of copulation between a male and a female on a bed while another male character, playing voyeur, masturbates underneath (*Vive l'amour*); a mysterious virus or disease that causes a young man's neck to hurt so badly that he cannot hold his head straight (*The River*); a gaping hole between two floors of an apartment building that leads to a strange friendship between a man and a woman in the midst of a contagious disease invading the island of Taiwan (*The Hole*); a young man trying to connect with a woman (who wants to buy a dual-time wristwatch from him on the street in Taipei one day before she goes off to Paris) by resetting every clock he comes across to Paris time (*What Time Is It There?*); unexpected or missed encounters during the last screening of a martial arts classic at an old movie theater the night before it closes down (*Goodbye, Dragon Inn*); and so forth.

As can be surmised from these odd assemblages of people and situations, Tsai's cinema has consistently explored the sense of a world caught up in inexplicable happenings, the eccentricity of which becomes magnified as a result of the lack of linguistic intervention, distraction, explanation, or simplification.[9] His scenes, albeit on the cinema screen, rather resemble those of a sparsely decorated stage set on which it is human bodies—their basic physical needs, automatized movements, and weird behaviors—rather than human minds that become the primary sites of drama (a genre in which Tsai received his early training). With reminders of Kafka's works (notably "The Metamorphosis"), being human in Tsai also verges on becoming animal in an environment in which authority over life is not at the rational disposal of the individual person. Tsai's characters move about, eat, pee, sleep, fuck, masturbate, get sick, and face problems with a mute mechanicity that at once draws attention to the mundaneness of their animal-like bodies and intensifies their unfulfilled emotional longings.[10]

Although these borrowings from and affinities with high modernist drama and fiction (as well as the postwar European cinemas of directors such as Michelangelo Antonioni and François Truffaut) position Tsai's works unmistakably as a series of contemporary filmic experiments with avant-garde aspirations,[11] it would be insufficient to view these works simply at this level. More pertinent and necessary, it seems to me, are the questions of what such easily recognizable high modernist elements are doing in his stories and how their obviously formal or aesthetic highlights can be—and are—articulated with sociological import.

Part of the difficulty here lies in the fact that Tsai's films are highly metaphorical and, as a result, offer multiple possible points of entry into them, leading to an irresolvable network of connotations. Consider *The Hole*: if the point is that of portraying human loneliness so that the accident of a hole between two apartments ironically serves as a way to bring two strangers into contact with each other, how do we explain all the other interesting but rather bizarre details, such as the image of the female character sitting on her toilet peeing while holding a plastic container atop her head to catch the water dripping from the floor above, the shots of the male character befriending a cat on a street where most shops are closed, and the colorful, fantasmatic scenes of dancing and singing (featuring the Westernized popular songs of a glamorous singer and actress of the 1950s and 1960s, Ge Lan [Grace Chang])? Alternatively, in *The River*, why does the story of a young man suffering from a neck disease also include a leaking ceiling in his father's bedroom? Are both events—the pain in the neck and the hidden internal leakage—simply "symbols of" anomie, estrangement, desperation, and general social malaise? While this kind of interpretation of Tsai's work does have some relevance and has been offered by critics,[12] it may be too constricting for an apprehension of the kinds of innovations he has made.

The rich connections that can indeed be established among these apparently disjointed characters, happenings, images, logics, and associations suggest that most interpretations, by drawing on various details, would likely be valid. Precisely for this reason, however, I believe that Tsai's cinema should be approached in a way that goes beyond what is usually termed the interpretation of meaning. Another method would need to be devised whereby the high modernist dramatic elements—together with their conjuring of existential crises and disasters—that seem so prominently present in his films would only serve as a beginning rather than as the conclusion of critical reading. A more focused discussion of *The River* will help clarify my point.

THE RIVER

This film begins when a young man, Hsiao Kang, runs into a woman friend outside a Taipei department store. An assistant on a film production, she brings him to an outdoor shooting session in which the director (played by

Hong Kong director Ann Hui) is filming a scene of a corpse floating along a river. As the dummy, the prop of the human figure facedown, fails to produce the desired effect after repeated takes, the director approaches Hsiao Kang. Reluctant at first because the water is so filthy, he ends up playing the floating corpse to her satisfaction. Hsiao Kang cleans himself in a hotel room afterward, noticing, as he finishes showering, that dirt from the river seems to be sticking to his body. His woman friend brings him something to eat; they eat together and then have sex.[13] At home, his parents have a nonsexual and noncommunicating relationship. His mother works as an elevator operator in a restaurant, from which she brings home leftovers for their meals. She has an extramarital affair with a fellow who makes illegal duplicates of pornographic videos. His father is gay (he is a regular customer at a *san wennuan* and is shown picking up a young male in a shopping arcade one day), but he keeps his sexual activities secret from his wife and son.

Soon after he has played the corpse, Hsiao Kang comes down with a mysterious pain in his neck and cannot hold his head straight. In one hilarious scene, his father is shown literally holding and steadying Hsiao Kang's head as he sits behind Hsiao Kang on a motorcycle ride (fig. 9.1). The rest of the story shows him and his parents seeking different methods of cure, from visiting a local religious healer to injections, chiropractic, Chinese medicine, acupuncture, massage, and hospitalization, all to no avail. His father finally takes him to consult a spiritual master in Taizhong. While waiting for the master to exercise his healing powers through meditation, father and son find their way separately to a local *san wennuan* and become physically involved in the scene I described earlier. When the light is turned on, reality sets in. They return to their motel and spend the night together in their room. In the morning, the father makes a phone call to the spiritual master as he has been instructed, only to be told that the spirits have asked them to return to Taipei to see a doctor. He goes out, as usual, to buy them some breakfast. Hsiao Kang gets up, opens the curtains, and steps out on to the balcony overlooking the neighborhood. His condition looks pretty much the same as before, with his head awkwardly tilted to one side.

As I mentioned, numerous possible metaphoric connections can be made with the collection of materials Tsai uses in this film: the river and water as a source both of life and death, with associations of intoxication, disease, and corruption; the leak in the ceiling as an objective correlative of things getting out of control, of the collapse of the family, and of an irrepressible and destructive libido. At the same time, as I also suggested, precisely the sheer proliferation or expandability of these metaphoric connections—which can and do validate most sensitive and sensible types of readings—should be taken as a sign that this film demands to be treated as more than just a collection of "meanings" to be interpreted. Instead, I propose that what Tsai has undertaken is a production of discursivity, one that is not exactly geared toward a centralizable and thus summarizable logic but that operates in the manner of an archaeological excavation. What is being excavated? The remnants of conventional social—and specifically kinship family—relations,[14] which are presented by Tsai as images with little or no interiority—in the form of bodies, gestures, movements, and looks. These remnants of conventional social and kinship relations are, in other words, laid bare and displayed as part of a visual assemblage, a repertoire that constitutes a (cinematic) discursivity in production and an investigative process that will probably never be completely finished.

Take the example of Hsiao Kang's home: an ordinary-looking urban apartment in which father, mother, and son reside, each in his or her own bedroom. As they each live their separate lives, their paths occasionally cross. The mother usually brings home leftovers from the restaurant where she works, and the father, when he needs to eat, warms them up in the rice cooker and chews on his food abjectly by himself. Similar homely scenes show the mother drinking water or cleansing her face in front of her bedroom mirror; the son or the father going to the bathroom; the father or the mother coming home, climbing the stairs by himself or herself; the mother and the son sharing some durian. As the characters make their regular appearances, repeating motions that we know must have been made innumerable times, they also tell us something more: the family has turned into a mere household, traversed daily by those who are supposed to be intimately related but are psychically estranged from one another. (When the father needs to call the mother to tell her their son is in the hospital, he has to look up the phone number printed on the restaurant takeout box that she has left in the refrigerator.) The activities of feeding, resting, and conversing that are normally part of the domestic scene of sharing are now performed in their raw physicality, stripped of any familiar and familial cover (story) of love and caring—and that is why we notice them. And, just as the material environment around these characters is reduced to simple items that serve the most basic needs—such as a table, chairs, beds, a refrigerator, a bathtub, a toilet, and other nondescript furnishings—so, too, are the characters themselves shorn of any serious signs of an inner life or subjectivity that can be effectively expressed or communicated. Instead, they come across as the human remains of some previous social arrangement, apparently long since defunct, that can now be glimpsed only from the nonrelations displayed before us. The household in Tsai's work is therefore a key archaeological find, its members being the walking exhibits of a collective order that has survived in the form of ruins. How did it all come to this? what happened? we feel compelled to ask. In their desolation, these ruins constitute the most important elements of Tsai's production of a discursivity in which the social—recast as *evacuated* family relations— becomes part of the cinematic.

At the core of this production is Tsai's distinctive approach to visuality/visibility. In contrast to the works of some of his fellow directors, Tsai's images are consistently and self-consciously still and minimalist. Be it in the form of a "corpse" in the river, the mother bringing up customers in the restaurant elevator, the father eyeing and picking up a young man in the shopping arcade, or Hsiao Kang riding his motorcycle, the visual/visible as deployed by Tsai has the eerie quality of allegory—sections, fragments, broken parts, whose whole has somehow been lost. Although, simply because they are concretely present on the screen, the images tend to invite readings of themselves as symbols (with full symbolic meanings), I'd argue that, in this case, precisely such visual concreteness becomes Tsai's paradoxical means of enlarging and dramatizing an ontological and social dysfunction whose origins, nonetheless, cannot immediately be seen. And, unlike many contemporary Chinese-language films (including those by masters such as Hou Hsiao-hsien, Ann Hui, Wong Kar-wai, Zhang Yimou, Stanley Kwan, and others) that typically introduce music at crucial moments in order to enhance the appeal of the visual/visible with an added, aural level of signification, so as consciously or unconsciously to influence and direct the audience's response, in Tsai, the visual/visible is most often left to stand alone without such external interference or reinforcement.[15] What this means, interestingly, is that the visual/visible, by itself, enacts a sense of isolation, a deliberate "disconnect" whose quiet, uncushioned presence gives rise to a fresh aesthetic potential. As much as they are ruins in the aftermath of a missing past, Tsai's images are at the same time runes to be deciphered and speculated on for an as-yet unknown future. This open temporality of Tsai's visual compositions, which at once scavenge materials from the chance situations of the everyday and assemble them as parts of a mesmerizing, artificial medium, one that points simultaneously to the past and the future, to melancholic disintegration and redemptive transformation, is what makes the discursivity in production that characterizes his works to date so fascinating to contemplate.[16]

In light of these observations, how are we to assess the significance of the "incest" episode? Let us compare this scene in Tsai's film with another scene of gay male sex in contemporary Chinese cinema, the scene of the two protagonists having anal intercourse toward the beginning of Wong Kar-wai's *Happy Together*, also made in 1997. In Wong's film, as discussed in chapter 2, the acts of intimacy and penetration take place in the private space of the two lovers, and there is nothing ambiguous about the identities of the two men involved. As I have argued, this scene may be seen as a fantasy origin of a relationship that keeps breaking down, a perfect togetherness the lovers want incessantly to recapture in vain. In Wong's film, it is the feeling of romance—expressed in the form of a climactic physical union—that lingers as the telos for nostalgic longing. The transience of this romance—its brief duration of happiness and its inevitable disappearance—is what lends its illusion of timelessness and plenitude a sense of magic, which is reinforced throughout the film by color and music. In the scene in *The River*, by contrast, the momentary physical pleasure and intimacy enjoyed by the two males are presented in darkness and silence and stand rather as the source of many viewers' horror. What feelings of homophobia might have been there to begin with are compounded by the disturbance caused by the conventional prohibition against incest. The locale for this scene, meanwhile, is not the relatively secure private space of cohabitants but one room (among many) in a public facility where, by paying a charge, men have access to the opportunity of having sex anonymously with other men. The rather seedy-looking interiors imbue the transient relationships that take place there with a strong sense of pathos—the pathos of people who move from room to room like faceless nomads seeking company and sustenance and whose behaviors are stigmatized, criminalized, and forbidden in broad daylight. There is no question of any idealized romance here.

And yet, in the midst of such pathos, in the midst of what is considered morally shameful and disgusting, there emerges a rare instant of connectivity that is the result not purely of the narcissistic pleasure of sex but also of a reciprocal tenderness. This tenderness is especially evident as the father holds the son from behind as he masturbates him, lets him reach orgasm, and then helps him clean himself off before the son takes his turn as the pleasure giver. This series of motions gives the impression first and foremost of a caring—rather than of sexual domination—and an effort to shelter and comfort the other rather than single-mindedly to gratify himself. The conveyance of this embrace of the other, an embrace that is discernible from within (the portrayal of) an aggressive and violent physical desire, makes this scene extraordinarily poignant to watch.[17] Although the sexual partners have transgressed against most known bounds of custom, culture, and civilization, the exchange we witness nonetheless commands sympathy and respect: as the two men caress and satisfy each other, just for a few moments, their mutuality touches some of us in a profound way.[18]

In this scene, the allegorical nature of Tsai's work can be clearly detected, in the enigmatic manner in which a utopian aperture unveils itself under the most oppressive and censorious of social conditions. After smashing the sacredness of the father-son relationship, which has devolved into an empty shell, he nonetheless rearranges the broken pieces in a boldly imaginative configuration. I am tempted to add that herein lies, perhaps, the uniqueness of Tsai's cinematic discursivity. Whereas in the hands of some other directors, the obvious destitution and deviance of his characters—lonesome, inarticulate, mysteriously ill, sexually perverse, morally anarchic—might have simply stopped at being stark portrayals of existential angst, in Tsai's works, such destitution and deviance, collected from an archaeology of contemporary urban human types—psychically defective and disabled, to be sure—become elements of a different sensorium and sociality, whereby it is precisely the limits, thresholds, prohibitions, and repressed intensities that are tracked, taken apart, and remolded into potentialities for remaking the world. In Fran Martin's words: "The scene in which father and son . . . find symbolic 'salvation' through sex together operates on one level as a utopian vision, in which the apparent deadlock between same-sex love and familial love is magically broken in a moment of apocalyptic rupture."[19]

To this extent, the characteristic quality of excess—all the deluges, breakdowns, and dead-ends, physical and social—we frequently encounter in Tsai's films is perhaps less a sign of the saddening collapse of traditional kin relations, as some critics have suggested with good reason,[20] than it is a sign of possible release (from such relations). A polluted river, a leak in the

ceiling, a hole between two apartments, a disease attacking an island country, and perhaps even an embarrassing pain in the neck are, in this regard,
means of transition, course changing, or temporary escape, despite the obvious inconvenience, danger, and chaos they cause. In the metaphoric excess of these multiple flows and blockages lies also *a dialectics of movement
and arrest*, whereby impasses, however constricting and catastrophic, need
to be understood as part of a vision of potential diversion, evacuation, and
deterritorialization toward an as-yet-unidentifiable elsewhere.

Might it not make sense, then, to think of the "incest" episode finally
with the help of anthropological language, in which father and son could
be seen as natives of an indigenous culture (to wit, the traditional kinship
family) that is on its way to extinction? As this culture becomes devoid of
its substance, practices, and values and degenerates into a stock stage set,
father and son—nomenclatures that are residues of the older sociality—
meet, by accident or by fate, as fugitives seeking asylum in a hideout with
very different customs and conventions. (Notably, as Hsiao Kang goes from
door to door trying to find a partner, the old man's room is the only one
that remains unlocked—as if it is awaiting him.)[21] And there, in the murky
shadows of an illicit enclave, away from their original homeland, they shed
their former identities and relate to each other as comrades, companions,
and fellow participants in a new kind of social contract, replete with its own
language and its own rules of communal sharing. Recast in this imaginary
perspective, the scene in question would take on the import of a collective
fleeing and crossing, a process of transculturation that demands not only
the reconstitution of identities but also—and more importantly—a new
metalanguage for accessing and registering such reconstituted identities.
To this end, would not an insistence on the two males' being father and
son—and on what has taken place between them as an unmistakable case
of incest—become an embarrassing instance of epistemic foreclosure, otherwise known as ethnocentrism?

SAME-SEX TROUBLE

Because the enigma at hand is so-called incest, Tsai's film also raises the
question of whether and how the scene can be read in relation to Oedipus.
In the classical mythical framework, Oedipus is the story of incest between
a mother and a son, and the tragedy is caused in large part by the two's lack

of awareness of what they have committed, so much so that knowledge (or revelation of the truth) can only result in suicide, physical blindness, and general destruction. When Freud adapted the myth to psychoanalysis, his point was to turn the truth of the story—that is, the possibility of sexual relations between parent and child—into the complex of modern human civilization. In Freud's work, that possibility is always lurking especially in the relationship between a mother and a son, both as a predilection and as a prohibition: incestuous desire is thus the paradigmatic case of a repressed desire that must at once be disavowed and displaced. Although Freud did distinguish between the positive and the negative Oedipus complex (with the latter involving a same-sex attraction, which the little boy feels toward his father, for instance),[22] in the bulk of his work, his attention remained focused on the heterosexual paradigm of sex, and it is reasonable to conclude that heterosexuality continues to shape most discussions about incest to this day.

Presuming this to be indeed the case, let me now reiterate the question I raised at the beginning of this chapter: is the act committed by the two males in Tsai's film really incest? Even in the Chinese language, in which the common term for incest is *luanlun*[23]—the overturning of kin or, more precisely, of hierarchically arranged social relations—this question is crucial. Although the ancient Chinese concept of *lun* does not exclusively involve blood relations and is therefore much more explicitly cultural in its rationale,[24] as long as that rationale is intertwined with a heterosexual paradigm of sex (whereby the moral emphases on seniority, order, and propriety that define *lun* also mean that *lun* can never possibly recognize same-sex sex relations as belonging anywhere inside the proper social hierarchy in the first place), what happens between Hsiao Kang and the old man ought to be read as an enigma—one that, moreover, we do not yet seem to have the analytical tools to resolve—rather than as a plainly intelligible incident of kinship violation or *luanlun*.

Furthermore, although Hsiao Kang may be the protagonist in this family drama, it is, I think, the old man who offers the more revealing clues to the dissolution of the kinship system based on seniority and hierarchy. Rather than being a patriarch in control of his woman, his offspring, and his household, the old man is a forlorn figure who at some point became consigned to a small room in the apartment, a room that obviously is not the master bedroom. He eats his meals alone (no one cooks for him), sweeps the apartment floors, and irons his own clothes. When there is a leak in the ceiling, at times with torrents coming down into his room, he does his best to accommodate and conceal the steadily deteriorating conditions, going to the ridiculous, elaborate extreme of picking up a large piece of plastic from a junkyard as a way to channel the water out of the window into a potted plant on the balcony. (Again, in contrast to Wong Kar-wai, such casual pickups in Tsai, whether the object is a piece of plastic or a young man in the mall, have nothing romantic attached to them.) Like other gay males at the *san wennuan*, the father turns himself into an object as well as a seeker of sexual transactions among strangers, going in and out of darkened rooms hunting or waiting for the interested partner to show up, taking chances with being rejected. His position is thus, as Chang Hsiao-hung writes, "dephallicized" and far removed from that of a father with authority.[25] Indeed, the title "father," which partakes of age-old conventions of sex and gender,[26] is now arguably just part of an automatized obligation left in him by a former social arrangement (that is why he still performs some fatherly functions, such as taking Hsiao Kang to various doctors, bringing him his medicine, making sure that he is not hungry, etc.).

More appropriately speaking, the old man is now an anonymous member of a clandestine sexual economy, in which his body, like others', is a token of exchange—his penis is just a penis—and in which his age, rather than giving him special status (as in the traditional order of *lun*), only means that he will become increasingly undesirable. Insofar as the old man enters the culture of the *san wennuan* as an agent of consensual sex transactions, he is, strictly speaking, no longer a father, with his traditional privileges and entitlements, but a (mere) peer to his "son." If women have been the objects of exchange in exogamous kinship relations,[27] here we have a situation in which men have become both the subjects and objects of exchange, their bodies serving as the very gifts regulating and sustaining an underground socius that does away with women altogether. The ultimate scandal, therefore, is not only a matter of same-sex sex and same-sex incest; it is also a fundamental rescripting of the conventional gender system, hitherto based rigidly on the binarism of exactly two differentiated sexes, male and female, and on the idea that they must both be present—however subordinate one (usually the female) might be—for social reproduction as such to materialize.[28] In this respect alone, the radical implications of Tsai's conceptualization of homosexuality have far exceeded the idealization of (two-partner) romance in Wong Kar-wai's *Happy Together* or the updating of kinship biopolitics through flexible inclusionism in Ang Lee's *Wedding Banquet*.

HUMAN LIFE AS A TRANSIENT ABODE

Tsai, who was born and raised in Malaysia and who now lives and works in Taiwan, is reported to have commented that the notion of *rensheng ru ji* 人生如寄 — literally, human life is a transient abode—is a good description of what he has tried to achieve with *The River*.[29] In the Chinese language, the connotations of the word *ji* are rich and wide-ranging. Used often to indicate "to send," "to depend on," or "to attach oneself to" something, it is also part of numerous idioms and expressions—such as *jisu* (to be at boarding school), *jiju* (to stay as a guest), *jiren lixia* (to live under someone else's roof), *jisheng* (to live parasitically), *jituo* (to entrust to the care of someone), and so forth—all of which share the spatial sense of displacement and the temporal sense of impermanence. For Tsai, who is interested in the teachings of Buddhism, this spiritual awareness of human life as (inherently) displaced and impermanent emerges in the midst of the most deeply entrenched and seemingly inalterable social organizations (such as the Chinese family) in contemporary urban Taiwan.

I'd like to suggest that this spiritual awareness can operate in two different directions: it can either become the source of despair, lament, and melancholy, or it can decode from displacement and impermanence a certain emancipatory method—the method precisely of detaching oneself from what appears to be an immovable and atrophied cultural situation. Because (as I have been trying to show throughout this book) this cultural situation derives so much of its strength from the sentimentalism based on attachment, this sense of detachment is, to say the least, subversive and controversial. As Meiling Wu writes (regarding some of the Taiwan films of the 1990s such as Tsai's): "The concept of displacement moves beyond the ethos of sadness, which focuses mostly on tragic, work-burdened, and politically victimized representation of Taiwanese family. Instead, Tsai Ming-liang envisions relationships among men and women in postsadness Taiwan as accidental and replaceable." And, precisely "because all the sentimental expressions have been suspended or filtered out, the characters' meaningless daily repetitious actions and routines arouse *antipathy* from the spectators."[30] "Antipathy" can also be read as another expression for detachment. Tsai's passing remarks on the notion of solitude (or aloneness) (*gudu*) are revelatory in this regard:

I try to reflect the sense of solitude inherent in human nature in a destructive and exaggerated manner because I don't know whether solitude is good or bad, though what the whole society and value system tell us is: "You cannot/must not be alone." The burden created by the Chinese's strong sense of family is especially hard to bear. Our society has never told us how to live freely. What it imposes on you is a set of formulas, with no one ever telling you what kind of distance there ought to be between human beings. That is why I want to push my films to extremes (to the limits) and see if human beings become capable of thinking only when there is a far enough distance between them.[31]

In ways similar to detachment and antipathy, in other words, solitude or isolation (from traditional family relations) is not necessarily a negative state of mind to be regretted and avoided at all costs; it can also bring forth a kind of space, gap, and distance in which observation can take place and the paths of (re)thinking can become perceptible. Understood in this manner, the notion of human life as a transient abode—as a way station, so to speak—may be seen as the conceptual or epistemic correlative to Tsai's aesthetically experimental method. Displacement and impermanence are now not so much conditions about which to become maudlin as the very essential means to an enlightened form of imagining. Being displaced and impermanent enables one to imagine the possibility of not staying on, of pursuing lines of flight from (the kinship family norms of) a human life world that has become uninhabitable (albeit without necessarily arriving at any safe destination).

The ending of *The River* seems to encourage such a reading. Although, when the light is turned on after the incident of "incest," the old man slaps the young man, who rushes out, the last part of the film gives no further elaboration of the fallout from the dreamlike sequence of mutual tenderness. It is as if, for the time being at least, these fugitives to that other world have returned to their indigenous abode, taking up once again their vestigial roles as father and son. Meanwhile, alone in the apartment in Taipei on a rainy night, the mother finally discovers the father's secret of the leaking ceiling (as water begins seeping under his bedroom door into the living room area). She manages to locate the source of the entire mystery—a tap that has been left running in the kitchen in the empty apartment upstairs—and turns it off.

Importantly, the significance of this anticlimactic and untraumatic ending lies not so much in its seeming return to familial normalcy and domestic security as in its explicit detour from the tragedy that, by the narrative rules set by the ancients, must follow the violation of the incest taboo. In the most quiet yet radical manner, as the discerning remarks by Chang cited at the beginning of this chapter remind us, the elimination of "the father" as such has taken the form not of patricide but rather of sexual intimacy with the old man, an intimacy that impedes the powerful flow of the classic oedipal plot, causing the latter to abandon its hitherto natural or naturalized course. The very final scene, in which father and son go about their unremarkable routines in the motel room, is thus utterly remarkable because of this emotional detachment (and deviation) from the oedipal logic of punitive inevitability. (This is one reason I have been reluctant to read this entire episode strictly by way of the interpretative nuances of Freudian psychoanalysis, as some critics have done with admirable—but to my mind misdirected—sophistication.) Even though the truth has been revealed—namely, that not only is same-sex sex possible but same-sex sex within the so-called kinship family has occurred—no death, suicide, or apocalypse needs to ensue from such revelation. The spectators are left with an ending that is suggestively introduced by the light let into the room as Hsiao Kang opens the curtains and the balcony door and steps outside. This closing—or opening, rather, which is placed visibly at the center of the scene—is as enigmatic in its indeterminacy as it is refreshing in its sidestepping of the classical-tragic/psychoanalytic-traumatic conclusion. It marks the discursivity of Tsai's film with one more evocative surprise, endowing his allegorical social figures with an unpredictable, rather than fatalistically (pre)determined, sense of the life still to come.[32]

Postscript
(Inspired by *Brokeback Mountain*)
"The Juice"; or, "The Great Chinese Theme"

In an interview with the *New York Times* during the publicity period for his blockbuster film *Wohu canglong* (*Crouching Tiger, Hidden Dragon*, 2000), director Ang Lee spoke of the enormous influence on his filmmaking of the Mandarin classic *Liang Sanbo yu Zhu Yingtai* (*Love Eterne*, directed by Li Hanxiang, 1963).[1] "I think that for every movie I make, I always try to duplicate that feeling of purity and innocence that I got when I saw this movie. . . . Whatever I bring into my own films, I am forever trying to update and recapture that feeling. *I call it juice—the juice of the film—the thing that moves people, the thing that is untranslatable by words.*"[2] The story in question, replete with suggestions of homosexual and homosocial bonding from today's perspectives, is built on what Lee called "the great Chinese theme," which, he said, is about "lovers who, because of the strictures of filial piety and duty, cannot speak openly about their romantic feelings."[3]

But what exactly is the great Chinese theme?

Although, as Lee's remarks indicate, it may strike many audiences as a paradigmatic case of a "repressed love" story, I believe *Liang Sanbo yu Zhu Yingtai* is, more accurately speaking, a story of romantic rebellion. The ending offers the most important clue to this point. Forced into an arranged marriage by her family, Yingtai, the young heroine, agrees on condition that the wedding procession pass by the place where her beloved Sanbo's gravesite lies. As she arrives, Yingtai rips open her wedding robe to reveal funereal clothes underneath. The heavens respond in sympathy with a cyclone; the crowd clears away and Sanbo's grave is cracked open. Yingtai dashes into the grave to rejoin her beloved; the grave is then buried under dirt by the cyclone. As calm is restored, we see two butterflies fluttering away across a rainbow, transcending the wicked human world that has caused the lovers so much misery.

For the doomed lovers, this ending signifies the shining path of escape: if they cannot be together in life, it says, it is life itself that should be given up, indeed abandoned, so that happiness and fulfillment can be sought in another world.[4] To the extent that the lovers are, through a kind of trans-species metamorphosis, reunited, their love is vindicated and triumphant. This unambiguous sense of revolutionary romanticism was perhaps the reason why, despite its traditional Confucian social setting, this classic tale was greeted by the Chinese Communists as an example of righteous revolt against the feudalist world order. As is evident in the famous popular musical work—*Liang Zhu xiaotiqin xiezouqu* (*The Butterfly Lovers Violin Concerto*)—composed in celebration of the heroism of the lovers,[5] the gist of this story is courageous folk resistance against an oppressive regime of power: repressed love is merely a vehicle.

By contrast, Lee's own more recent and internationally acclaimed film *Brokeback Mountain* (2005; based on a short story by Annie Proulx) may be a bona fide reincarnation of the great Chinese theme of not being able to speak openly or directly about romantic feelings. At one level, indeed, *Brokeback Mountain* seems to have many ingredients similar to those of *Liang Sanbo yu Zhu Yingtai*: a love that begins as two young people, far away from home, become bonded in a memorable locale of shared daily activities; class as well as gender tensions; family pressures and social strictures; the untimely and shattering death of one lover; a tragic ending. Yet I would also contend that *Brokeback Mountain* is unlike *Liang Sanbo yu Zhu Yingtai* in one remarkable respect: it is a sentimental story in that it involves no act of social revolt or rebellion.

In and of itself, to be sure, the bond between Ennis Del Mar and Jack Twist is a romantic union, but it is their obligatory participation in society—their separate lives in the midst of hostile and uncomprehending gazes, emanating from that impersonal "they" that constitutes the only communities they know—that makes this film so incomparably heart-wrenching. To use Ang Lee's own vocabulary, the "juice" of the film—and the reason for its wide-ranging impact—flows not only in the mutual pas-

sion between the two men but also, and more crucially, in the webs of familial, reproductive, and social entanglements into which the they must
reinsert themselves over the decades after stumbling on their own sexuality and intimacy one brief summer.[6] These webs of entanglement give their
(socially unmentionable) relationship the emotional charge of self-imposed
restraint and containment and lead, eventually, to Ennis's destitution and
forlornness. The only thing he has left to keep him company for the rest
of his life are the two old shirts, soiled, entwined, and quietly closeted for
years, that he salvages from Jack's sparse belongings.

Obviously, since it uses white actors and the setting of an American
western, I cannot get away with categorizing *Brokeback Mountain* as an
example of contemporary Chinese cinema. Nevertheless, it seems appropriate, as contemporary Chinese directors have so noticeably contributed
to and transformed the production of global cinematic culture since the
1980s, to conclude the present study with a brief reflection on this film. To
my mind, the film's affective mode—conveyed in a unique combination of
the most expansive elemental spaces and the most oppressive, human cultural forces—seems entirely in tune with the workings of the sentimental I
have tried to analyze in some of the foregoing chapters. With filiality as its
keel,[7] this is an affective mode whose intensity is distinguished most of all
by its tendency toward accommodation and thus, ultimately, toward what
in Chinese idiom is known as *weiqu qiuquan* 委曲求全—literally, stoop-
ing/bending to make compromises out of consideration for the general interest. The pejorative connotations (such as weakness, cowardliness, and
defeatism) conjured by the notion of compromise notwithstanding, where
Brokeback Mountain succeeds is that it dare focalize on compromise as an
important emotional event. As a result, it is able to give full play to the
sense of vulnerability that accompanies attempts to settle differences by
the making of concessions (as Ennis and Jack do for the better part of their
lives) when, for various reasons, the problems at hand cannot be fixed simply by migration or relocation.

As the affect of accommodation, compromise, and settlement, the sentimental—what I myself consider to be the great Chinese theme, with the
specifications I have provided in this book—is a form of thinking-cum-living
that, to put it forthrightly, is the opposite of nomadism. Hence its potency,
paradoxically, to move (us).[8] Accordingly, the scenarios most effectively
dramatized in the sentimental mode are often other than those of defiance,
rebellion, flight, or absolute departure. More typically, even where effects

of critical staging, distancing, and detachment have been introduced (arguably, as in the films discussed in part 3, for instance), they tend in the end to be scenarios of reserve, indirection, submission, entrapment, and enslavement. As Lee has said of his own work: "I think one thing I have always been exploring through my work is the concept of freedom against social propriety. It is not merely someone putting a force upon you, but you putting a force upon yourself. But there is no such thing as absolute freedom. Unless, of course, you jump off a cliff to get away from it all! (*Laughs*) Other than that, as long as you are still dealing with people, you are enslaved in a relationship."[9] In terms of tone, sentimentalism is all about adaptation and resilience: if the romantic rebellion is a matter of announcing "I have to be/ assert myself, whatever it costs and whomever it may sacrifice"; sentimentalism is much more a matter of gesturing, with sadness as much as with humor: "I assimilate; I eat bitterness; I efface myself if I have to."

In underscoring this predominant epistemic, as much as affective, orientation of the sentimental as it has surfaced in some contemporary Chinese films, the point of this book is not to endorse or condemn the sentimental as such but rather to show how it continues to signify as a mode—how it fabulates its logics and effects, discursively as well as aesthetically, across the movie screen. If, as some have predicted, the twenty-first century turns out to be the Chinese century, the tremendous powers of staying, of enduring, and of holding (things and people) together that have figured so prominently in these films may have something significant to tell us about the forms of attachment that are likely to persist—and evolve—in the age of global visibility. "Sentimental fabulations": clearly a theme to be continued.

Notes

INTRODUCTION

1. Dudley Andrew, "The 'Three Ages' of Cinema Studies and the Age to Come," *PMLA* 115.3 (2000): 348. Andrew offers this information as part of a discussion of the history of cinema studies.

2. Christine Gledhill and Linda Williams, introduction to *Reinventing Film Studies*, ed. Christine Gledhill and Linda Williams (London: Arnold, 2000), 1.

3. See my discussion of Lu Xun's famous reactions to a slide show of an execution of a Chinese man (which he happened to watch during 1904–5 in Japan), reactions that led him to abandon medical studies and become a writer, at the beginning of part 1 of *Primitive Passions: Visuality, Sexuality, Ethnography, and Contemporary Chinese Cinema* (New York: Columbia UP, 1995). Tanizaki, for his part, noted how, in contrast to Western faces, Japanese faces appeared hideous and repulsive on film. For in-depth commentaries on as well as translations of some of Tanizaki's film essays and stories (written during the 1910s and 1920s), see Thomas LaMarre, *Shadows on the Screen: Tanizaki Junichiro on Cinema and "Oriental" Aesthetics* (Ann Arbor: Center for Japanese Studies, University of Michigan, 2005), in particular chaps. 7 and 8. It should be added, however, that Tanizaki's emphases were largely aesthetic—indeed, synesthetic, as LaMarre argues—in orientation, whereas Lu Xun's emphases were motivated by his sense of shock at his countrymen's apathy as bystanders and geared toward the urgency of national reform. For a major historical study of early East Asian cinema that elaborates the sensorial aspects of cin-

ematic modernity, see Zhang Zhen, *An Amorous History of the Silver Screen: Shanghai Cinema, 1896–1937* (Chicago: U of Chicago P, 2005).

4. See Walter Benjamin, "The Work of Art in the Age of Mechanical Reproduction" and "On Some Motifs in Baudelaire," in *Illuminations*, trans. Harry Zohn, ed. Hannah Arendt (New York: Schocken, 1969), 217–51, 155–200. For more recent English translations of the first, widely reprinted essay, see Walter Benjamin, "The Work of Art in the Age of Its Technical Reproducibility: Second Version," in *Walter Benjamin: Selected Writings*, vol. 3, 1935–1938, trans. Edmund Jephcott et al., ed. Howard Eiland and Michael W. Jennings (Cambridge: Harvard UP, 2002), 101–33; and Walter Benjamin, "The Work of Art in the Age of Its Technological Reproducibility: Third Version," in *Walter Benjamin: Selected Writings*, vol. 4, 1938–1940, trans. Edmund Jephcott et al., ed. Howard Eiland and Michael W. Jennings (Cambridge: Harvard UP, 2003), 251–83. The essay "On Some Motifs in Baudelaire" can also be found, with slight modifications, in *Walter Benjamin: Selected Writings*, vol. 4: 1938–1940, 313–55.

5. Tom Gunning, "'Animated Pictures': Tales of Cinema's Forgotten Future, After 100 Years of Films," in *Reinventing Film Studies*, 326.

6. An example is the French filmmaker and film theorist Jean Epstein's notion of *photogénie*, the essence of film that he defines as beyond verbalization and definition. For an informative discussion, see Leo Charney, "In a Moment: Film and the Philosophy of Modernity," in *Cinema and the Invention of Modern Life*, ed. Leo Charney and Vanessa R. Schwartz (Berkeley: U of California P, 1995), 285–88.

7. See Benjamin, "What Is the Epic Theatre?" *Illuminations*, 147–54; and idem, *Understanding Brecht*, trans. Anna Bostock, intro. Stanley Mitchell (London: New Left, 1973). For a version with slight modifications, see also idem, "What Is the Epic Theater? (II)," in *Walter Benjamin: Selected Writings*, vol. 4, 1938–1940, 302–9. The notion of defamiliarization—intimately linked to the notion of art as a technique or device—can be traced to the Russian formalists, who had strongly influenced Brecht. For the work of the most well-known Russian formalists, see, for instance, *Readings in Russian Poetics: Formalist and Structuralist Views*, ed. Ladislav Matejka and Krystyna Pomorska (Cambridge, Mass.: MIT Press, 1971); and *Russian Formalism: A Collection of Articles and Texts in Translation*, ed. Stephen Bann and John E. Bowlt (New York: Barnes and Noble, 1973). See also the chapter "Russian Formalism and the Bakhtin School," in Robert Stam, *Film Theory: An Introduction* (Malden, Mass.: Blackwell, 2000), 47–54.

8. See Walter Benjamin, *The Arcades Project*, trans. Howard Eiland and Kevin McLaughlin (Cambridge: Harvard UP, 1999).

9. Benjamin's contemporary Ernst Bloch developed this forward-looking potential into a principle of hope, and his utopian argument about film and mass culture significantly influenced subsequent generations of cultural theorists, such as, notably, Fredric Jameson. See Ernst Bloch, *The Principle of Hope*, vol. 1, trans. Neville Plaice, Stephen Plaice, and Paul Knight (Cambridge, Mass.: MIT Press, 1986). See Jane Gaines's discussion of this genealogy in her "Dream/Factory," in *Reinventing Film Studies*, 100–13. For another contemporary of Benjamin's who wrote substantially on film, see Siegfried Kracauer, *Theory of Film: The Redemption of Physical Reality* (Oxford: Oxford UP, 1960). For interesting comparisons with a non-Western author's observations about cinematic shock, see Tanizaki's film writings in LaMarre, *Shadows on the Screen*.

10. André Bazin, *What Is Cinema? Essays Selected and Translated by Hugh Gray*, foreword Jean Renoir (Berkeley: U of California P, 1967), 1:14–15.

11. In this regard, Bazin, like many early film theorists, still conceptualized the cinematic in terms of its affinity with and dependency on photography. For a discussion of this tendency, see Gunning, "'Animated Pictures,'" 322–25.

12. See André Bazin, "The Stalin Myth in Soviet Cinema" (1950), trans. Georgia Gurrieri, intro. Dudley Andrew, in *Movies and Methods*, ed. Bill Nichols (Berkeley: U of California P, 1985), 2:29–40.

13. Christian Metz, *Film Language: A Semiotics of Cinema*, trans. Michael Taylor (New York: Oxford UP, 1974); idem, *Language and Cinema*, trans. Donna Jean Umiker-Sebeok (The Hague: Mouton, 1974).

14. See Christian Metz, *The Imaginary Signifier: Psychoanalysis and the Cinema*, trans. Celia Britton, Annwyl Williams, Ben Brewster, and Alfred Guzzetti (Bloomington: Indiana UP, 1982).

15. For an illuminating historical account of the complicated tensions between semiotics and psychoanalysis within the theorizing of film, see Teresa de Lauretis, *Alice Doesn't: Feminism, Semiotics, Cinema* (Bloomington: Indiana UP, 1984). Drawing on the work of fellow feminist theorists such as Laura Mulvey, de Lauretis highlights the sexual politics inscribed in those tensions, and her own work provides a fine example of how the two models can be made to work together in film analysis. For two exemplary studies in feminist film theory during the 1980s that built on Mulvey's contributions, see Mary Ann Doane, *The Desire to Desire: The Woman's Film of the 1940s* (Bloomington: Indiana UP, 1987); and Kaja Silverman, *The Acoustic Mirror: The Female Voice in Psychoanalysis and Cinema* (Bloomington: Indiana UP, 1988).

16. Andrew, "The 'Three Ages' of Cinema Studies," 344.

17. Laura Mulvey, "Visual Pleasure and Narrative Cinema," in *Visual and Other Pleasures* (Bloomington: Indiana UP, 1989), 14–26. Mulvey was not alone in

her effort to theorize narrativity in relation to film. Among her fellow travelers were Jean-Louis Baudry, Christian Metz, Stephen Heath, and Paul Willemen, who each did substantive work with film narrative during the same period. See Jean-Louis Baudry, "The Apparatus," in *Narrative, Apparatus, Ideology: A Film Theory Reader*, ed. Philip Rosen (New York: Columbia UP), 1986, 299–319; Christian Metz, *Film Language* and *Language and Cinema*; Stephen Heath, "Narrative Space," *Screen* 17.3 (1976): 68–112, and *Questions of Cinema* (Bloomington: Indiana UP, 1981); and Paul Willemen, *Looks and Frictions: Essays on Cultural Studies and Film Theory* (Bloomington: Indiana UP, 1994). Mulvey, however, was the one who raised the issue of sexual politics.

18. Mulvey, "Visual Pleasure and Narrative Cinema," 16.

19. Maggie Humm, *Feminism and Film* (Bloomington: Indiana UP, 1997), 17. Humm's book offers a thoughtful account that places Mulvey's essay in its historical context of the United Kingdom in 1960s and 1970s, when the British intellectual left encountered the burgeoning of feminist theory.

20. Martin Jay, *Downcast Eyes: The Denigration of Vision in Modern French Thought* (Berkeley: U of California P, 1993).

21. Many criticisms of Mulvey's polemic piece, including feminist criticisms of the 1980s, revolve around her point about destroying pleasure and, as a counterargument, attempt to recuperate the positive value of pleasure, especially for women spectators. My argument is quite different in that it is about the intellectually and institutionally productive—that is, reproducible—nature of Mulvey's original negative move (of deconstructing the image) and how this is thought-provokingly bound up with the iconophobia of our (image-studded) culture at large.

22. See Michel Foucault, *The History of Sexuality*, vol. 1, trans. Robert Hurley (New York: Pantheon, 1978).

23. Mulvey, "Visual Pleasure and Narrative Cinema," 14.

24. To her credit, Mulvey herself has, with historical hindsight, critiqued the binarism of her earlier polemical argument and revised her observations. See the chapter "Changes: Thoughts on Myth, Narrative and Historical Experience" (first published in 1985), in *Visual and Other Pleasures*, 159–76.

25. Bill Nichols, "Film Theory and the Revolt Against Master Narratives," in *Reinventing Film Studies*, 42.

26. See, for instance, essays in the following collections: *Unthinking Eurocentrism: Multiculturalism and the Media*, ed. Ella Shohat and Robert Stam (New York: Routledge, 1994); *Fugitive Images: From Photography to Video*, ed. Patrice Petro (Bloomington: Indiana UP, 1995); *The Image in Dispute*, ed. Dudley Andrew with Sally Shafto (Austin: Texas UP, 1997); *The Oxford Guide to Film Studies*, ed. John Hill and Pamela Church Gibson (Oxford: Oxford UP,

1998); *Visual Culture: The Reader*, ed. Jessica Evans and Stuart Hall (London: Sage, 1999); and *Popular Film and Cultural Studies*, ed. Matthew Tinkcom and Amy Villarejo (New York: Routledge, 2001).

27. Nichols, "Film Theory and the Revolt Against Master Narratives," 40.

28. As Nancy Armstrong writes: "The sixties saw an important shift in the theater of political activism from the plane of physical action and conflicts that we persist in designating as real to the plane of discourse, representation, and performance, where conflicts determine how we imagine our relation to the real" ("Who's Afraid of the Cultural Turn?" *differences* 12.1 [Spring 2001]: 42). Her essay offers an interesting discussion of the linkage between the iconophobic legacy of Victorianism and the so-called cultural turn set off by the media-oriented activist events of the 1960s in the United States.

29. The field of Chinese film scholarship in English provides perhaps one of the best instances of such an academic migration. To my (obviously incomplete) knowledge, with the exception of a few—Chris Berry, Esther C. M. Yau, Emilie Yeh Yueh-yu, Zhang Zhen—many of those who have published on film since the early 1990s are scholars who hold doctoral degrees in literature.

30. Gilles Deleuze, *Foucault*, trans. Seán Hand, foreword by Paul Bové (Minneapolis: U of Minnesota P, 1988), 52, 58, and 59.

31. See, for instance, Charles Tesson, "L'Asie majeure," *Cahiers du cinema* 553 (January 2001): 5; Dave Kehr, "In Theaters Now: The Asian Alternative," *New York Times*, January 14, 2001, 2:1, 30. Apart from being featured at film festivals around the world, at which they have been receiving major awards, East Asian films, directors, and actors and actresses have also steadily made their way into mainstream cinematic venues in Western Europe and North America. For a few examples of interesting book publications on East Asian cinema in recent years, see *Cinematic Landscapes: Observations on the Visual Arts and Cinema of China and Japan*, ed. Linda C. Erlich and David Desser (Austin: U of Texas P, 1994); David Bordwell, *Planet Hong Kong: Popular Cinema and the Art of Entertainment* (Cambridge: Harvard UP, 2000); Mitsuhiro Yoshimoto, *Kurosawa: Film Studies and Japanese Cinema* (Durham, N.C.: Duke UP, 2000); *At Full Speed: The Transnational Cinema of Hong Kong in a Borderless World*, ed. Esther C. M. Yau (Minneapolis: U of Minnesota P, 2001); Eric Cadzdyn, *The Flash of Capital: Film and Geopolitics in Japan* (Durham, N.C.: Duke UP, 2002); Kyung Hyun Kim, *The Remasculinization of Korean Cinema* (Durham, N.C.: Duke UP, 2004); and *South Korean Golden Age Melodrama: Gender, Genre, and National Cinema*, ed. Kathleen McHugh and Nancy Abelmann (Detroit: Wayne State UP, 2005). For informed discussions of Asian cinemas in the discursive contexts among contemporary Asian cultures, see

some of the essays in the special issue "Chinese Culture in Inter-Asia," guest ed. Kwai-cheung Lo and Laikwan Pang, *Modern Chinese Literature and Culture* 17.1 (Spring 2005).

32. For an account of the study of Chinese cinema in the West, see the chapter "The Rise of Chinese Film Studies in the West," in Yingjin Zhang, *Screening China: Interventions, Cinematic Reconfigurations, and the Transnational Imaginary in Contemporary Chinese Cinema* (Ann Arbor: U of Michigan P, 2002), 43–113.

33. Notable examples of films include Godard's *La chinoise* (1967), *Le vent d'Est* (*Wind from the East*) (1969), and *Tout va bien* (1972), while Chris Marker's *Sunday in Peking* (1956) was among the first European documentaries to chronicle China under Mao (even though Marker is not considered a representative of the nouvelle vague). Among the more well-known publications by members of *Tel quel* on China, see, for instance, Julia Kristeva, *About Chinese Women*, trans. Anita Barrows (New York: Urizen, 1977); and Roland Barthes, *Alors la Chine?* (Paris: C. Bourgois, 1975). Among other well-known European endeavors to engage with China during this period and not too long afterward, see Jacques Derrida, *Of Grammatology*, trans. Gayatri Chakravorty Spivak (Baltimore: Johns Hopkins UP, 1976); the film *Chung Kuo/Cina*, directed by Michelangelo Antonioni (1972); and the film *The Last Emperor*, directed by Bernardo Bertolucci (1987).

34. It should, however, be noted that although the Chinese Communist Party was always eager to emphasize that loyalty to the party and the state must come before the family (in case of contradiction), efforts were often made to ensure that the patriarchal family system and the party could coexist in harmony. In other words, communism in China did not in actuality supplant or eradicate loyalty to the patriarchal family.

35. See, for instance, some of the essays by Mulvey in *Visual and Other Pleasures*; Tania Modleski, *Loving with a Vengeance: Mass-Produced Fantasies for Women* (Hamden, Conn.: Archon, 1982); Ien Ang, *Watching Dallas: Soap Opera and the Melodramatic Imagination*, trans. Della Couling (London: Methuen, 1985); Doane, *The Desire to Desire*; Thomas Elsaesser, "Tales of Sound and Fury: Observations on the Family Melodrama," in *Movies and Methods*, ed. Bill Nichols (Berkeley: U of California P, 1985), 2:165–89; Geoffrey Nowell Smith, "Minnelli and Melodrama," in *Movies and Methods*, 2:190–94; and Christine Gledhill, "Genre and Gender: The Case of Soap Opera," in *Representation: Cultural Representations and Signifying Practices*, ed. Stuart Hall (London: Sage in association with the Open University, 2003), 337–85. See also some of the essays in the following collections: *Home Is Where the Heart Is: Studies in Melodrama and the Woman's Film*, ed. Christine Gledhill (London: British Film In-

stitute, 1987); *Melodrama: Stage, Picture, Screen*, ed. Jacky Bratton, Jim Cook, and Christine Gledhill (London: British Film Institute, 1994); and *Feminism and Film*, ed. E. Ann Kaplan (Oxford: Oxford UP, 2000). For an informative account that argues melodrama's close affiliations to genres of action and suspense (in contrast to the standard view that sees it as primarily linked to genres of passion and femininity), see Steve Neale, *Genre and Hollywood* (London: Routledge, 2000), 179–204.

36. Before the 1980s, a large number of Chinese films had been produced during various time periods—for example, the silent films from the late 1890s to the early 1930s; the nation-building patriotic films of the 1930s and beyond; films produced on the mainland during and after the reign of Mao Zedong; films in Cantonese, Chaozhouhua (Chiu Chow), Xiamenhua (Amoy), and Minnanhua (Taiwanese) as well as in Mandarin, produced in Shanghai, Taiwan, Hong Kong, and southeast Asia in the decades of the 1940s to the early 1980s. For discussions of these earlier periods, see Jay Leyda, *Dianying: An Account of Films and the Film Audience in China* (Cambridge, Mass.: MIT Press, 1972); Zhang, *The Amorous History of the Silver Screen*; Laikwan Pang, *Building a New China in Cinema: The Chinese Left-Wing Cinema Movement, 1932–1937* (Lanham, Md.: Rowman and Littlefield, 2002); Hu Jubin, *Projecting a Nation: Chinese Cinema Before 1949* (Hong Kong: Hong Kong UP, 2003); Paul Clark, *Chinese Cinema: Culture and Politics since 1949* (Cambridge: Cambridge UP, 1987); Ying Zhu, *Chinese Cinema During the Era of Reform: The Ingenuity of the System* (Westport, Conn.: Praeger, 2003); Poshek Fu, *Between Shanghai and Hong Kong: The Politics of Chinese Cinemas* (Stanford: Stanford UP, 2003); Chris Berry, *Postsocialist Cinema in Post-Mao China: The Cultural Revolution after the Cultural Revolution* (New York: Routledge, 2004); and Yingjin Zhang, *Screening China* and *Chinese National Cinema* (New York: Routledge, 2004). Many of these films were targeted at local audiences, though some, such as the Mandarin films produced in Taiwan and Hong Kong during the post–Second World War period, were typically subtitled in both Chinese and English and had circulations in overseas Chinese-speaking communities, such as those in Southeast Asia and North America. Before the 1980s, it was not uncommon for Chinese films to be shown at regional (especially Asian) film festivals, but few participated in international film festivals involving European and American audiences—some notable exceptions being, for instance, Tang Shuxuan's *Dong furen* (*The Arch*) (produced in 1966–67 but premiering in Hong Kong in 1969), which was invited to the Cannes Film Festival's Directors' Fortnight Section; and King Hu's *Xianü* (*A Touch of Zen*) (1975), which won a prize at the Cannes Film Festival of that year. For discussions of Tang and Hu, see Yau Ching, *Filming Margins: Tang Shu Shuen, a Forgotten Hong*

Kong Woman Film Director (Hong Kong: Hong Kong UP, 2004); and Stephen Teo, *Hong Kong Cinema: The Extra Dimensions* (London: British Film Institute, 1997), in particular 138–40, 87–100. Although this concrete and substantial historical record has begun to attract serious academic research efforts, my point is simply that none of these former periods and film productions received the scope and scale of international attention that Chinese cinema began to command as a phenomenon beginning in the mid-1980s. I believe it is this international attention, rather than the historical record itself, that has made the study of Chinese film in English so popular these days.

37. In the Chinese language, various publications have debated the becoming-visible of Chinese cinema in sophisticated terms, though, understandably, these publications tend not to take into consideration the history of film studies in the English-speaking world in which I am locating my inquiry. See, for instance, some of the essays in *Wenhua piping yu huayu dianying* (*Cultural Criticism and Chinese Cinema*), ed. William Tay, intro. Liao Ping-hui (Taipei: Ryefield, 1995); and *Houzhimin lilun yu wenhua rentong* (*Postcolonial Criticism and Cultural Identity*), ed. Zhang Jingyuan (Taipei: Ryefield, 1995). For some of the essays by the well-known mainland Chinese film scholar Dai Jinhua that have been translated into English, see *Cinema and Desire: Feminist Marxism and Cultural Politics in the Work of Dai Jinhua*, ed. Jing Wang and Tani E. Barlow (London: Verso, 2002). For related interest, see also various discussions in the following publications: *Transnational Chinese Cinemas: Identity, Nationhood, Gender*, ed. Sheldon Hsiao-peng Lu (Honolulu: U of Hawaii P, 1997); David Bordwell, *Planet Hong Kong*; Ni Zhen, *Memoirs of the Beijing Film Academy: The Genesis of China's Fifth Generation*, trans. Chris Berry (Durham, N.C.: Duke UP, 2002); June Yip, *Envisioning Taiwan: Fiction, Cinema, and the Nation in the Cultural Imaginary* (Durham, N.C.: Duke UP, 2004); Paul Clark, *Reinventing China: A Generation and Its Films* (Hong Kong: Chinese UP, 2005); and Chris Berry and Mary Farquhar, *China on Screen: Nation and Cinema* (New York: Columbia UP, 2005).

38. For an informed reappraisal, based on knowledge of the Chinese language as well as of German and French, of the work of Brecht and the journal *Tel quel* in relation to Chinese art and politics, see Eric Hayot, *Chinese Dreams: Pound, Brecht, Tel Quel* (Ann Arbor: U of Michigan P, 2004), 54–102, 103–75.

39. John Frow, referring to Alastair Fowler's *Kinds of Literature: An Introduction to the Theory of Genres and Modes* (Cambridge: Harvard UP, 1982), has provided a succinct formulation of the term "mode" that I find helpful: "What I would . . . like to suggest is that the term 'mode' be reserved for use

in . . . the 'adjectival' sense . . . , in which modes are understood as the extensions of certain genres beyond specific and time-bound formal structures to a broader specification of 'tone'" (*Genre* [London: Routledge, 2006], 65).

40. Sir Leslie Stephen defined the sentimental as "the name of the mood in which we make a luxury of grief" in *English Thought in the Eighteenth Century* (London: Smith, Elder, 1902), 2:436, quoted in Janet Todd, *Sensibility: An Introduction* (London: Methuen, 1986), 7.

41. Friedrich Schiller, *On Naïve and Sentimental Poetry* (1795–96), trans. Julius A. Elias (slightly modified), excerpted in *The Origins of Modern Critical Thought: German Aesthetic and Literary Criticism from Lessing to Hegel*, ed. David Simpson (Cambridge: Cambridge UP, 1988), 148–73; the quoted statements can be found on 155, 156, 158.

42. Ibid., 170.

43. See Raymond Williams, *Keywords: A Vocabulary of Culture and Society*, rev. ed. (London: Fontana, 1983), 280–83, for a brief account of the evolution of the word "sensibility," including its important relation to the word "sentimental" in the eighteenth and nineteenth centuries. In the English-speaking world, a classic treatise is Adam Smith, *The Theory of Moral Sentiments* (1759), ed. Knud Haakonssen (Cambridge: Cambridge UP, 2002), in which Smith, extending the work of moral-sense philosophers such as Francis Hutcheson and David Hume, elaborated the notions of sympathy—an imaginative sharing or agreement of feelings that is not simply benevolence—and of the mental construct of an impartial spectator as bases for his theory of conscience and moral judgment.

44. For an informative study of the controversy of sentimentalism in British writings, see Markman Ellis, *The Politics of Sensibility: Race, Commerce and the Sentimental Novel* (Cambridge: Cambridge UP, 1996).

45. For a comparative study that discusses the English, French, and German literary and philosophical contributions to these debates, see James A. Steintrager, *Cruel Delight: Enlightenment Culture and the Inhuman* (Bloomington: Indiana UP, 2004).

46. The sentimental in Anglo-American narrative fiction is an extensively researched and debated topic area, and it would be presumptuous of a nonspecialist to try to offer a list of the representative works concerned. For starters, interested readers may consult some of the following: Ann Douglas, *The Feminization of American Culture* (1977; reprint, New York: Avon, 1978); Jane Tompkins, *Sensational Designs: The Cultural Work of American Fiction, 1790–1860* (New York: Oxford UP, 1985), in particular the chapter "Sentimental Power: *Uncle Tom's Cabin* and the Politics of Literary History" (122–46); Todd, *Sensibility*; Nancy Armstrong, *Desire and Domestic Fiction: A Politics of*

the Novel (Oxford: Oxford UP, 1987); *The Culture of Sentiment: Race, Gender, and Sentimentality in Nineteenth-Century America*, ed. Shirley Samuels (New York: Oxford UP, 1992); Barbara M. Benedict, *Framing Feeling: Sentiment and Style in English Prose Fiction, 1745–1800* (New York: AMS, 1994); Nancy Armstrong, "Why Daughters Die: The Racial Logic of American Sentimentalism," *Yale Journal of Criticism* 7, no. 2 (1994): 1–24; and Ellis, *The Politics of Sensibility*. For sentimentalism and the related generic issues of melodrama in film and television, see, in addition to the works on film melodramas and television soap operas listed in n. 35, above, Jane Gaines, *Fire and Desire: Mixed Race Movies in the Silent Era* (Chicago: U of Chicago P, 2001); Linda Williams, *Playing the Race Card: Melodramas of Black and White from Uncle Sam to O. J. Simpson* (Princeton: Princeton UP, 2001); and Ben Singer, *Melodrama and Modernity: Early Sensational Cinema and Its Contexts* (New York: Columbia UP, 2001) (see in particular chap. 2, in which the author elaborates five primary features as characteristic of melodrama—pathos, emotionalism, moral polarization, nonclassical narrative form, and graphic sensationalism).

47. As Ellis puts it in regard to the sentimental novel: "Paradoxically, . . . by addressing an audience that was disenfranchised and lacking power in political life, the sentimental novel effectively created a new political role for literature" (*The Politics of Sensibility*, 3).

48. For comparative interest, see Ben Singer, *Melodrama and Modernity: Early Sensational Cinema and Its Contexts* (New York: Columbia UP, 2001), in particular chap. 2. Singer defines melodrama as a "cluster concept"—"a term whose meaning varies from case to case in relation to different configurations of a range of basic features or constitutive factors" (44). The five basic features Singer elaborates are listed in n. 46, above. Although I have found the melodramatic and the sentimental to intersect on some occasions, I do not consider them to be identical phenomena.

49. This interesting reading was suggested by one of the anonymous reviewers of the manuscript. Obviously, a full-fledged discussion of the (re)turn to medium and ontology will have to be saved for another occasion, but let me, to follow the advice of this reviewer, note some of the works that are of relevance: Linda Williams, "Film Bodies: Gender, Genre, and Excess," *Film Genre Reader II*, ed. Barry Keith Grant (Austin: U of Texas P, 1995), 140–58; "Reading: Body Genres," *The Oxford Guide to Film Studies*, ed. John Hill and Pamela Church Gibson, consultant ed. Richard Dyer, E. Ann Kaplan, and Paul Willemen (Oxford: Oxford UP, 1998), 339–41; Leo Charney, *Empty Moments: Cinema, Modernity, and Drift* (Durham, N.C.: Duke UP, 1998); Jonathan Crary, *Suspensions of Perception: Attention, Spectacle, and Modern Culture* (Cambridge, Mass.: MIT Press, 1999); Mary Ann Doane, *The Emergence*

of *Cinematic Time: Modernity, Contingency, the Archive* (Cambridge: Harvard UP, 2002); and Sean Cubitt, *The Cinema Effect* (Cambridge, Mass.: MIT Press, 2004).

50. Probably the result of a common conflation of sentimentalism with romanticism as well as the result of the influence of German and English romantic writings, the word "sentimental" has been translated into the Chinese language as *ganshang* (sorrowful, melancholy) or *duochou shangan* (excessive sadness and sensitivity), among other idioms. During the period in the early twentieth century when some (mostly male) Chinese intellectuals, such as those associated with the Creation Society (Chuangzao she), were inspired by works such as Goethe's *The Sorrows of Young Werther*, the term "sentimentalism" was translated as *ganshang zhuyi*. For an example by a notable author, see Yu Dafu's essay (narrated in the first person) "Ganshang de xinglü" (Sentimental journey—a title that seems to be a reference to Laurence Sterne's work) (1928), collected in *Chunlun: Yu Dafu wenji* (Hong Kong: Longzu wenhua shiye gonsi, n.d.), 223–44. For critical works that have dealt with sentimentalism—typically understood as the profusion of emotions, as emotionalism—in the context of modern Chinese literature (including the popular Mandarin Ducks and Butterfly fiction), especially with respect to the vexed relation between sentimentalism and gender, see the following (partial) list: Leo Ou-fan Lee, *The Romantic Generation of Modern Chinese Writers* (Cambridge: Harvard UP, 1973); Rey Chow, *Woman and Chinese Modernity: The Politics of Reading Between West and East* (Minneapolis: U of Minnesota P, 1991), in particular chaps. 2 and 4; Sally Taylor Lieberman, *The Mother and Narrative Politics in Modern China* (Charlottesville: U of Virginia P, 1998); Wendy Larson, *Women and Writing in Modern China* (Stanford: Stanford UP, 1998); Liu Jianmei, *Revolution Plus Love: Literary History, Women's Bodies, and Thematic Repetition in Twentieth-Century Chinese Fiction* (Honolulu: U of Hawaii P, 2003), in particular chap. 3; and Jin Feng, *The New Woman in Early Twentieth-Century Chinese Fiction* (West Lafayette, Ind.: Purdue UP, 2004), in particular her discussions of the politics of emotionality and the sentimental biographies by women writers. See also Laikwan Pang's analysis of the leftist films of the 1930s, in which she associates sentimentalism with populism and the entertainment value of mass culture (*Building a New China in Cinema*, 141–64). As I will go on to argue, however, the term *wenqing zhuyi* tends to be more thought-provoking because it is ambiguous: while its standard explanation is that of excessive tenderheartedness, the rather opposite meaning of moderation is simultaneously present.

51. Although it is conceivable to trace the notion of *qing* (alternately translated as sinner experience, emotion, sentiment, or personal nature) in Chinese

usage all the way back to the ancients, such a genealogy of ideas is not exact-ly the point of my discussion, which is to come to grips with the sentimental-ism in some contemporary Chinese films as a noticeable affective symptom emerging both from global modernity and from cinematic mediation. My in-terest, in other words, is not in the elaboration of the nuances of *qing* in the sense of a natural or cultivated form of interiority (or self) but rather in sen-timentalism or *wenqing* as a manifestation, in the context of global visibility, of evolving inter- as well as intracultural politics. For authoritative studies of the expressive-affective theories of writing throughout the Chinese dy-nasties (in what is generally called the premodern period), see James J. Y. Liu, *Chinese Theories of Literature* (Chicago: U of Chicago P, 1975), especially 16–87 for the discussions of *qing* as it appears in metaphysical, deterministic, and expressive theories; and Qian Zhongshu, *Limited Views: Essays on Ideas and Letters* (1979–80), ed. and trans. Ronald Egan (Cambridge: Harvard UP, 1998), in particular the chapters related to the emotions. For related inter-est, see also Stephen Owen, *Readings in Chinese Literary Thought* (Cambridge: Harvard UP, 1992). Cao Xueqin's novel *The Dream of the Red Chamber* (edited by Gao E and published in the 1790s) is regarded by many scholars as the epitome of China's culture of *qing* or sentiment. For an account of the Chi-nese sentimental novel tradition from the *The Dream* to late imperial and early republican Butterfly fiction, see C. T. Hsia, "Hsu Chen-ya's *Yu-li hun*: An Essay in Literary History and Criticism," *Renditions*, nos. 17 and 18 (1982): 199–240. Because the debates about *qing* in the vast subfield of *Hong xue* (*The Dream of the Red Chamber* studies) are quite a remove from the current study, I will refrain from giving an extensive bibliography here.

52. See my remarks and references in n. 39, above.

53. Harry Harootunian, "Time's Envelope," forthcoming in his book-in-progress *Borrowed Time: History in Search of Temporality*, MS page 37.

54. For two fairly recent, informative studies of the Fifth Generation direc-tors and their works that place them in historical perspective, see Ni, *Mem-oirs of the Beijing Film Academy*, and Clark, *Reinventing China*.

55. These four examples are taken respectively from the films *Song of the Exile*, *Comrades, Almost a Love Story*, *The Wedding Banquet*, and *Not One Less*.

56. In using the terms "residual" and "emergent," I am indebted to Ray-mond Williams's influential discussion of the categories residual, dominant, and emergent, pertaining to what he has famously called "structures of feel-ing" in *Marxism and Literature* (Oxford: Oxford UP, 1977). Although both the residual and the emergent contain elements that can be incorporated within the dominant, Williams argues that they also signify experiences and prac-tices that have an alternative or oppositional relation to the dominant cul-

ture. Whereas the residual refers to meanings and values that were formed in the past but are still active in the present cultural process, the emergent "is never only a matter of immediate practice; indeed it depends crucially on finding new forms or adaptations of form" (126). In the context of contemporary Chinese films, I see the residual and the emergent as thoroughly entangled categories.

57. For a different view, see Shu-mei Shih's distinction between "Chinese" and "sinophone" in her work *Visuality and Identity: Sinophone Articulations Across the Pacific* (Berkeley: U of California P, 2006). For discussions that problematize Chineseness in relation to literature, film, and other media, as well as in relation to different languages and localities, see my introduction and some of the essays in *Modern Chinese Literary and Cultural Studies in the Age of Theory: Reimagining a Field*, ed. Rey Chow (Durham, N.C.: Duke UP, 2000); Yip, *Envisioning Taiwan*; and Kwai-cheung Lo, *Chinese Face/Off: The Transnational Popular Culture of Hong Kong* (Urbana: U of Illinois P, 2005).

58. This reference to Friedrich Nietzsche's notion of the world becoming a fable is in part a continuation of my discussion toward the end of *Primitive Passions*, in particular 195–98. For Nietzsche's original discussion, see the chapter "How the 'Real World' at Last Became a Myth (Fable)," in his *Twilight of the Idols/The Anti-Christ* (1889), trans. R. J. Hollingdale (Harmondsworth: Penguin, 1968), 40–41. Deleuze's notion of fabulation, which he adopted from Henri Bergson, is closely related to his own thinking on minor language, minor literature, and minor cinema. See the chapter "Literature and Life," in *Essays Critical and Clinical*, trans. Daniel W. Smith and Michael A. Greco (Minneapolis: U of Minnesota P, 1997), 1–6; and *Cinema 2: The Time-Image*, trans. Hugh Tomlinson and Robert Galeta (Minneapolis: U of Minnesota P, 1989), 215–24. For a helpful discussion, see also Daniel W. Smith, "Introduction—'A Life of Pure Immanence': Deleuze's 'Critique et Clinique' Project," in *Essays Critical and Clinical*, in particular xliii–li.

1. THE SEDUCTIONS OF HOMECOMING

1. A good case in point is Zhang Yimou's blockbuster *Hero* (2002), which was criticized by some Chinese audiences in the PRC and elsewhere (in particular intellectual audiences) for downplaying the fact that Qin Shihuang, the emperor who was the target of various assassins in the story, was a dictator and a tyrant.

2. This is a problematic the politics of which I consider in detail in *Primitive Passions: Visuality, Sexuality, Ethnography, and Contemporary Chinese Cinema* (New York: Columbia UP, 1995); see in particular part 2, chap. 4.

3. Story and filmscript by Chen and Wang Anyi, with the involvement of Ye Zhaoyan, Lu Wei, and Shu Qi at various stages. In the Chinese idiom, *fengyue*, literally "wind, moon," is a euphemism for eroticism or matters of sex.

4. This reference to Diderot has been made famous by Michel Foucault, *The History of Sexuality*, vol. 1, *An Introduction*, trans. Robert Hurley (New York: Vintage, 1980), 77–80.

5. For an authoritative discussion of the problematic of seduction in psychoanalysis, see Jean Laplanche, *New Foundations for Psychoanalysis*, trans. David Macey (Cambridge: Basil Blackwell, 1989), chap. 3: "Foundations: Towards a General Theory of Seduction" (89–151).

6. In his response to the initial version of this chapter (when it was presented as a keynote speech at the annual conference of the journal *Narrative*, University of Florida, Gainesville, April, 1997), Lee Edelman commented thoughtfully that Zhongliang cannot reach Beijing because he has, literally from the outset, been shanghaied. Hence, for Zhongliang, Beijing remains nothing more than a fantasy. This is evident in a revealing scene in which he interrogates Ruyi about her ignorance of the outside world. In his pretentious attempt to educate her, he describes Beijing in lyrical, revolutionary, but entirely bookish terms—as a place where the sky is blue, the walls are high, the girl students all have short hair and wear long black skirts, and so forth. While he has thus succeeded in seducing Ruyi with his professed enlightenment, he is painfully aware that he is, in effect, performing his own lack.

7. In *Farewell My Concubine*, Chen takes pains to show the process in which Cheng Dieyi "becomes" the character of the concubine in the opera of the same title. As a boy apprentice in the Beijing opera troupe with which his mother left him, Dieyi is for a long time unable to accept his role as a woman and unable to speak his lines correctly. Because of this failure, he is severely punished, and he tries to run away. He would have successfully escaped, but on his way he unexpectedly comes across a street performance of none other than the opera *Farewell My Concubine*. Completely absorbed and moved by what he sees, he changes his mind and returns to the troupe. From then on, he accepts, performs, and identifies with his assigned role—and fate—of concubine to the end.

8. For instance, the typical scenario in some of Lu Xun's short stories is that of a male narrator emotionally shocked by a spectacle of social injustice, regarding which he feels impotent; in spite of his sympathies for the victim(s), such a narrator usually takes flight in one form or another. Likewise, in Ba Jin's 1931 classic *Jia* (*The Family*) (Hong Kong: Tiandi tushu, 1985), the predominant narrative action is placed with the characters who, feeling indignant at the corrupt nature of the feudalist patriarchal family system, attempt to

rebel and take leave. See a more detailed discussion of this connection with May Fourth writings in my essay "Bulunbulei de youhuo," in *Comparative Literature and Cultural Studies*, vol. 1 (Taipei: Fu Jen University, 1997), also on *Temptress Moon*, which complements the present discussion. Insofar as Chen associates home and countryside with backwardness, he is modernist (that is, modernist in the proper May Fourth tradition) in his authorial/directorial perspective, a perspective that is different from the romanticization of the countryside as the place of simple and eternal truths that also runs throughout modern and contemporary Chinese literary culture. An example of this latter tendency is found in Zhang Yimou's 1995 film *Shanghai Triad*, in which the point-of-view character, a child fascinated by Shanghai, nonetheless sees truth at the end through his experience in the countryside.

9. This can perhaps be described by way of the phrase "motion and emotion" (first used by Wim Wenders); see Tony Rayns, "Motion and Emotion," *Sight and Sound* (March 1996): 11–13. Rayns's brief discussion was based on some of the rushes rather than on the finished film. According to Paul Clark, "The distinguishing feature of the film suggested that fifth-generation experimentation still fascinated Chen. The camera is constantly mobile . . . , sweeping and gliding throughout the rooms and gardens of the family mansion, suggesting the swirling uncertainty of an hallucination and the instability of this world" (*Reinventing China: A Generation and Its Films* [Hong Kong: Chinese UP, 2005], 161). The actors' performances also correlate to the dramatic nature of the camera movements, as one critic puts it: "Both Leslie Cheung . . . and Gong Li . . . join the rest of the cast in displaying extreme emotions in the most extreme manner. . . . They shout, scream, and weep, often in sudden, unexpected and unjustified outbursts, while striking each other, breaking furniture or porcelain or *objets d'art*, so that everyone seems always poised on the brink of some stylized hysteria" (George Grella, "Sex, Drugs, and Violence in China," *City* 26.45 [July 30–August 5, 1997]: 24). In "Bulunbulei de youhuo," I offer a related discussion of the over-the-top effects generated by Chen's use of motion and hysteria in terms of melodrama.

10. Chen Kaige himself sees this distribution of flight and staying-put in these terms: "I have always adopted a rather uncooperative attitude toward my own culture. And that's partly what I was expressing through *Temptress Moon*. I feel that everyone, on one level or another, is trying to run away. So the main theme of *Temptress Moon* is running away, that is really what the film is about. However, Ruyi, the character played by Gong Li, does not run away, and thus her destruction is inevitable" (interview with Chen in Michael Berry, *Speaking in Images: Interviews with Contemporary Chinese Filmmakers*, foreword by Martin Scorsese [New York: Columbia UP, 2005], 97).

11. Please see my more elaborate discussions of Chen's handling of women characters in the relevant sections in *Primitive Passions*. Chen told Rayns that in
April 1993, when his previous film, *Farewell My Concubine*, had been completed and was about to be shown at the Cannes Film Festival, he "suddenly
felt [he] wanted to make a film about a woman" (see "Motion and Emotion,"
12). Chen's (sentimental) sympathies, however, lie ultimately with boys and
men: see, for instance, *He ni zai yi qi* (*Together*, 2002), in which the urban,
talented girl violinist is the one leaving (or abandoning) China for the West,
whereas the boy violinist from the countryside, equally talented, chooses to
stay home. Unlike the case of Ruyi in *Temptress Moon* (see Chen's remarks
cited in n. 10, above), his staying home is not presented in this film as an
inevitable destruction.

12. For an insightful analysis of the allegorical significance of Duanwu's character—as the younger, lower-class man who is unburdened by modern enlightenment or by the history of his own suffering, whose ruthless behavior
toward the woman he loves suggests a rejection of psychologized Western
subjectivity, and whose ascension to power comes with staying home—see
Wendy Larson, "Duanwu Goes Home: Chen Kaige's *Temptress Moon* and the
Politics of Homecoming," in *Cross-Cultural Readings of Chineseness: Narratives, Images, and Interpretations of the 1990s*, ed. Wen-hsin Yeh (Berkeley:
Center for Chinese Studies, Institute of East Asian Studies, University of
California, Berkeley, 2000), 27–52. Larson's essay was a response to a version
of this chapter delivered at a workshop held at the Center for Chinese Stud-
ies, University of California, Berkeley, in January 1998.

13. Although a systematic study of this point must wait, I'd like to note that
contemporary Chinese film directors have borrowed frequently from other
Asian directors as well as from oft-noted European directors such as François
Truffaut and Jean-Luc Godard. For instance, the aesthetically pleasing shots,
in a film such as *In the Mood for Love*, of fashionably clad women wearing
high heels, taken from behind as they walk away from the camera, suggest
the strong influence of Yasujiro Ozu's 1950s and 1960s films (about domestic life and relationships) on Wong Kar-wai, while the multiperson narrative
perspectives, the use of distinct sets of colors for purposes of dramatic differentiation and coordination, and the striking image of a besieged soldier
being pinned to the gate, surrounded by arrows fired at him by the enemies
in Zhang Yimou's *Hero* indicate clear borrowings from Akira Kurosawa's classics *Rashomon*, *Ran*, and *Throne of Blood*.

14. This is one of a series of films made by Li during the 1970s and 1980s
on the political events of the late Qing. Others include *Qingguo qingcheng*
(*The Empress Dowager*, 1975), *Yingtai qixue* (*The Last Tempest*, 1976), *Chuilian*

tingzheng (*Reign Behind the Curtain*, 1983), *Huo long* (*The Last Emperor*, 1986), and *Xi taihou* (*The Empress Dowager*, 1989). Li, a director who left mainland China in the 1950s, worked both in Taiwan and Hong Kong. He died in 1996 in the midst of making a film in Beijing. Li first became well-known in the 1960s with films he made for Shaw Brothers Ltd. (in Hong Kong) and for his own company Guolian/Grand Motion Picture Studio (in Taiwan). When box office trends no longer favored the styles of his early works, he made a series of pornographic films in order to stay in the business, and it was in part due to the success of these pornographic films that he made his comeback by receiving funding for his major historical films featuring the late Qing. One of his pornographic films, entitled *Fengyue qitan* (*Legends of Lust*, 1972), makes use of the Chinese idiom *fengyue*, which, as mentioned in n. 3, above, is a euphemism for matters of sex. Since Li's film, I believe, pornographic films have often been referred to as "*fengyue pian*" in Chinese. Is it a coincidence that Chen adopted *Fengyue* as the title of his film?

15. Rayns offers the following account: "In Beijing in 1993, while he was still searching for a scriptwriter for *Temptress Moon* and trying to deal with the Film Bureau's demands for cuts in *Farewell My Concubine*, Chen joked to me that he would definitely set his next film in 1920—a year before the Chinese Communist Party held its first (underground) congress in Shanghai. That way, he implied, his scenario couldn't possibly be accused of misrepresenting the Party's role. So much for jokes in present-day China: the film is indeed set in 1920" ("Motion and Emotion," 13). For related interest, see Chen's comments on the unresolved problems with film production (as well as with the reception of his films) in the People's Republic of China, in the interview conducted on April 27, 1993, "The Narrow Path: Chen Kaige in Conversation with Tony Rayns," *Projections 3: Film-makers on Film-making*, ed. John Boorman and Walter Donohue (London: Faber and Faber, 1994), 47–58.

16. Slavoj Žižek, *Looking Awry: An Introduction to Jacques Lacan through Popular Culture* (Cambridge, Mass.: MIT Press, 1991), 112, 114.

2. NOSTALGIA OF THE NEW WAVE

1. Jacques Lacan, "Of Structure as an Inmixing of an Otherness Prerequisite to Any Subject Whatever," in *The Structuralist Controversy: The Languages of Criticism and the Sciences of Man*, ed. Richard Macksey and Eugenio Donato (Baltimore: Johns Hopkins UP, 1970), 191; emphases in the original.

2. See Jacques Derrida, "Structure, Sign, and Play in the Discourse of the Human Sciences," in *The Structuralist Controversy*, pp. 247–72.

3. Wong himself was apparently sickened by the questions about July 1, 1997, and saw the making of *Happy Together*, with its story about two Hong Kong men in Argentina, as an escape, though he confessed to discovering that Hong Kong seemed inescapable everywhere he went. See his interview in Cannes with Peng Yiping, "*Chunguang Zhaxie*: 97 qian rang women kuaile zai yiqi" (*Happy Together*: Let's be happy together before '97), *Dianying shuangzhoukan (City Entertainment)*, no. 473 (1997): 41.

4. Interested readers are asked to see Rey Chow, "Introduction: On Chineseness as a Theoretical Problem," *boundary 2* 23.3 (Fall 1998): 1–24. In this essay, I analyze the manners in which certain kinds of ethnicity (such as Chineseness) are explicitly or implicitly imposed on non-Western literary or cultural texts, as if such texts make sense only if they can be shown to speak in a documentary mode—from within their a priori ghettoized backgrounds. Instead of simply focusing on identity politics per se, my point is to underscore the way identity politics is, in such contexts, already embedded in habits of literary criticism and reading that may be termed "coercive mimeticism."

5. Stephen Teo, for instance, writes of Wong's work in the following terms: "As the latest new wave auteur, Wong may be said to have brought the Hong Kong new wave into the 90s by combining postmodern themes with new wave stylistics." In Wong's films, "the accent on style conveys a feeling of sharp-edged excitement and a sense of high-octane elation recalling the impact of the French new wave in Europe" (*Hong Kong Cinema: The Extra Dimension* [London: British Film Institute, 1997], 196, 197). See also Teo's thoughtful discussion of *Happy Together*, including details of the film's production, in his *Wong Kar-wai* (London: British Film Institute, 2005), 98–113. Emphasizing the literary qualities of Wong's work in general, Teo's book on Wong offers informative appraisals of his other films as well.

6. Some critics in Hong Kong consider *Happy Together* to be a love story rather than a love story between two gay men. Wong Kar-wai himself shares this view. When asked during an interview the reason he had chosen to deal with the theme of male homosexual love in this film, he said: "As far as I am concerned, this was not planned in advance . . . in fact, homosexual love is not any different from heterosexual love" (interview with Peng, "*Chunguang Zhaxie*," 42). Naturally, other critics disagree. For instance, Jiang Yingsheng writes: "*Happy Together* takes homosexual love as a point of departure but also tends to idealize paternal power. For the character Lai Yiu-fai, traditional family values and his own homosexual identity constitute two incompatible forces" ("Let's Start Over Again—A Brand New Wong Kar-wai," *Dianying shuangzhoukan*, no. 473 [1997]: 70; my translation).

7. See Teo, *Wong Kar-wai*, 100–105, for the film's interesting Argentinian con-
   nections. See also Jeremy Tambling, *Wong Kar-wai's Happy Together* (Hong
   Kong: Hong Kong UP, 2003), for a discussion of the relevance of some Latin
   American literary works as one of the sources that inspired Wong.

8. The version of the song "Happy Together" Wong had in mind was the one by
   Frank Zappa. See Zhong Yitai, "From The Turtles to Wong Kar Wai," *Dianying
   shuangzhoukan*, no. 474 (1997): 71.

9. To avoid confusion, I will hereafter follow the lead of the film's English subtitles and refer to the two main characters as Fai and Bo-wing. Although
   Bo-wing's name is usually given (as in his passport) as "Po-wing," however, I prefer the spelling of "Bo-wing" because it is a slightly more accurate
   transliteration of the name's pronunciation in Cantonese. All such transliterations are, of course, merely atonal approximations of the sounds of the
   Chinese words.

10. For nuanced discussions of some of these films, see, for instance, the
    following essays in "Eros on the Move: Wong Kar-wai's Cinematic Charting
    of Desire," a special focus issue on Wong Kai-wai, *Chung Wai Literary Monthly*
    35.2 (July 2006), guest ed. Shuan-hung Wu: Shuan-hung Wu, "'Love Is to
    Give What One Does Not Have': Lateral Desire in Wong Kar-wai's Films"
    (7–10); Chia-chin Tsai, "Wong Kar-wai's Trilogy of Desire: On *Days of Being
    Wild*, *In the Mood for Love* and *2046*" (12–40); Yung Hao Liu, "The Lost Langue
    Phenomenon in Wong Kar-wai's *Fallen Angel*: The Lost and Found, the Moth-
    er Tongue and the Home Movie" (62–84); and Yung-chao Liao, "Touching
    Wong Kar-wai's *In the Mood for Love*: Embodied Form, Haptic Visuality, and
    History-as-Surface" (86–110).

11. Wong, interview with Peng, "*Chunguang Zhaxie*," 44; my translation.

12. The contrast between the two characters has been well noted by critics. See,
    for instance, Xu Kuan, "*Happy Together* as a Continuation of *Days of Being
    Wild*": "The male characters of Wong Kar-wai's works all follow a consistent
    pattern, which can be divided into the killer-type and the policeman-type.
    The former is decadent, unruly, and highly sexed; the latter is innocent,
    straight, and nearly platonic by inclination. In the film which brought him
    fame at Cannes, this principle continues to hold" (*Xin bao [Hong Kong Eco-
    nomic Journal]*, overseas edition, May 27, 1997, 9). Similarly, Shi Qi writes
    that the typical subjectivity explored in Wong's films is "actually a journey
    of self-exploration . . . there is often an introverted, conservative character
    as opposed to an unruly and decadent one. This can be regarded as two faces
    of a single person" ("The 'I' in Wong Kar-wai—A Third Discussion of *Happy
    Together*," *Ming Pao Daily News*, June 5, 1997, entertainment section; my

translation). As Song Hwee Lim writes, however, the two domains embodied by Fai and Bo-wing "are not mutually exclusive, as each can be the repressed desire of the other" (*Celluloid Comrades: Representations of Male Homosexuality in Contemporary Chinese Cinemas* [Honolulu: U of Hawaii P, 2006], 113).

13. Shi Qi, "The Home in Wong Kar-wai—A Second Discussion of *Happy Together*," *Ming Pao Daily News*, June 4, 1997, entertainment section; my translation.

14. Sigmund Freud, "The 'Uncanny,'" in *Collected Papers*, authorized translation under the supervision of Joan Riviere (New York: Basic, 1959), 4:368–407.

15. Ibid., 397–99.

16. Pan Liqiong, "Ordinary Life Murders Love—*Happy Together*," *Ming Pao Daily News*, June 1, 1997, C3; my translation.

17. For a somewhat different (because less sympathetic) reading of Fai's character, see Lim's thoughtful chapter on *Happy Together* in *Celluloid Comrades*, 99–125. Lim insightfully points out that underlying Fai's domestic inclinations is a certain violence, which manifests itself in possessiveness and a desire for control. Such violence is, of course, inherent to sentimentalism as an affective mode. For related interest, see also Marc Siegel, "The Intimate Spaces of Wong Kar-wai," in *At Full Speed: Hong Kong Cinema in a Borderless World*, ed. Esther C. M. Yau (Minneapolis: U of Minnesota P, 2001), 277–94. Siegel argues for a reading of *Happy Together* not only in terms of a sexual relationship between two men but also in terms of the behaviors, spaces, and images of a sexual ghetto where intimacy between people, rather than being understood exclusively as private or domestic, often happens in public situations and places.

18. For a sensitive reading of the tango sequence, see Helen Hok-sze Leung, "Queerscapes in Contemporary Hong Kong Cinema," *positions: east asia cultures critique* 9.2 (Fall 2001): 437–38.

19. Shi Qi, "*Happy Together*—Straightforward and Stylistically Unusual," *Ming Pao Daily News*, June 2, 1997, entertainment section; my translation.

20. In the words of Charlotte O'Sullivan: "Foaming like a chocolate malt milkshake—a calm maelstrom, whose spiralling steam the camera respectfully trails" ("*Happy Together/Chunguang Zhaxie*," *Sight and Sound* 8.5 [May 1998]: 49).

21. Some critics in Hong Kong consider the character of Chang to be an inspired creation and suggest that what takes place around this character could easily lead to the making of another film. Indeed, if the love story of Fai and Bo-wing can be said, in the conventional manner of describing romance, to form a single unit, then what Chang's presence stands for is precisely the

"1+," the "one more" that carries with it the unpredictable possibilities of an open-ended structuration. It is in this light that the suggestive use of sound and voice brought by Chang (who likes to understand people through listening), in contrast to the dominance of the image within the diegesis, may be understood. Be that as it may, as a character, Chang remains, as I already mentioned, underdeveloped and lacks the vitality of the mutually implicated affinities of Fai and Bo-wing.

22. When the initial version of this chapter was first presented at the symposium "Visualizing Eros" at the University of California, Irvine, in May 1998, some members of the audience commented that Chang has a family to return to in Taipei, whereas Fai's acceptance by his father is uncertain and Bo-wing does not seem to have any family links at all. These familial reminders, they suggested, could be interpreted in conjunction with the announcement of the death of Deng Xiaoping (which is made during Fai's brief stay in Taiwan at the end), with Fai's return to Hong Kong, and with Hong Kong's return to China in 1997. As I indicated at the beginning of this chapter, I tend not to be enthusiastic about this line of inquiry because it would require one to reduce narrative and imagistic significations more or less to a national allegory type of reading and thus, by implication, to confine the film work within an ethnic ghetto. For an interestingly argued reading of the film that disagrees with my view, see Leung, "Queerscapes in Contemporary Hong Kong Cinema," in particular 435–39.

23. "[The waterfall] represents the sexual energy of this city. In this country [Argentina], there are fifteen women to one man" (Wong Kar-wai, interview with Peng, "*Chunguang Zhaxie*," 44; my translation). Wong apparently used the English words "sexual energy" in the interview.

3. THE EVERYDAY IN *THE ROAD HOME* AND *IN THE MOOD FOR LOVE*

1. Pier Paolo Pasolini, "The 'Cinema of Poetry,'" in *Heretical Empiricism*, ed. Louise K. Barnett, trans. Ben Lawton and Louise K. Barnett (Bloomington: Indiana UP, 1988), 168. Hereafter references to this collection of essays will be indicated with the abbreviation *HE* and included in parentheses in the text.

2. Ferdinand de Saussure, *Course in General Linguistics*, intro. Jonathan Culler, ed. Charles Bally and Albert Sechehaye in collaboration with Albert Reidlinger, trans. Wade Baskin (Glasgow: Collins, 1974), 120; emphasis in the original.

3. Apart from the two previous chapters, see my arguments about nostalgia in "A Souvenir of Love," in *Ethics after Idealism: Theory—Culture—Ethnic-*

ity—Reading (Bloomington: Indiana UP, 1998), 133–48 (originally published in *Modern Chinese Literature* 7.2 [Fall 1993]: 59–78). For related discussions pertaining to Hong Kong cinema, see also Leung Ping-kwan, "Urban Cinema and the Cultural Identity of Hong Kong" and Natalia Chan Sui Hung, "Rewriting History: Hong Kong Nostalgia Cinema and Its Social Practice," both in *The Cinema of Hong Kong: History, Arts, Identity*, ed. Poshek Fu and David Desser (Cambridge: Cambridge UP, 2000), 227–51, 252–72. Chan's essay offers an extended examination of the history, features, and critical analyses of nostalgia film. In the present chapter, my interest is less in making the argument again about nostalgia than in exploring the place of the everyday in the general sentimentalism affined with nostalgia and the theoretical implications this has for the study of mediatized culture.

4. According to Zhang Yimou, "There were a lot of personal elements that went into the making of *The Road Home*, because it was shot just after the passing of my father" (interview with Zhang in Michael Berry, *Speaking in Images: Interviews with Contemporary Chinese Filmmakers*, foreword by Martin Scorsese [New York: Columbia UP, 2005], 127).

5. In an interview conducted in New York, Wong is reported to have said: "The child we see with Maggie Cheung may be Tong Leung's, or may be not" (*Ming Pao Daily News* [North American edition], October 4, 2000, A3; my translation).

6. Shuqin Cui describes Zhang's film as a return to "the nostalgia of romantic melodrama" (*Women Through the Lens: Gender and Nation in a Century of Chinese Cinema* [Honolulu: U of Hawaii P, 2003], 122).

7. In a film review, Zhao Di is described in the following manner: "This is a woman who, on recognizing her destiny, will let nothing stand in the way of her seizing it" (Stephen Holden, "Two Lives in China, with Mao Lurking," *New York Times*, May 25, 2001, B14).

8. I thank Christopher Lee for this important point.

9. Tao Jie attributes this to Zhang's reaching middle age. By this, he means that Zhang's film demonstrates a worldview that can be summarized as "what is lost can finally be found"—in other words, a worldview that stresses harmony, unity, and togetherness ("Da tuanyuan de Zhang Yimou," *Ming Pao Daily News* [North American edition], January 8, 2001, B18). Paul Clark is more critical, describing the film as "an empty celebration of the sunny days of yore, despite the cloud of a suggestion that political problems in the Anti-Rightist campaign of 1957 have detained the school teacher in the city" (*Reinventing China: A Generation and Its Films* [Hong Kong: Chinese UP, 2005], 184).

10. Su Lizhen is also the name of one of the two young female characters in Wong's earlier film *Days of Being Wild*, which is set in 1960. *In the Mood for*

Love may hence be seen as a kind of sequel to the earlier film. For informative discussions of Wong's earlier work, see Jean-Marc Lalanne, David Martinez, Ackbar Abbas, and Jimmy Ngai, *Wong Kar-wai* (Paris: Dis Voir, 1997).

11. For a discussion of the connotations of role-playing in the film, see Stephen Teo, *Wong Kar-wai* (London: British Film Institute, 2005), 114–33.

12. Wong said in an interview: "From the very beginning I knew I didn't want to make a film about an affair. That would be too boring, too predictable. . . . What interested me was the way people behave and relate to each other in the circumstances shown in this story, the way they keep secrets and share secrets. . . . The central characters were going to enact what they thought their spouses were doing and saying. In other words, we were going to see both relationships—the adulterous affair and the repressed friendship—in the one couple" (Tony Rayns, "In the Mood for Edinburgh: Wong Kar-Wai Talks About His Most Difficult Film-Making Experience with Tony Rayns," *Sight and Sound* 10.8 [August 2000], 14–19). The doubling of Su and Zhou's relationship is part and parcel of what Audrey Yue describes as the device of intersection in Wong's work in general, which, as she and others have pointed out, is filled with parallels, repetitions, and interchangeability of characters and narrative elements; see her *"In the Mood for Love*: Intersections of Hong Kong Modernity," in *Chinese Films in Focus: 25 New Takes*, ed. Chris Berry (London: British Film Institute, 2003), 128–29. Wong is obviously drawn to the formal patterns, perhaps more so than he is to the human contents involved.

13. This disappearance of a distinct personality is also characteristic of Wong's films; it recalls, for instance, Fai's becoming indistinguishable from Bo-wing toward the end of *Happy Together*.

14. Leslie Camhi, "Setting His Tale of Love Found in a City Long Lost," film section, *New York Times*, January 28, 2001, 11.

15. The columnist and novelist in question is the well-known Liu Yichang, whose novel *Duidao* (Hong Kong: Holdery Publishing Enterprises, 2000; first serialized in 1972, rewritten in 1981, and expanded into a full-length novel in 1993) gave Wong the inspiration for his film (in which some lines from Liu's work are cited). For a perceptive analysis of the conceptual connections between the two works, see Pan Guoling, "'Huayang nianhua' yu 'Duidao,'" *Ming Pao Daily News* (North American edition), October 28, 2000, 22. See also Thomas Y. T. Luk, "Novels into Film: Liu Yichang's *Tête-Bêche* and Wong Kar-wai's *In the Mood for Love*," in *Chinese-Language Film: Historiography, Poetics, Politics*, ed. Sheldon H. Lu and Emilie Yueh-yu Yeh (Honolulu: U of Hawaii P, 2005), 210–19.

16. For an interesting discussion of the scenes of Su ascending and descending the staircase in the hotel where Zhou is waiting for her in room 2046, see Teo, *Wong Kar-wai*, 129–33.

17. Wong is reported to have indicated that he did not have to do any research on Su's wardrobe "because our mothers dressed like this" (Liza Bear, "Wong Kar-wai," *Bomb Magazine*, no. 75 [Spring 2001], cited in Teo, *Wong Kar-wai*, 11). Obviously, Hong Kong women did not all dress like that in the 1960s; Su's stylish appearance rather reminds one of famous female stars in Hong Kong Mandarin and Cantonese films of that period (for example, Li Lihua, Lin Dai, Bai Yan, Le Di, Ge Lan, Ye Feng, Lin Feng, Bai Luming, and their cohort).

18. See Yue, "*In the Mood for Love*," 128–36, for a discussion of the signifi-cance of claustrophobic spaces in this and other films by Wong.

19. By contrast, Luk sees this nostalgia as the nostalgia specifically for a chronologically earlier time. Comparing Liu's novel and Wong's film, Luk writes: "Both Liu's novel and Wong's film are about desire and its repression. To a certain extent, they touch on a kind of subtle emotional expression, characterized by reserve and delicacy that has since gone out of vogue. . . . The mood of nostalgia in the film highlights an era when people were used to expressing their emotion with a sense of delicacy" ("Novels into Film," 212–13).

20. 旺角卡門，阿飛正傳，東邪西毒，重慶森林，墮落天使，花樣年華，天下無雙, 2046.

21. Actress Maggie Cheung's description gives a good idea of Wong's improvisa-tory method: "'At the beginning, we were given a four-page short story by a Japanese writer from the 1960s, about an affair between two neighbors,' Ms. Cheung said. 'There was not a lot of detail. Then, during every hair and makeup session, we would receive a still-warm fax with some lines of dia-logue to be shot later that day, and which Kar-wai had clearly written that morning.'" "'Sometimes we would shoot the same scenes with the dialogues between myself and Tony reversed,' she said. 'Or we would film the same dialogues but on a different set'" (Camhi, "Setting His Tale of Love Found In a City Long Lost," 26).

22. I am thinking in particular of Wong's *Dongxie xidu/Ashes of Time* (1994), a film that generically resembles a martial arts legend but foregrounds the theme of unfulfilled longing (and dislocated or mismatched identities) that underlies all his stories. For a detailed study of this film, see Wimal Dissanay-ake, *Wong Kar-wai's Ashes of Time* (Hong Kong: Hong Kong UP, 2003).

23. *Yuan* can be translated as affinity, link, or connection; the important point is that such affinity, link, or connection is predestined or predetermined (in a previous life) in ways that defy or exceed conscious human decision or present human understanding. Wong's remarks were in part in response to a question about the titling of his previous film *Chunguang zhaxie* (*Happy*

Together); see his interview in Cannes with Peng Yiping, "*Chunguang Zhaxie*: 97 qian rang women kuaile zai yiqi" (*Happy Together*: Let's be happy together before '97), *Dianying shuangzhoukan* (*City Entertainment*), no. 473 (1997): 44; my translation.

24. See, for instance, Fredric Jameson, *Postmodernism; or, The Cultural Logic of Late Capitalism* (Durham, N.C.: Duke UP, 1991), in particular chaps 1 (1–54), 8 (260–78), and 9 (279–96), which deal respectively with culture, postmodernism and the market, and film.

25. Prasenjit Duara, "Leftist Criticism and the Political Impasse: Response to Arif Dirlik's 'How the Grinch Hijacked Radicalism: Further Thoughts on the Postcolonial,'" *Postcolonial Studies* 4.1 (2001): 81–88; the quoted passage is on 87.

26. I am thinking, for instance, of the rituals of winemaking, of transporting the bride in a wedding, of raising lanterns in a rich household, and so forth. See a more extended discussion of such (inauthentic) "ethnographic details" in Zhang's early works in part 2, chapter 4 of my book *Primitive Passions: Visuality, Sexuality, Ethnography, and Contemporary Chinese Cinema* (New York: Columbia UP, 1995). For related interest, see Zhang's remarks on his various films in Berry, *Speaking in Images*, 109–40.

4. AUTUMN HEARTS

1. For discussions of biographical and autobiographical writings in modern Chinese literature, including those in relation to women's experiences, see Wendy Larson, *Literary Authority and the Modern Chinese Writer: Ambivalence and Autobiography* (Durham, N.C.: Duke UP, 1991); Jin Feng, *The New Woman in Early Twentieth-Century Chinese Fiction* (West Lafayette, Ind.: Purdue UP, 2004); Lingzhen Wang, *Personal Matters: Autobiographical Practice in Women's Writing in Twentieth-Century China* (Stanford: Stanford UP, 2004).

2. *Bing Xin xiaoshuo ji* (Shanghai: Kaiming shudian, 1943), 296–313. Translations from the Chinese are mine. Henceforth references will be included in parentheses in the text.

3. On the theme of loneliness in this story, see C. T. Hsia, *A History of Modern Chinese Fiction* (New Haven: Yale UP, 1961), 76–77. Hsia's view is that the recurrence of this theme indicates Bing Xin's "inability to develop further" as a writer (77). See also Gloria Bien, "Images of Women in Bing Xin's Fiction," in *Women Writers of 20th-Century China*, ed. Angela Jung Palandri (Eugene: Asian Studies Program at the U of Oregon, 1982). For a discussion of the problem with seeing women's writings as underdeveloped and immature, see chapter 4 of my *Woman and Chinese Modernity: The Politics of Reading Between West and East* (Minneapolis: U of Minnesota P, 1991).

4. "Hueyin" is the spelling of the character's name (based on its Cantonese pronunciation) in the film's English subtitles, though a more accurate transliteration of the Cantonese would be "Hugh-yun." In *pinyin*, the name would be Xiaoen.

5. Hueyin's astonishment at hearing about her mother's ethnic origins at this point is, I believe, a flawed detail in the film because Aiko's Japaneseness has been introduced numerous times during the flashbacks to the Macao period, when Hueyin is present as a child. Even if the repression of such an important piece of information is possible, it is not probable or convincing.

6. For a substantive discussion of Hui's works, including the implications of memory, see Elaine Yee-lin Ho, "Women on the Edges of Hong Kong Modernity: The Films of Ann Hui," in *At Full Speed: Hong Kong Cinema in a Borderless World*, ed. Esther C. M. Yau (Minneapolis: U of Minnesota P, 2001), 177–206. For brief general discussions of Hui's contributions to Hong Kong cinema, see Stephen Teo, *Hong Kong Cinema: The Extra Dimensions* (London: British Film Institute, 1997), 149–52, 211–15, 212–13, 265–66. For an analysis of *Song of the Exile*, see Patricia Brett Erens, "Crossing Borders: Time, Memory, and the Construction of Identity in *Song of the Exile*," in *Between Home and World: A Reader in Hong Kong Cinema*, ed. Esther M. K. Cheung and Chu Yiu-wai (Hong Kong: Oxford UP, 2004), 177–95 (this essay was originally published in *Cinema Journal* 39.4 [Summer 2000]: 43–59). See also Erens, "The Film Work of Ann Hui," in *The Cinema of Hong Kong: History, Arts, Identity*, ed. Poshek Fu and David Desser (Cambridge: Cambridge UP, 2000), 176–95 (this essay overlaps in part with "Crossing Borders"). Additional relevant information on Hui and her work, including references to Chinese-language materials, can be found in Michael Berry, *Speaking in Images: Interviews with Contemporary Chinese Filmmakers*, foreword by Martin Scorsese (New York: Columbia UP, 2005), 423–39.

7. Ho, "Women on the Edges of Hong Kong Modernity," 180.

8. For an example of Bing Xin's use of the flashback in literary writing, see my discussion of her story "Di yi ci yanhui" (The first dinner party) in chapter 4 of *Woman and Chinese Modernity*.

9. Gilles Deleuze, *Cinema 2: The Time-Image*, trans. Hugh Tomlinson and Robert Galeta (Minneapolis: U of Minnesota P, 1989), 19.

10. "The question of the flashback is this: it has to be justified from elsewhere" (ibid., 48). Although I do not find Deleuze's qualification to be entirely useful in the present discussion, I have benefited from his philosophically rich argument about the centrality of time in post–Second World War cinema.

11. For a detailed historical and theoretical study of the flashback, see Maureen Turim, *Flashbacks in Film: Memory and History* (London: Routledge, 1989),

especially chap. 6, in which she discusses the renovation of the flashback as an element of modernism in film after the Second World War.

12. A contemporary Hong Kong film in which flashbacks take on a fantastical status (because they are the memories of a ghost) is Stanley Kwan's *Rouge*. See my discussion in the chapter "A Souvenir of Love," in *Ethics after Idealism: Theory—Culture—Ethnicity—Reading* (Bloomington: Indiana UP, 1998). The chapter was originally published in *Modern Chinese Literature* 7.2 (Fall 1993): 59–78.

13. This is what leads Erens to write: "The past is seen only in terms of its relevance to the present. A present consciousness pervades the representation of the past" ("Crossing Borders," 186).

14. Erens provides such a final, stable referent by reading the film as Ann Hui's autobiography. Accordingly, she suggests distinguishing between Ann Hui's past and her memories of her past: "I am going to refer to the scenes in Macau and the years before her third birthday as memories or recollections rather than flashbacks because I feel that Hui has consciously constructed a subject in the present (Hueyin as narrator who addresses us in the first person). Despite the so-called ever 'present tense' of cinema, we never literally return to the past in *Song of the Exile*. Rather, Hueyin, in the present, tells us her memories of various stages of her life" ("Crossing Borders," 185). Erens's proposed solution is reasonable, but it works only insofar as the film's significations are rerouted to the consciousness of the author (in this case, director) as the ultimate determinant. Such a rerouting would seem to defeat the point of engaging with the material/semiotic complexity of the representations of the past in the first place. Another way of putting all this would be to say that, while autobiographical elements are undoubtedly present in the film, the film does not have to be read exclusively as autobiography.

15. Some critics refer to the non-character-specific flashback as the impersonal flashback and attribute it to an "omniscient camera" or "omniscient filmmaker." See Bernard F. Dick, *Anatomy of Film*, 3d ed. (New York: St. Martins, 1998), 194.

16. For this insight, I am indebted to Turim's discussion of Roland Barthes on pages 10–12 of *Flashbacks in Film*.

17. Leung Ping-kwan's remarks on Hui's earlier film *Fengjie* (*The Secret*) are relevant here: "All these different forces cannot be harmonized, just as the divergent perspectives and fragmented narratives refuse to be easily unified, but it is exactly through their conflicts that the complex hybrid nature of the urban space and the cultural identity of Hong Kong are revealed" ("Urban Cinema and the Cultural Identity of Hong Kong," in *The Cinema of Hong Kong*, 227–51; the quotation is from 241).

18. This is a consistent feature of Hui's films, many of which thematize people crossing cultures—for example, *Touben nuhai* (*Boat People*), *Hu Yue de gushi* (*The Story of Woo Viet*), *Shanghai jiaqi* (*My American Grandson*), *Shujian enchou lu* (*Romance of Book and Sword*), and *Xiangxiang gongzhu* (*Princess Fragrance*), among others. As Erens writes: "Throughout her career, she has focused on the lives of characters who find themselves exiles in a foreign land: Vietnamese in Hong Kong and the Philippines, Japanese in Vietnam, Mainlanders in Hong Kong, Hong Kongers in England and Japan, Americans in China, foreigners in Macau, and even Han Chinese under the Manchus" ("The Film Work of Ann Hui," 179). Teo writes that "the burden of the quest for ethnic purity was a theme never better treated by a Hong Kong director" (*Hong Kong Cinema*, 151).

19. Claude Lévi-Strauss, *The Raw and the Cooked*, trans. John Weightman and Doreen Weightman (New York: Harper and Row, 1969).

20. In her own reflections on the film, Ann Hui has said:

> My main feeling was about my mom's experience and the irony of her journey. When she was in Hong Kong, all she did was scream for her homeland, but when she finally went back to Japan she didn't appreciate it at all. . . . The concept that we should unconditionally love our homeland was just an idea that had been drummed into our heads, and I was beginning to grow skeptical of such concepts. But my skepticism was not just about the concept of one's homeland, but about all conceptions of identity and nationality. The definition of these concepts can be very different for different individuals based on their own background and experiences.
>
> (interview with HUI, in BERRY, *Speaking in Images*, 431)

21. The song is also featured in *Rouge*; see my brief discussion of its connotations in the context of that film in "A Souvenir of Love."

22. Ho, "Women on the Edges of Hong Kong Modernity," 186. Ho's remarks are intended as reflections on Hui's earlier films (from 1979 to 1982), but they are, in my opinion, relevant to Hui's works as a whole.

5. BY WAY OF MASS COMMODITIES

1. This has not always been the case. For an account of Chinese mainlanders' negative attitudes toward Hong Kong in the context of the history of cinema, see Poshek Fu, "Between Nationalism and Colonialism: Mainland Émigrés, Marginal Culture, and Hong Kong Cinema, 1937–1941," in *The Cinema of Hong Kong: History, Arts, Identity*, ed. Poshek Fu and David Desser (Cambridge: Cambridge UP, 2000), 199–226.

2. Michael Curtin, "Sweet Comrades: Historical Identities and Popular Culture," in *In Search of Boundaries: Communication, Nation-States, and Cultural Identities*, ed. Joseph M. Chan and Bryce T. McIntyre (Westport, Conn.: Ablex, 2002), 277.

3. For a rich and detailed account of the significance of commodities in contemporary Hong Kong cinema, see Gina Marchetti, "Buying American, Consuming Hong Kong: Cultural Commerce, Fantasies of Identity, and the Cinema," in *The Cinema of Hong Kong*, 289–313. Marchetti's essay, which focuses on Wong Kar-wai's *Chungking Express*, has a final section on *Comrades, Almost a Love Story*.

4. See, for instance, Linda Chiu-han Lai, "Film and Enigmatization: Nostalgia, Nonsense, and Remembering," in *At Full Speed: Hong Kong Cinema in a Borderless World*, ed. Esther C. M. Yau (Minneapolis: U of Minnesota P, 2001), 231–50; see in particular the brief reference on 241–42 to *Comrades*. See also the informative and thoughtful discussion in Curtin, "Sweet Comrades," 264–90. Curtin's thesis is that the film "explores the unstable nature of contemporary political and social boundaries within the framework of a commercial, romantic melodrama" (265).

5. It should be noted, however, that director Chan himself also offers this type of reading of the film. See, for instance, the interview conducted with him by Zhang Liangbei, recorded in "Chen Kexin *Tian mi mi*," in *Dangdai zhongguo dianying, 1995–1997*, ed. Huang Wulan (Taipei: Shibao shuxi, 1998), 171–85.

6. Kwai-cheung Lo, "Transnationalization of the Local in a Circular Structure," in *Chinese Face/Off: The Transnational Popular Culture of Hong Kong* (Urbana: U of Illinois P, 2005), 112. This chapter is a revised version of Lo's essay "Transnationalization of the Local in Hong Kong Cinema of the 1990s," in *At Full Speed*, 261–76. Citations of Lo's text are taken from the more recently published book chapter.

7. In Hong Kong, as is shown in the film, rentals of wedding garments are often supplied by such studios, whose customers tend to want their wedding portraits taken indoors on a day other than the official wedding day.

8. As Lo writes: "Even in a Western metropolis, the trajectory of the Chinese-food delivery bike ridden by Xiaojun becomes a lifeline, rescuing Li Qiao from the hands of foreigners" ("Transnationalization of the Local in a Circular Structure," 121). Lo has provided an elegant analysis of the two significant bike rides in the film in terms of the characters' negotiations of transnational space (see 120–21). (The other significant bike ride is the one taken daily by Xiaojun delivering slaughtered chickens to Chinese restaurants, to make a living as a new immigrant in Hong Kong.)

9. For this reason, the film's significance has been dismissed—and unfortunately missed—by some critics. Yingjin Zhang, for instance, writes: "The problem with *Comrades*, I suggest, lies in its overindulgence in melodrama, in a romantic narrative whose initial attention to issues of identity and ethnicity is carried away or taken over by the overwhelming melody of Deng Lijun's songs" (*Screening China: Critical Interventions, Cinematic Reconfigurations, and the Transnational Imaginary in Contemporary Chinese Cinema* [Ann Arbor: U of Michigan P, 2002], 276).

10. Some critics have pointed out that the film's presentation of Teng's popularity should be seen more as a narrative device than as historical fact. See Curtin, "Sweet Comrades," 279 and 288 n. 10. For an account of how the soft, romantic music from Hong Kong and Taiwan such as Teng's played an important role in challenging officially sanctioned discourses, practices, and ideologies in the late 1970s and 1980s in China, well before the emergence of so-called revolutionary rock and roll, see Nimrod Baranovitch, *China's New Voices: Popular Music, Ethnicity, Gender, and Politics, 1978–1997* (Berkeley: U of California P, 2003), 10–18.

11. Lo, "Transnationalization of the Local in a Circular Structure," 120.

12. This is what leads Darrell Wm. Davis to comment harshly: "Li Chiao was always 'a real Hongkie' even before she arrived. She is an innate Hong Konger even though she is also 'Uncle China.' For though she too is a mainlander, she doesn't hesitate to screw others to get ahead. This habit dies hard; it persists even after she has gotten rich" ("Comrades, People on the Make," in *Cinedossier: The 34th Golden Horse Award-Winning Films* [Taipei: Golden Horse Film Festival, 1998], 60). Davis is trying to emphasize the point—a valid one—that Li Qiao is an opportunistic character, though I find his essentialist stigmatization of Hong Kong people unnecessary. See also Yueh-Yu Yeh, "Xinglixiang li de tian mi mi: Meiguo meng, tangrenjie, Deng Lijun," also in *Cinedossier*, 50–55. Yeh's and Davis's essays duplicate each other in some spots.

13. See, for instance, Sheldon H. Lu:

> Yet, even in eternal diaspora, China looms large in [the immigrants'] lives, perhaps not in the narrow sense of the modern sovereign nation-state, but in the realm of private, emotional attachment, as revealed, for instance, in their love for the songs of Deng Lijun. It is the popular, deterritorialized, pan-Chinese songs of a Taiwanese singer more than the national anthem that unite ethnic Chinese and Hong Kongers into some sense of communal bonding. As the TV broadcast states, there is a Chinese saying: "wherever there are Chinese people, you will hear the songs of Deng Lijun."
>
> ("Filming Diaspora and Identity: Hong Kong and 1997,"
> in *The Cinema of Hong Kong*, 278)

Davis makes a similar point: "Those who recognize her voice are the new China, united not by ideology, but by sentiment. Coming from Taiwan, itself an orphan island, Teng was a wanderer all over Asia, winning over Japanese, Hong Kong, SE Asian and especially mainland Chinese audiences. This sentimental Chinese identity, then, is or depends on a condition of exile bound by fellow feeling, nostalgia, and homesickness" ("Comrades, People on the Make," 60). Peter Chan himself echoes both Lu's and Davis's views: "Teresa Tang [*sic*] . . . is such an icon for all three Chinas, Hong Kong, Taiwan, and the mainland. She is really the one who pulled everyone together. If you were from China in 1985, there was nobody else but Teresa Tang [*sic*]. And she herself also represents that through her own diasporic background. She herself is the incarnation of the rootless Chinese" (interview with Chan in Michael Berry, *Speaking in Images: Interviews with Contemporary Chinese Filmmakers* [New York: Columbia UP, 2005], 499).

14. Lo, "Transnationalization of the Local in a Circular Structure," 120, 122.
15. Jean Baudrillard, "The System of Objects," *Jean Baudrillard: Selected Writings*, ed. Mark Poster (Stanford: Stanford UP, 1988), 21; emphasis in the original. Some of Baudrillard's other writings—notably, *For a Critique of the Political Economy of the Sign*, trans. Charles Levin (1972; reprint, St. Louis, Mo.: Telos, 1981); and *The Mirror of Production*, trans. Mark Poster (1973; St. Louis, Mo.: Telos, 1975)—are also germane to the present topic.
16. Baudrillard, "Consumer Society," in *Jean Baudrillard*, 46.
17. Marchetti writes that "Commodities—culturally mediated, tainted, fetishistic certainly, but concrete—remain the most certain conduit for the communication of personal feelings and desires" ("Buying American, Consuming Hong Kong," 304). My reading differs from Marchetti's in that I do not consider the commodities in question as mere "conduits" for "communication." In other words, the understanding of commodities as offered by this film, I suggest, goes considerably beyond an instrumentalist one.
18. Peter Chan uses the Chinese expression *baorong* (magnanimity, forgiveness) to describe Bao, comparing him to the husband of the character played by Ingrid Bergman in *Casablanca*. See "Chen Kexin *Tian mi mi*," 181.
19. For Davis, even this decision is caused less by Li Qiao's loyalty to Bao than by her fear of acknowledging her emotional ties to, or need for, a fellow mainlander. See "Comrades: People on the Make," 58.
20. Director Chan's own interpretation of the emotions involved in this scene is also noteworthy, as he explained to actress Maggie Cheung before they shot the scene: "This woman went through so many experiences and ended up with Bao, even though this was not her first preference. For the sake of having a bit of stability in life, she threw away many of her past ide-

als and instead traveled with a much older man for such long distances, only to lose everything at the end. How would you respond if you were she? You would cry, but perhaps not necessarily for Bao; it could be for yourself" ("Chen Kexin *Tian mi mi*," 183; my rough translation). See also the opening pages of Miriam Bratu Hansen, "Benjamin and Cinema: Not a One-Way Street," *Critical Inquiry* 25 (Winter 1999): 306–43, for a brief reference to this scene as an example of Walter Benjamin's theory about the recovery of sensory affect through film practice.

21. See Guy Debord, *Society of the Spectacle*, unauthorized translation (Detroit: Red and Black, 1970; reprint, *The Society of the Spectacle* [New York: Zone, 1994]); and *Comments on the Society of the Spectacle*, trans. Malcolm Imrie (London: Verso, 1990). I respect the moral severity of Debord's critique but do not find it entirely useful in analyzing contemporary Chinese cinema—unless, of course, my goal were to produce predictable readings aimed at a wholesale condemnation of spectacular society, including film itself.

22. Reading the film with Chinese patriotic interest, Lu understands it instead as a story about Hong Kong's love for China: "Indeed, the film is also indirectly an allegory of the relationship between Hong Kong and China. The love-hate relationship of Hong Kong to the mainland has been 'almost a love story.' The ostensible identification of the Hong Kong people with the fate of the mainland is all too touchingly evident in recent history" ("Filming Diaspora and Identity," 279).

6. ALL CHINESE FAMILIES ARE ALIKE

1. Sigmund Freud, *Three Essays on the Theory of Sexuality*, trans. and rev. James Strachey, with a new introduction by Steven Marcus (New York: Basic, 1975), 97.

2. Ibid., 15.

3. Jean Laplanche, *New Foundations for Psychoanalysis*, trans. David Macey (Oxford: Blackwell, 1989), 29–30; emphasis in the original.

4. Michel Foucault, *The History of Sexuality*, vol. 1, *An Introduction*, trans. Robert Hurley (New York: Vintage, 1980), 8–9.

5. Ibid., 103.

6. In particular, he discussed four types of institutional practices that together form "strategic unities" in enforcing "normal" sexuality: hysterization of women's bodies, pedagogization of children's sex, socialization of procreative behavior, and psychiatrization of perverse pleasure. See *The History of Sexuality*, 104–105.

7. Ibid., 141.

8. Originally published in 1961, the novel was reissued in 1979. See Louis Chu, *Eat a Bowl of Tea*, intro. Jeffrey Chan (Seattle: U of Washington P, 1979). For related interest, see David Shih, "*Eat A Bowl of Tea* by Louis Chu," in *A Resource Guide to Asian American Literature*, ed. Sau-ling Cynthia Wong and Stephen H. Sumida (New York: Modern Language Association of America, 2001), 45–53. My discussion in this chapter, however, will be of the film rather than the novel.

9. David L. Eng, *Racial Castration: Managing Masculinity in Asian America* (Durham, N.C.: Duke UP, 2001), 170. Eng's analysis is based on Chu's novel (though he has included a couple of stills from Wayne Wang's picture), but I believe his argument about male hysteria is intended as a general argument about Asian American culture.

10. Ibid., 179. For another reading of the film that emphasizes Asian American sexuality as colonized and deformed by mainstream white culture, see Darrell Y. Hamamoto, "The Joy Fuck Club: Prolegomenon to an Asian American Porno Practice," in *Countervisions: Asian American Film Criticism*, ed. Darrell Y. Hamamoto and Sandra Liu (Philadelphia: Temple UP, 2000), 62–71. Hamamoto's argument may be glimpsed in a passage such as this: "Out of the legal, legislative, and moralistic strategies brought to bear in the regulation of Asian American sexuality, a system of psychosocial dominance has evolved that, to varying degrees, has been internalized by the objects of social control" (63).

11. Eng, *Racial Castration*, 181.

12. See Eng's discussions in *Racial Castration*, 169, 180, 182, and 190. In the film, the historical consequences of the Chinese Exclusion Act and its subsequent amendment are referred to by the president of the North American branch of the Wang Family Association in the speech he makes at Ben Loy and Mei Oi's wedding banquet.

13. When Ben Loy teases his mother about having boyfriends, she laughs and reprimands him for having crazy ideas—ideas about sex—that she associates with "America." When it comes to the elderly women left behind in China, in other words, sexual gratification and fulfillment, which otherwise seem to occupy such a central place in the story, are conveniently brushed aside as a culturally specific preoccupation.

14. In the novel, Ben Loy's recovery results, after their move to San Francisco, from repeated visits to an herbalist who prescribes the special tea. In the film, however, Mei Oi is the agent delivering the magic potion.

15. In the novel, one reason Wah Gay wants to get his son a wife in China is that he does not like or trust American-born Chinese girls. Yet despite this belief in Chinese and suspicion of American values, Wah Gay obviously has

no intentions of ever returning to China. In the film, his wife has a kitchen cupboard full of American electric cookware items he keeps sending her over the years even though she has no use for such "fancy junk." In another scene, as the news of the Korean War is announced on the radio, Wah Gay tells Lee Gong: "The truth is, we were never meant to go back." This implicit ambivalence about both China and the United States on the part of the Chinatown inhabitants is, it seems to me, crucial to any reading of this story.

16. Interpreters of Chu's novel have suggested that the illegitimacy of Mei Oi's child may be seen as a sign of hope for future legitimate participation within the American system. See Shih, "*Eat a Bowl of Tea* by Louis Chu," 49; Jeffrey Chan, "Introduction to the 1979 Edition," in Chu, *Eat a Bowl of Tea*, 5.

17. See Eng, *Racial Castration*, 220.

18. Lee describes the evolution of his screenplay as coming from his dramatic and social background. "My dramatic background taught me how to create a situation so all the issues and circumstances collide. You throw people into a situation in which they are not in harmony, but in conflict. . . . Through this process you examine humanity and our human situation" (interview in Michael Berry, *Speaking in Images: Interviews with Contemporary Chinese Filmmakers* [New York: Columbia UP, 2005], 331). Chris Berry has argued that the film should be seen as a Chinese family drama that combines features of Hollywood-style melodrama with the Chinese *jiating lunlipian* (family ethics film). See his "*Wedding Banquet*: A Family (Melodrama) Affair," in *Chinese Films in Focus: 25 New Takes*, ed. Chris Berry (London: British Film Institute, 2003), 183–90. For other discussions of the question of genre and classification, see Sheng-mei Ma, "Ang Lee's Domestic Tragicomedy: Immigrant Nostalgia, Exotic/Ethnic Tour, Global Market," *Journal of Popular Culture* 30.1 (1996): 191–201; and Gina Marchetti, "*The Wedding Banquet*: Global Chinese Cinema and Asian American Experience," in *Countervisions*, 275–97.

19. See Mark Chiang, "Coming Out into the Global System: Postmodern Patriarchies and Transnational Sexualities in *The Wedding Banquet*," in *Q & A: Queer in Asian America*, ed. David Eng and Alice Y. Hom (Philadelphia: Temple UP, 1998), 374–95, for a persuasive argument of how the visibility of homosexuality represented in the film should not be seen as subversion or resistance but rather be recognized as an "ideological mirage of transnational capital," one that is implicated in the reconstitution of nationalist patriarchy and its subordination of women. See also Song Hwee Lim's thoughtful discussion, in which an analysis of the film is accompanied by a fundamental critique of the pitfalls of the liberationist imperative of coming out as inscribed in Western leftist cultural romanticism, in *Celluloid Comrades: Repre-*

sentations of Male Homosexuality in Contemporary Chinese Cinemas (Honolulu: U of Hawaii P, 2006), 41–68.

20. See Cynthia W. Liu, "'To Love, Honor and Dismay': Subverting the Feminine in Ang Lee's Trilogy of Resuscitated Patriarchs," *Hitting Critical Mass: A Journal of Asian-American Cultural Criticism* 3.1 (1995): 1–60, for an engaging argument of how Mr. Gao is the primary vehicle of identification—the omniscient character through whom the audience's sympathies are channeled. By contrast, she writes, the narratives of Lee's trilogy "exhibit a punitive tendency in his constructions of the feminine" (9). Similarly, Emilie Yueh-yu Yeh and Darrell William Davis have used the phrase "latent misogyny" to characterize Ang Lee's treatment of women characters. See their *Taiwan Film Directors: A Treasure Island* (New York: Columbia UP, 2005), 199.

21. Lee's remarks on his own relationship with his parents are noteworthy:

I think the influence of the father is something that weighs heavy on most male Chinese filmmakers. On *Pushing Hands* and *The Wedding Banquet*, [my father had] a very heavy impact. Although I'm not gay, much of the dialogue in *Wedding Banquet* between the gay son and his father was taken directly from my father's mouth. My mother was also a model of sorts for the mother figure in those films, but to a lesser degree. I think the father figure represents the Chinese patriarchy, the social and psychological structure of society. I am the first son, so I took in a lot of those ideas that women are not important. . . . I didn't know what I wanted from life, but I knew I had to please my father.

(interview in BERRY, *Speaking in Images*, 329)

In relation to his 1994 film *Eat Drink Man Woman*, Lee said in jest about the father figure: "Well, he is already gone. He is just a paper tiger. He has a poker face but doesn't know what to do. I think I must have had a plan to weaken my father movie by movie. It is funny, by *The Hulk* [2003] I end up blowing him up. (*Laughs*) Like some Greek myth, I blew him up like a jellyfish. It is funny that after that movie my father passed away" (336).

22. Regarding the first incident, Sister Mao, the ideal match found by Wai Tung's parents through a marriage agency, reports on her arrival in New York that his father has been hospitalized because of an episode of "fa xinzangbing" (a heart attack), which is mistranslated in the English subtitles as "a stroke."

23. Wei Ming Dariotis and Eileen Fung, "Breaking the Soy Sauce Jar: Diaspora and Displacement in the Films of Ang Lee," in *Transnational Chinese Cinemas: Identity, Nationhood, Gender*, ed. Sheldon Hsiao-peng Lu (Honolulu: U of Hawaii P, 1997), 207.

24. Ibid., 217–18.
25. Shu-mei Shih, "Globalisation and Minoritisation: Ang Lee and the Politics of Flexibility," *New Formations: A Journal of Culture/Theory/Politics* 40 (Spring 2000): 96, 98.
26. Berry, "*Wedding Banquet*," 189.
27. See Chris Berry and Mary Farquhar, *China on Screen: Cinema and Nation* (New York: Columbia UP, 2006), 175–79.
28. For a scholarly study in English on this topic, see Bret Hinsch, *Passions of the Cut Sleeve: The Male Homosexual Tradition in China* (Berkeley: University of California P, 1990). For the controversy over the originality of Hinsch's book and the allegations that much of it was derived, without due acknowledgment, from Samshasha (Xiaomingxiong), *History of Homosexuality in China (Zhongguo tongxingai shilu)* (Hong Kong: Pink Triangle: 1984; rev. ed. 1997), see the interview with Samshasha (reportedly the first Hong Kong gay rights activist), as conducted and presented by Mark McLelland, at wwwsshe.murdoch.edu.au/intersections/issue4/interview_mclelland.html. I am indebted to one of the anonymous reviewers of the manuscript of this book for the information about this controversy.
29. Liu, "'To Love, Honor and Dismay,'" 27.
30. As Jeroen de Kloet writes: "The insistence put on harmony, hierarchy, patriarchy, and filial piety indicates that what may at first appear to be a daring cinematic project, including an interracial gay couple in potential conflict with the Chinese parents, 'fails' to spread much dirt on Chinese family ideology" ("Saved by Betrayal? Ang Lee's Translations of 'Chinese' Family Ideology," in *Shooting the Family: Transnational Media and Intercultural Values*, ed. Patricia Pisters and Wim Staat [Amsterdam: Amsterdam UP, 2005], 124).
31. Dariotis and Fung offer a slightly different formulation of the same idea: "The kitchen scenes where Wei-wei and Simon cook (or in Wei-wei's case, attempts to cook) show two potential 'daughters-in-law,' where one fulfills the expectations of the traditional Chinese parents and the other satisfies the sexual desires of the gay husband" ("Breaking the Soy Sauce Jar," 205).
32. As Berry comments, "Although his [Simon's] motivation for suggesting marriage to Wei-Wei is selfish—getting Wai-Tung's parents off their backs—this act mimics the ideal behaviour of a barren daughter-in-law in suggesting a second wife to enable her husband to produce an heir" ("*Wedding Banquet*," 186).
33. Chiang, "Coming Out into the Global System," 383.
34. Fran Martin, "Globally Chinese at *The Wedding Banquet*," in *Situating Sexualities: Queer Representation in Taiwan Fiction, Film and Public Culture* (Hong Kong: Hong Kong UP, 2003), 145.
35. Chiang, "Coming Out into the Global System," 384.

36. Gayatri Chakravorty Spivak, "French Feminism in an International Frame," in *In Other Worlds: Essays in Cultural Politics* (New York: Methuen, 1987), 152. See also the critique of patriarchal and procreative imperatives in Liu, "'To Love, Honor, and Dismay.'"

37. Chiang, "Coming Out into the Global System," 376.

38. For related interest, see the account of Chinese diaspora cinema and its interesting ties to American independent film production in Gina Marchetti, "Guests at *The Wedding Banquet*: The Cinema of the Chinese Diaspora and the Rise of the American Independents," in *Contemporary American Independent Film: From the Margins to the Mainstream*, ed. Chris Holmlund and Justin Wyatt (London: Routledge, 2005), 211–25.

39. In a parallel move, Mrs. Gao busies herself with tidying up the young people's garden.

40. For a sensitive and original analysis of Mr. Gao's various features and gestures—his secret knowledge and tolerance of his son's homosexuality, his insistence on maintaining silence, and his raising his arms to the airport official at the end—see Martin, "Globally Chinese at *The Wedding Banquet*," 143–61. Martin argues that the multicoding of such features and gestures that characterizes Ang Lee's global cinema (one that attempts to be legible to audiences from different cultures at the same time) is what allows for the reconsolidation of Mr. Gao's authority as a traditional Chinese patriarch, paradoxically, through the inclusion and reproduction of a contemporary, liberal model of homosexuality.

41. Spivak, "French Feminism in an International Frame," 153.

42. See Dariotis and Fung, "Breaking the Soy Sauce Jar," 203–206, for an analysis of the ambivalence of Wei Wei's characterization. See also Marchetti, "*The Wedding Banquet*," for a discussion of the implications of Wei Wei's "embourgeoisement" (288); Marchetti's conclusion is that, insofar as women are expected to sacrifice themselves for men and children, the film's happy ending is "constructed on the ruins of feminism." (290).

43. Chiang puts it this way: "Wei Wei's desire is understood by Wai Tung (and the film) only as ventriloquizing the father's imperative, a conflation that effectively excludes any possibility of autonomy for Wei Wei or release from the dictates of the international sexual division of labor" ("Coming Out into the Global System," 383).

7. THE POLITICAL ECONOMY OF VISION IN *HAPPY TIMES* AND *NOT ONE LESS*

1. See in particular part 2, chapter 4 of *Primitive Passions: Visuality, Sexuality, Ethnography, and Contemporary Chinese Cinema* (New York: Columbia UP, 1995).

2. This point, which necessitates a detailed discussion of the history of modern Chinese literature and its study, is obviously one that I can only mention but not substantiate here.

3. Outside academia, there is the additional problem, perpetrated by international film audiences, including organizers of international film festivals, of viewing films from China categorically as being either antigovernment or representing government propaganda. This was the reason Zhang Yimou withdrew *Not One Less* and *The Road Home* from the Cannes International Film Festival in 1999 (see the brief mention of this in the *New York Times*, April 21, 1999, B8). In his letter to the festival organizers, excerpted in the Chinese-language media during that period, Zhang indicated that *Not One Less* was intended as an expression of his love for children and his concern for the current and future conditions of his people's culture as a whole and that *The Road Home* was meant to be a celebration of pure, innocent love.

4. See, for instance, the discussions of Zhang's evolving work in the group of essays devoted to *Not One Less* under the title *Yige dou buneng shao yingpian gean fenxi*, in *Zhongguo dianying meixue: 1999 (Aesthetics of Chinese Film: 1999)*, ed. Hu Ke et al. (Beijing: Beijing Broadcasting Institute, October 2000); and various discussions of the film in *Dianying yishu (Film Art)*, no. 5 (September 10, 1999), no. 3 (May 5, 2000), and no. 1 (January 5, 2001).

5. See Zhang Yiwu, "Zaidu xiangxiang zhongguo: quanqiuhua de tiaozhan yu xin de 'neixianghua'" (Once again imagining China: The challenge of globalization and the new "inward-looking tendency"), *Dianying yishu*, no. 1 (January 5, 2001): 16–21. According to Zhang Yiwu, films made by the Fifth Generation directors in the 1980s represented a brief period in which the directors reacted against the inward-looking tradition in Chinese cinema (a cinema that concerns itself primarily with Chinese history and society) to create an outward-looking one intent on drawing the attention of the rest of the world. With most of the world in economic recession and the overseas market for Chinese film dwindling in recent years, however, that outward-looking moment, argues Zhang, has passed. Globalization, he suggests, has led paradoxically to a renewal of the tradition of inward-looking cinema, centered on China's internal problems and produced for a predominantly Chinese audience. He writes: "Globalization is not just a background but a problem internal to film" (19; my translation).

6. Zhang himself sums up these reactions in good humor: "I always feel that there are two schools of criticism out there when it comes to my films. They say that I'm trying to kiss either foreigners' asses or the Chinese government's ass. I always jokingly respond that I'm actually kissing my own ass! . . . In the

eyes of many, I am an opportunist. They think I sit around all day devising schemes to win the approval of foreigners or the Chinese government. . . . It is a big source of uneasiness for me, but what can I do?" (quoted in Michael Berry, *Speaking in Images: Interviews with Contemporary Chinese Filmmakers* [New York: Columbia UP, 2005], 126). For discussions related to the implications of orientalism in Zhang's work, including Zhang's responses to some of his critics, see, for instance, the interviews with Zhang regarding the making of *Not One Less* in the following: *Zhongguo dianying meixue: 1999*, 29–35; *Jiushi niandai de diwudai (The Fifth Generation of Chinese Filmmakers in the 1990s)*, ed. Yang Yuanying (Beijing: Beijing Broadcasting Institute, November 2000), 121–27. For general interest, see also *Zhang Yimou: Interviews*, ed. Frances Gateward (Jackson: U of Mississippi P, 2001).

7. See Shi Wenhong, "Yige dou buneng shao de aichou" (The sadness of *Not One Less*), *Yingpingren jikan (Film Critics Quarterly)*, no. 6 (2000): 7.

8. For a sustained critique of the periodical's politics of representing non-Western cultures, see Catherine A. Lutz and Jane L. Collins, *Reading National Geographic* (Chicago: U of Chicago P, 1993).

9. The cast of *Not One Less*, for instance, was made up of amateur actors, many of whom were actual villagers from the film's location. Some of these villagers' names were used for characters' names in the film. As Xiaoling Zhang points out, however, "the whole suggestion of reality is entirely artificial: the school was chosen from a few dozen schools in that area, the eighteen pupils were selected from among thousands of pupils, and the girl playing Wei Minzhi was picked from twenty thousand girls, in an auditioning process which lasted more than half a month" ("A Film Director's Criticism of Reform China: A Close Reading of Zhang Yimou's *Not One Less*," *China Information* 25.2 (2001): 138.

10. As Zhang puts it forthrightly:

> [The critics] think I have no passion for cinema and everything I do is driven by a certain objective. You can say all I care about is kissing up to foreign audiences or the Chinese government. Fine, I don't care. But saying I have no love for the art of cinema and accusing me of using cinema as a tool to achieve my own personal objective is a fundamental negation of my commitment to the art form. Although I don't like it, I don't bother explaining myself. You can hate my films, but no one can accuse me of not loving the art of film. As a filmmaker that is the greatest insult one can receive.
>
> (BERRY, *Speaking in Images*, 127)

11. As one critic, Zeng Guang, writes: "Under the current political system, he [Zhang Yimou] feels that the biggest difference between himself and direc-

tors from foreign countries, Hong Kong, and Taiwan lies in the fact that 'when I receive a film script, the first thing I think about is not whether there will be an investor for the film, but how I can make the kind of film I want with the approval of the authorities.'" This passage is cited as the epigraph in Sheldon H. Lu, "Understanding Chinese Film Culture at the End of the Twentieth Century: The Case of *Not One Less* by Zhang Yimou," *Journal of Modern Literature in Chinese* 4.2 (January 2001): 123–42.

12. For an earlier, perhaps even more remarkable example of such a cinematic staging method, see my discussion of Zhang's 1994 film *Huo zhe* (*To Live*) in the chapter "We Endure, Therefore We Are: Survival, Governance, and Zhang Yimou's *To Live*," in *Ethics after Idealism: Theory—Culture—Ethnicity—Reading* (Bloomington: Indiana UP, 1998), 113–32. This chapter is a revised version of an essay initially published in the *South Atlantic Quarterly* 95.4 (Fall 1996): 1039–64. Zhang considers *To Live* as "the film closest to [him]"; see his remarks in Berry, *Speaking in Images*, 127–29.

13. Zhang also made an alternative ending, in the version of the film officially released outside the People's Republic, that averts attention from the big economic picture by focusing on the personal stories. In this version, after writing the fake letter to the blind girl, Lao Zhao is hit by a truck and goes into a coma. The blind girl, not knowing what has happened, decides to move on so that she will no longer be a burden. She leaves behind a tape on which she thanks Lao Zhao for what he has done for her, explaining that she has known all along about the lies but appreciates the intentions behind them. As Lao Zhao's friends listen to the tape while reading aloud Lao Zhao's fake letter, the final scene shows the blind girl walking down the street alone. In his interview with Michael Berry, Zhang Yimou indicates that he was dissatisfied with both endings and classifies *Happy Times* as "a weaker work," in which "neither the style nor the inner philosophical underpinnings of the film ever really came out" (Berry, *Speaking in Images*, 126).

14. Naomi Schor, "Blindness as Metaphor," *differences* 11.2 (Summer 1999): 88; emphasis in the original. In this semiautobiographical essay, Schor argues for seeing blindness (and other forms of physical deprivation) as part of a human sensorium in its full range of complexity and not simply as a negative version of a normal, healthy body: "The realm of the senses must . . . be extended to include all manner of sensual deprivation: lack of vision, lack of hearing, lack of speech, lack of taste, lack of smell, lack of touch" (83).

15. See Dave Kehr, "Beyond Glamour There's Humor," "At the Movies" sec., *New York Times*, July 26, 2002, B11. Since Zhang does not speak English, the quoted remarks are most likely a loose translation of what he actually said in Chinese.

16. Michael Dutton, "Street Scenes of Subalternity: China, Globalization, and Rights," in *Whither China? Intellectual Politics in Contemporary China*, ed. Xudong Zhang (Durham, N.C.: Duke UP, 2001), 355, 358. This essay is based on arguments excerpted from Dutton, *Streetlife China* (Cambridge: Cambridge UP, 1998).

17. Note that although the film was adopted from Shi Xiangsheng's story "Tian shang you ge taiyang" (A sun in the sky), *Feitian*, no. 6 (1997) (as cited in Zhang, "A Film Director's Criticism of Reform China," 136 n. 13), Zhang Yimou changed the title to one that highlights the act of counting (bodies).

18. Wang Yichuan, "Wenming yu wenming de yeman" (Civilization and civilized barbarity), *Zhongguo dianying meixue*, 1999, 67–75; the cited passages are on 71 and 73; the loose translation from the Chinese is mine. Among the readings that were published shortly after the film's release in China in 1999, this is the only one I have come across that pointedly identifies money and the media as what constitute the decisive structural significance of the narrative. For an account of the success of *Not One Less* in the People's Republic and the related issue of television's popularity in China today (including how the television episode in the film was modeled after two popular television programs on CCTV in the 1990s), see Laikwan Pang, "Piracy/Privacy: the Despair of Cinema and Collectivity in China," *boundary 2* 31.3 (Fall 2004): 117–22.

19. As Jacques Derrida has written, "What the accelerated development of teletechnologies, of cyberspace, of the new topology of 'the virtual' is producing is a practical *deconstruction* of the traditional and dominant concepts of the state and citizen (and thus of 'the political') as they are linked to the actuality of a territory" (Jacques Derrida and Bernard Stiegler, *Echographies of Television: Filmed Interviews*, trans. Jennifer Bajorek [Cambridge: Polity, 2002], 36; emphasis in the original).

20. Hu Ke writes that Zhang's narrative method is like an "ad for charity." See his "Jishi yu xugou" (Documentary record and fictional construct), *Zhongguo dianying meixue: 1999*, 41–49; the point about "ad for charity" is on 42. This view is shared by other critics: see, for instance, Wang Ailing, "Tinghua de haizi" (Obedient children), in *1999 Xianggang dianying huigu* (A look back at Hong Kong cinema of 1999) (Hong Kong: Xianggang dianying pinglun xuehui, 2000), 301–302; Valerie Wong, "*Not One Less*," *Cinemaya*, no. 45 (1999): 20–21. This type of reading is not incorrect, but the main problem I have with it is that these critics tend to read Zhang's film as a *completed* realist message rather than as a process and a structure in which a dialectical understanding (of the changes brought to Chinese society by the new media) is being actively and aesthetically produced. While they are undoubt-

edly right about the explicit propaganda at the end of the film, they tend to miss the significance of the presence of other propaganda messages (including the moral virtues of frugality and hard work and the rationalistic logic, internalized by poor people, of equating units of physical labor with units of financial reward), a presence that is staged throughout the entire film. For an opposite type of reading that approaches Zhang's film not as propaganda but as a laudable piece of social criticism, See Zhang, "A Film Director's Criticism of Reform China."

21. For a discussion of this point as well as an informative discussion of Zhang's film in relation to recent conditions of film production and reception in mainland China, see Lu, "Understanding Chinese Film Culture at the End of the Twentieth Century."

8. "HUMAN" IN THE AGE OF DISPOSABLE PEOPLE

1. Martin Heidegger, "Letter on Humanism," in *Martin Heidegger, Basic Writings from* Being and Time *(1927) to* The Task of Thinking *(1964)*, rev. ed., ed. David Farrell Krell (New York: HarperCollins, 1977, 1993), 217–65; the quotation is from 243. Hereafter references to this essay will be included in parentheses in the text.

2. See Liu Qingbang, "Shen mu," in *Buding jia gei shui* (Changchun: Shidai wenyi chubanshe, 2001), 359–448. In an interview conducted in April 2003, Li Yang mentions that this story was given the Lao She Prize, the highest literary award in China; see Stephen Teo, "'There Is No Sixth Generation!' Director Li Yang on *Blind Shaft* and His Place in Chinese Cinema," *Senses of Cinema*, June 2003, www.sensesofcinema.com/contents/03/27/li_yang.html, 4.

3. See Guan Jingsong, "Jing mang, xin bu mang: Zhuanfang dianying *Mang Jing* daoyan Li Yang," *Cream* 14 (November 2003): 114–15. In this interview (conducted at the end of September 2003, when *Blind Shaft* was shown in Hong Kong for the second time that year), Li indicated that because of the film, which had initially been banned in the People's Republic, he was prohibited by the Chinese authorities from all film-, television-, and commercial-making activities. He also mentioned his experience of being surrounded and threatened by gun-carrying mine owners and policemen when he visited a coal mine. Reportedly, however, in late 2003 the Chinese Film Bureau "suddenly approved what had previously been labeled an 'illegal film' for release and distribution"—apparently, by removing all explicit sex scenes and the subversive version of the song "Shehuizhuyi hao" (Socialism is good). For this update, see Michael Berry, *Speaking in Images: Interviews with Contemporary Chinese Filmmakers* (New York: Columbia UP, 2005), 210, 551 n. 1 (of the

chapter "Li Yang"). Berry's interviews with Li Yang were conducted in May and November 2003.

4. David Farrell Krell, introduction to Heidegger, *Martin Heidegger, Basic Writings*, 216; emphasis in the original.

5. This is presented as a fact rather than a suspicion in the original narrative. Li Yang explains the alteration as follows: "In the film I left it a bit hazy. Maybe Fengming is his [the first victim's] son, and maybe he is not. In the novel Liu Qingbang makes it clear that they are indeed father and son, but with a population of 1.3 billion people in China, I thought that was a bit too much of a coincidence. So in the film, I intentionally left this detail open-ended" (Berry, *Speaking in Images*, 217).

6. *Blind Shaft*, DVD (Hong Kong: Star Treasure Holdings Ltd, 2003), back cover; my translation from the Chinese.

7. See, for instance, details given in the investigative reports in *Zhonghua tansuo*, November 13, 2004, 2, 4. A report in English sums it up this way: "Two forces driving Chinese industrial development—cheap, poorly protected labor and rapid, some say even reckless, growth—fall especially heavily on China's coal mines. They are often small, poorly equipped and poorly ventilated, but owners have been profiting from China's strong demand for energy. . . . Work safety officials acknowledge that the hunger for profit and tax revenues among mine owners and local governments often outweighs safety concerns" (Chris Buckley, "166 Still Missing from China Mine Blast," *New York Times*, November 29, 2004, A8).

8. "Orgasm" is also "(sexual) high tide" in Chinese, a pun on which the lyrics play. These versions of the lyrics are from the Chinese and English subtitles of the film, with my slight modifications of the English translations. According to Li Yang, he and his crew found the lyrics on the Internet; see Berry, *Speaking in Images*, 226. His point is that Tang and Song, like most people in China who received a socialist education, have been left behind by China's new social situation.

9. Ban Wang, "Documentary as Haunting of the Real: The Logic of Capital in *Blind Shaft*," *Asian Cinema*, Spring/Summer 2005, 10.

10. Li Yang's account of his use of cinematic language is noteworthy: "I intentionally kept the camera at eye level throughout the shoot, so there are hardly any shots above what would be a normal person's perspective. By doing away with all high and low shots, I wanted to strip the film down to the simplest possible cinematic language. I didn't rely on any bird's-eye view shots or experiment with any other shooting angles. The audience is forced to see the film as if they are watching a documentary" (Berry, *Speaking in Images*, 224). The only exceptions, he emphasizes, are the opening scene and the closing shot.

11. See Liu Qingbang, "Shen mu," 430–31.

12. Martin Heidegger, *The Question Concerning Technology and Other Essays*, trans. William Lovitt (New York: Harper Colophon, 1977), 16.

13. There are copious references to kin relations in the original narrative.

14. Teo, "'There Is No Sixth Generation!'" 7–8; my emphases.

15. Li explains: "When I asked coal miners about what kept them going regardless of the dangers of working in the mines, the response I got over and over was that they needed to send their kids to school. They would often tell me that the only way their situation can change is by making sure their children have a good education. It is this belief that often leads them to risk their lives" (Berry, *Speaking in Images*, 222).

16. Teo, "'There Is No Sixth Generation!'" 9.

17. I thank Brian Rotman for this important question.

18. Étienne Balibar, *Politics and the Other Scene*, trans. Christine Jones, James Swenson, and Chris Turner (New York; Verso, 2002), 144; emphases in the original.

9. THE ENIGMA OF INCEST AND THE STAGING OF KINSHIP FAMILY REMAINS IN *THE RIVER*

1. Gayle Rubin, "The Traffic in Women: Notes on the 'Political Economy' of Sex," in *The Second Wave: A Reader in Feminist Theory*, ed. Linda Nicholson (New York: Routledge, 1997), 32. This essay was originally published in *Toward an Anthropology of Women*, ed. Rayna R. Reiter (New York: Monthly Review Press, 1975).

2. Howard Hampton, "Rainmaker," *Artforum*, Summer 2001, 162.

3. See, for instance, Judith Butler, "Quandaries of the Incest Taboo," in *Whose Freud? The Place of Psychoanalysis in Contemporary Culture*, ed. Peter Brooks and Alex Woloch (New Haven: Yale UP, 2000), 39–46.

4. To this extent, Claude Lévi-Strauss's classic *The Elementary Structures of Kinship* (1949) is, according to Rubin, "the boldest twentieth-century version of the nineteenth-century project to understand human marriage. It is a book in which kinship is explicitly conceived of as an imposition of cultural organization upon the facts of biological procreation. . . . The human subject in Lévi-Strauss's work is always either male or female, and the divergent social destinies of the two sexes can therefore be traced" ("The Traffic in Women," 34–35). For a discussion of how Lévi-Strauss's structuralist views on kinship are now considered anachronistic by some scholars, see Judith Butler, "Is Kinship Always Already Heterosexual?" *differences* 13 (Spring 2002): 14–44. Butler's essay offers, among other things, an analysis of the political stakes

involved in gay people's fight for the state's legitimation of same-sex marriage and other related issues.

5. Noting that some critics have read the scene in Tsai's film by comparing it to well-known scenes of mother-son intimacy, thus turning the father into a mother, Chang Hsiao-hung wrote that there seems to be "another taboo within the incest taboo." See her illuminating discussion in "Guaitai jiating luomanshi: *Heliu* zhong de yuwang changjing," in *Guaitai jiating luomanshi* (Taipei: Shibao, 2000), 117–18.

6. See "Repérages," an interview with Tsai conducted by Danièle Rivière and translated into Chinese by Wang Paizhang, in *Tsai Ming-liang*, trans. Chen Suli, Lin Zhiming, and Wang Paizhang (Taipei: Yuanliou, 2001), 73–75. (For the French original of the entire book, see Jean-Pierre Rehm, Olivier Joyard, and Danièle Rivière, *Tsai Ming-liang* [Paris: Dis Voir, 2001].) Tsai indicated that this scene had met with pernicious and oftentimes insulting criticisms from some audiences. In the main, there were three types of objections: that against the "incest," that against the dark and pessimistic portrayals of gay people's world, and that against the seemingly total rejection of women.

7. See the following works for various critical discussions of these films and/ or interviews with Tsai: Rehm, Joyard, and Rivière, *Tsai Ming-liang*; Chris Berry, "Tsai Ming-liang: Look At All the Lonely people," *Cinemaya* 30 (1995): 18–20; "Where Is the Love? The Paradox of Performing Loneliness in Ts'ai Ming-Liang's *Vive l'Amour*," in *Falling for You: Essays on Cinema and Performance*, ed. Lesley Stern and George Kouvaros (Sydney: Power, 1999), 147–75; Shelley Kraicer, "Interview with Cai Mingliang," *positions* 8.2 (Fall 2000): 579–88; Howard Hampton, "Rainmaker," *Artforum*, Summer 2001, 160–63; Wen Tianxiang, *Guangying dingge: Tsai Ming-liang de xinning changyi* (Taipei: Heng Sing, 2002); the special section on Tsai Ming-liang in *Jiaofeng* 489 (December 2002), in particular Kien Ket Lim, "Tsai Ming-liang yuedu," 5–21; Fran Martin, "*Vive l'Amour*: Eloquent Emptiness," in *Chinese Films in Focus: 25 New Takes*, ed. Chris Berry (London: British Film Institute, 2003), 175–82; Yomi Braester, "If We Could Remember Everything, We Would be Able to Fly: Taipei's Cinematic Poetics of Demolition," *Modern Chinese Literature and Culture* 15.1 (Spring 2003): 47–54; Carlos Rojas, "'Nezha Was Here': Structures of Dis/placement in Tsai Ming-liang's *Rebels of the Neon God*," *Modern Chinese Literature and Culture* 15.1 (Spring 2003): 63–89; Ban Wang, "Black Holes of Globalization: Critique of the New Millennium in Taiwan Cinema," *Modern Chinese Literature and Culture* 15.1 (Spring 2003): 90–119; and Meiling Wu, "Postsadness Taiwan New Cinema: Eat, Drink, Everyman, Everywoman," in *Chinese-Language Film: Historiography, Poetics, Politics*, ed. Sheldon H. Lu and Emilie Yueh-yu Yeh (Honolulu: U of Hawaii P, 2005), 76–95.

8. Kien Ket Lim has argued that humans have become part of a world of things in Tsai's films; see "Gai yizuo fangzi," *Chungwai Literary Monthly* 30.10 (March 2002): 42–74. A short version of this essay can be found in Kien Ket Lim, "To Build a House," unpublished MS.

9. Tsai explained in a conversation about *Vive l'amour*: "I didn't plan for there to be no dialogue. I cut a lot out just because it seemed natural to me. In life, people's motivations are complex and unclear. But in film, dialogue often makes motivation too direct and simple" (Berry, "Tsai Ming-Liang: Look At All the Lonely People," 20).

10. But, as in Kafka also, becoming animal is not necessarily just a negative event in Tsai. As the rest of this chapter will try to demonstrate, Tsai's tendency to portray his characters at times as animal-like can be seen as part of a visionary pursuit of ways out of an oppressive system. For an inspiring discussion of this point in relation to Kafka's work, see Gilles Deleuze, *Kafka: Towards a Minor Literature*, trans. Dana Polan, foreword by Réda Bensmaïa (Minneapolis: U of Minnesota P, 1986), in particular 9–42.

11. For discussions of Tsai's noticeably high modernist techniques and his work's relation to European modernism and avant-garde cinema, see Chang Aizhu, "Piaobo de zaiti: Tsai Ming-liang dianying de shenti juchang yu yuwang changyu," *Chungwai Literary Monthly* 30.10 (March 2003): 75–98; and Mark Betz, "The Cinema of Tsai Ming-liang: A Modernist Genealogy," in *Reading Chinese Transnationalisms: Society, Literature, Film*, ed. Maria N. Ng and Philip Holden (Hong Kong: Hong Kong UP, 2006), 161–72.

12. See, for instance, Fiona A. Villella, "Notes on Tsai Ming-liang's *The River*," *Senses of Cinema*, January 2001, www.sensesofcinema.com/contents/01/12/river.html. See also Elvis Mitchell, "A Fragmented Family Struggling to Reconnect," *New York Times*, January 11, 2002, B32. (This is an excerpt of a film review published in the *New York Times* on September 29, 2001; it deals more specifically with *What Time Is It There?* but offers a good example of the kind of existentialist reading that Tsai films often invite.) For a different kind of reading of these films, one that emphasizes hope-filled, homosexual connections that occur concurrently with the emptying-out of relationships defined by *jia* (home/house/family), see the nuanced analysis in Martin, "*Vive l'Amour*," which offers brief discussions of *The River* in relation to Tsai's other films.

13. For a discussion of parallel body activities and the close links between eating and having sex in the film, see Song Hwee Lim's chapter on Tsai's work in *Celluloid Comrades: Representations of Male Homosexuality in Contemporary Chinese Cinemas* (Honolulu: U of Hawaii P, 2006), in particular 144–46.

14. See Fran Martin's excellent analysis of the significance of these relations in *Situating Sexualities: Queer Representation in Taiwanese Fiction, Film*

and Public Culture (Hong Kong: Hong Kong UP, 2003), 163–84. Martin argues—persuasively, I think—for seeing The River as the instance of a "perverse utopia" or "queering of jia," whereby the breakdown of the patriarchal family coincides with the emergence of a (post)modern sexual subject.

15. When addressing the question of the general absence of music in his films, Tsai remarks: "It all comes down to whether the addition of music is going to make the film stronger or weaker—and for me, I usually feel that it makes the film weaker. When you watch an unscored scene in a film, the possibilities for interpretation are wide open because there is not music there helping you digest the visuals or instructing you how to read the scene. Without music there is no clear-cut map of how to read any given scene" (Michael Berry, Speaking in Images: Interviews with Contemporary Chinese Filmmakers [New York: Columbia UP, 2005], 373). For an interesting discussion of the rare cases of a use of diegetic sound in Tsai's work, see Lim, Celluloid Comrades, 149–50.

16. As in some of my other writings, the reading of the allegorical and the visual/visible here has been influenced by the work of Walter Benjamin, in particular The Origin of German Tragic Drama, trans. John Osborne (London: New Left, 1977), and Understanding Brecht, trans. Anna Bostock, intro. Stanley Mitchell (London: New Left, 1973; reprint, Verso, 1983).

17. Various critics have written eloquently about the cultural complexity of this scene. See, for instance, the essays in Heliu, ed. Jiao Xiongping (Taipei: Huangguan, 1997).

18. Tsai's personal investment in this scene can be glimpsed in these remarks: "In the entire twelve years of my career as a feature filmmaker, the most exciting moment for me was just after shooting that scene. . . . In virtually all of my films . . . I always felt as if all I was doing was carrying out some ideas. But the true excitement of artistic creation really made itself clear during the shooting of The River, and it was all because of that scene. That was truly one of the happiest moments in my filmmaking career" (Berry, Speaking in Images, 384).

19. Martin, Situating Sexualities, 183. She has written similarly of the several films featuring the character Hsiao Kang: "In one sense, the queer plenitude of these films seems the opposite of the existential emptiness critics frequently read in Tsai's oeuvre; yet this plenitude is also fixed in a dialectical relationship with emptiness insofar as it is the unravelling of older social systems that at once occasions existential crisis and creates space for new ways of being" ("Vive l'Amour," 180).

20. See, for instance, the reference to the meaning of the family as being disintegrated, eroded, and so on, in Wen, Guangying dingge, 134.

21. See Martin, *Situating Sexualities*, 169–71, for an interesting discussion of the frequent use of doors (and other types of frames) to suggest the compartmentalization of spaces in Tsai's works.

22. For a lucid and persuasive discussion of the negative Oedipus complex and its ramifications for sexual politics, see Kaja Silverman, *The Acoustic Mirror: The Female Voice in Psychoanalysis and Cinema* (Bloomington: Indiana UP, 1998).

23. In the Chinese sources I have consulted, this term is invariably used to describe the scene in question.

24. According to the teaching of the ancients in Chinese feudal society, the five main types of *lun* relations are those between father and son, emperor and official, husband and wife, elder and younger person, and friend and friend. Each type of relation is to be regulated by a specific moral principle.

25. Chang, "Guaitai jiating luomanshi," 134; the English word "dephallicized" is used in the original.

26. "In my view, there is no symbolic position of Mother and Father that is not precisely the idealization and ossification of contingent cultural norms" (Butler, "Quandaries of the Incest Taboo," 44).

27. This is a famous/notorious argument made by Lévi-Strauss in *The Elementary Structures of Kinship*. See Rubin, "The Traffic in Women," for a methodical and illuminating critique of Lévi-Strauss's argument, a critique that has been greatly enabling for subsequent discussions of women and the politics of gender and sexuality.

28. For this reason, it would be insufficient simply to append a discussion of the women and female bodies in Tsai's works to the present one, in order to complete a picture based, conventionally, on two differentiated sexes. Instead, women and female bodies in these films require a separate, full-fledged discussion of their own. For one such discussion with insights, see Feng Pinjia, "Yuwang shenti: Tsai Ming-liang dianying zhong de nüxing xingxiang," *Chungwai Literary Monthly* 30.10 (March 2002): 99–112.

29. For this suggestive piece of information, see Wen, *Guangying dingge*, 159, 227.

30. Wu, "Postsadness Taiwan New Cinema," 78–79, 93; my emphasis. By "postsadness," Wu is referring to the general cinematic/cultural ambience in Taiwan after Hou Hsiao-hsien's classic *Beiqing chengshi/City of Sadness* (1989). For a set of discussions of Hou's work in the historical context of contemporary Taiwan, see, for instance, June Yip, *Envisioning Taiwan: Fiction, Cinema, and the Nation* (Durham, N.C.: Duke UP, 2004).

31. "Wo xihuan suiyue de bianhua: Tsai Ming-liang tan *Ni nabian jidian?*" *Ming Pao Daily News* (North American edition), September 28, 2001, A7; my rough translation from the Chinese.

32. My reading of this ending is indebted to Wen Tianxiang's perceptive analysis in *Guangying dingge*, 160. See also Martin's comparable reading in *Situating Sexualities*, 176–84.

POSTSCRIPT (INSPIRED BY *BROKEBACK MOUNTAIN*)

1. Rick Lyman, "Watching Movies with Ang Lee; Crouching Memory, Hidden Heart," "Movies, Performing Arts/Weekend Desk" section, *New York Times*, March 9, 2001. In Lyman's article, the Mandarin classic Lee described at some length (the video cassette tape of which he played for Lyman during the interview) was obviously *Liang Sanbo yu Zhu Yingtai* (*Love Eterne*), though for some reason the title was mistakenly given as *Qicai Hu Bu Gui* (*Eternal Love*), a 1966 Cantonese production. The confusion was possibly caused by the similarity between the two films' translated titles in English. The *New York Times* issued a correction of this and other mistakes in Lyman's article on March 21, 2001. (Both the original article and the appended correction are accessible online at http://select.nytimes.com/search/restricted/. Page numbers of the article given hereafter are from the online version of the text.) For a discussion of the Mandarin classic (one that offers a critique of Ang Lee's reading of the film as homophobic), see Tan See Kam and Annette Aw, "*Love Eterne*: Almost a (Heterosexual) Love Story," in *Chinese Films in Focus: 25 New Takes*, ed. Chris Berry (London: British Film Institute, 2003), 137–43; see 143 n. 7 for a clarification of the two films as originally mixed up in Lyman's article. I should add (in good humor), however, that the confusion seems to continue on page 139 of Tan and Aw's article, too, because any audience who has seen Li Hanxiang's 1963 film or knows what the actresses actually looked like will recognize that the two characters in the picture are definitely not, as the caption says, Betty Loh Ti (Le Di) and Ivy Ling Po (Ling Bo)!

2. Lyman, "Watching Movies with Ang Lee," 1; my emphasis.

3. Ibid., 8, 7. Lee equated this theme with the repressed emotional wish, which he named the "hidden dragon" (8). This point was reiterated in his more detailed comments on the character of Jen Yu (Yu Jiaolong) in *Crouching Tiger, Hidden Dragon*; see Michael Berry, *Speaking in Images: Interviews with Contemporary Chinese Filmmakers* (New York: Columbia UP, 2005), 343–44. Lee obviously feels strongly about repression as a characteristic of Chinese society: in the banquet scene of *The Wedding Banquet*, he even made a cameo appearance as a guest who comments that the rowdy games inflicted on the newlyweds are the outcome of five thousand years of sexual repression.

4. Lee associated this ending with the ending of his own *Crouching Tiger, Hidden Dragon*, when Jen Yu (Yu Jiaolong) leaps off the bridge high in the moun-

tain and flies away through the clouds; see Lyman, "Watching Movies with Ang Lee," 7.

5. The concerto was composed by the musicians He Zhanhao and Chen Gang in 1959, when they were students at the Shanghai Academy of Music.

6. For a discussion of how, for Lee, it is virtually impossible to portray a love story in isolation from its social background, see Luo Feng (Natalia Chan), "Xunzhao yi zuo shan de ren ying" (an essay based on an interview with Ang Lee at the time of the release of *Brokeback Mountain* in Hong Kong), "Shiji" page, *Ming Pao Daily News* (North American edition), January 27, 2006.

7. One of the unforgettable scenes in *Brokeback Mountain* is the one in which Ennis recalls how, as a child, he was led by his own father to see the corpse of a man who had obviously been killed for being gay and left to rot. Jack's father, whom we meet at the end of the film, suggests an equally stern, uncomprehending paternalistic presence in Jack's life.

8. Not surprisingly, Tsai Ming-liang, whose work is clearly critical of this form of thinking-cum-living, is skeptical of the assumed virtue of a film's being moving. His remarks, reminiscent of the anticonvention tendencies of modern avant-garde artists and theorists, are noteworthy if only for the minority perspective they represent in contemporary Chinese cinema: "I don't believe that it is necessarily the role of films to move an audience. What does it mean to be moved, anyway? I think we have already grown accustomed to what it feels like to be 'moved' by a film; it is just like listening to music or anything else" (Berry, *Speaking in Images*, 374).

9. Berry, *Speaking in Images*, 355.

Index

Andrew, Dudley, on feminist film theory, 7

Anti-Rightist campaign of 1957, 71

Antonioni, Michaelangelo, 184: *Blow Up*, 49–50

Argentina in *Happy Together* (1997), 50, 54, 56, 62, 63

Armstrong, Nancy, on political activism of the 1960s, 205*n*28

Ashes of Time (*Dongxie xidu*) (1994, dir. Wong Kar-wai), 224*n*22

Asianness, 12. *See also* Chineseness

Balibar, Étienne: on inevitability of violence, 179; on superfluity of humans, 167, 168

Baudrillard, Jean, on consumption, 112

Bazin, André, on ontology of filmic image and Soviet propaganda, 5–6

Beijing: in *Burning of the Imperial Palace* (1983), 41; Forbidden City in, 42; and modernization of China, 32–33, 45; opera of, 52; Puccini's operas in, 149; in *Temptress Moon*, 32, 33, 35, 38, 53, 214*n*6

Benjamin, Walter, 247*n*16; *The Arcades Project*, 4; on Charles Baudelaire, 3, 4; on cinematic spectacle, 3; "The Work of Art in the Age of Mechanical Reproduction," 2–3, 202*n*4

Berry, Chris, on *The Wedding Banquet*, 139

Bertolucci, Bernardo, directs *The Last Emperor*, 41–43, 206*n*33

Bing Xin, "Xifeng," 86–89, 92, 94, 99, 100–101, 102

Blind Shaft (*Mang Jing*) (2003, dir. and prod. Li Yang): awards for, 168; banned by PRC authorities, 242*n*3; camera shots in, 243*n*10; coal mining in, 166 (fig. 8.1), 169–70, 170–71, 173; desolate landscape in, 172; documentary-like film language of, 175; DVD of, 170; education in, 176, 177, 178, 179; female characters in, 176; hope in, 172, 177; kinship family in, 170, 174–75, 176; main characters in, 169–70, 243*n*5; migration in, 168, 170, 172; murder and fraud in, 169–70, 174; music in, 172; names of characters in,

FILM AND CULTURE

A Series of Columbia University Press
Edited by John Belton